Society

Second Edition
Society

READINGS TO ACCOMPANY
SOCIOLOGY
A Down-to-Earth Approach
CORE CONCEPTS
Third Edition

Edited by
James M. Henslin
Southern Illinois University, Edwardsville

PEARSON

Boston ■ New York ■ San Francisco
Mexico City ■ Montreal ■ Toronto ■ London ■ Madrid ■ Munich ■ Paris
Hong Kong ■ Singapore ■ Tokyo ■ Cape Town ■ Sydney

Executive Editor: Jeff Lasser
Senior Editorial Assistant: Lauren Macey
Senior Marketing Manager: Kelly May
Editorial Production Service: Omegatype Typography, Inc.
Manufacturing Buyer: Debbie Rossi
Electronic Composition: Omegatype Typography, Inc.
Cover Administrator: Jenny Hart

For related titles and support materials, visit our online catalog at www.ablongman.com.

Between the time website information is gathered and then published, it is not unusual for some sites to have closed. Also, the transcription of URLs can result in typographical errors. The publisher would appreciate notification where these errors occur so that they may be corrected in subsequent editions.

ISBN-13:   978-0-205-57871-9
ISBN-10:   0-205-57871-3

Library of Congress Cataloging-in-Publication Data
Society : readings to accompany Sociology : a down to earth approach :
core concepts, third edition / edited by James M. Henslin.—2nd ed.
    p. cm.
    Includes index.
    ISBN-13: 978-0-205-57871-9 (pbk.)
    ISBN-10: 0-205-57871-3 (pbk.)
    1. Sociology. I. Henslin, James M. II. Henslin, James M. Sociology.
HM586.S626 2009
301—dc22   2008004380

Printed in the United States of America

10 9 8 7 6 5 4 3 2 1   12 11 10 09 08

Contents

Preface

■ ■

Sociology: A Down-to-Earth Approach: Core Concepts focuses on the main topics, ideas, research, and concepts in sociology. Since many instructors want to give their students the opportunity to read original sociological research, I have designed this brief anthology as a companion for *Sociology.* Because the readings follow the text's outline chapter for chapter and I have chosen two readings for each chapter, it is easy to incorporate them into the course.

As always, a selection may have several subthemes. This allows a reading to be incorporated into a different chapter than the one I have assigned it, or to be included in the course even though a particular chapter is not assigned. I have also written a short introduction to each selection.

If you have any suggestions for the next edition of this reader, please let me know. As always, I look forward to hearing from you.

Jim Henslin
Henslin@aol.com

Society

Invitation to Sociology

Peter L. Berger

introduction

To grasp *the sociological perspective* is to see the social world in a new light. As your angle of vision changes, no longer do things look the same. When you peer beneath the surface of human relationships, other realities begin to emerge. The taken-for-granted may take on unfamiliar hues. For example, if you place the sociological lens on something as familiar as friendship, you find that rather than being a simple matter, friendship is based on complex rights and obligations. As you analyze friendship, the implicit understandings on which it is based begin to emerge. Reciprocal obligations become visible—how you acquire a social debt when your friend does something for you, and in what way you are expected to repay this debt. Although seldom stated, these implicit understandings inhabit the background that rules the relationship. Violate them and you risk severing the friendship.

Uncovering realities that lie beneath the surface and attaining a different understanding of social life are part of the fascination of sociology. Regardless of a sociologist's topic—whether as familiar as friendship or as unfamiliar as the Yąnomamö, a fierce tribe in the jungles of South America (Reading 3)—as Berger points out in this selection, the sociologist's overriding motivation is curiosity, a desire to know more about some aspect of social life, to discover what is really going on in some setting.

Thinking Critically

As you read this selection, ask yourself:

1. What is the difference between a sociologist and a pollster?

2. What does Berger mean by this statement: "Statistical data by themselves do not make sociology"?

3. What does Berger mean when he says that sociology is a game? If it is a game, can it be taken seriously?

It is gratifying from certain value positions (including some of this writer's) that sociological insights have served in a number of instances to improve the lot of groups of human beings by uncovering morally shocking conditions or by clearing away collective illusions or by showing that socially desired results could be obtained in more humane fashion. One might point, for example, to some applications of sociological knowledge in the penological practice of Western countries. Or one might cite the use made of sociological studies in the Supreme Court decision of 1954 on racial segregation in the public schools. Or one could look at the applications of other sociological studies to the humane planning of urban redevelopment. Certainly the sociologist who is morally and politically sensitive will derive gratification from such instances. But, once more, it will be well to keep in mind that what is at issue here is not sociological understanding as such but certain applications of this understanding. It is not difficult to see how the same understanding could be applied with opposite intentions. Thus the sociological understanding of the dynamics of racial prejudice can be applied effectively by those promoting intragroup hatred as well as by those wanting to spread tolerance. And the sociological understanding of the nature of human solidarity can be employed in the service of both totalitarian and democratic regimes....

One image [of the sociologist is that of] a gatherer of statistics about human behavior.... He* goes out with a questionnaire, interviews people selected at random, then goes home [and] enters his tabulations [into computers].... In all of this, of course, he is supported by a large staff and a very large budget. Included in this image is the implication that the results of all this effort are picayune, a pedantic restatement of what everybody knows anyway. As one observer remarked pithily, a sociologist is a fellow who spends $100,000 to find his way to a house of ill repute.

This image of the sociologist has been strengthened in the public mind by the activities of many agencies that might well be called parasociological, mainly agencies concerned with public opinion and market trends. The pollster has become a well-known figure in American life, inopportuning people about their views from foreign policy to toilet paper. Since the methods used in the pollster business bear close resemblance to sociological research, the growth of this image of the sociologist is understandable.... The fundamental sociological question, whether concerned with premarital petting or with Republican votes or with the incidence of gang knifings, is always presumed to be "how often?" or "how many?"...

Now it must be admitted, albeit regretfully, that this image of the sociologist and his trade is not altogether a product of fantasy.... [A good] part of the sociological enterprise in this country continues to consist of little studies of obscure fragments of social life, irrelevant to any broader theoretical concern. One glance at the table of contents of the major sociological journals or at the list of papers read at sociological conventions will confirm this statement....

From *An Invitation to Sociology* by Peter L. Berger. Copyright © 1963 by Peter L. Berger. Reprinted by permission of Doubleday, a division of Random House, Inc.

*Some classic articles in sociology that are reprinted in this anthology were written when "he" and "man" were generic, when they referred to both men and women. So it is with "his," "him," and so on. Although the writing style has changed, the sociological ideas have not.

Statistical data by themselves do not make sociology. They become sociology only when they are sociologically interpreted, put within a theoretical frame of reference that is sociological. Simple counting, or even correlating different items that one counts, is not sociology. There is almost no sociology in the Kinsey reports. This does not mean that the data in these studies are not true or that they cannot be relevant to sociological understanding. They are, taken by themselves, raw materials that can be used in sociological interpretation. The interpretation, however, must be broader than the data themselves. So the sociologist cannot arrest himself at the frequency tables of premarital petting or extramarital pederasty. These enumerations are meaningful to him only in terms of their much broader implications for an understanding of institutions and values in our society. To arrive at such understanding the sociologist will often have to apply statistical techniques, especially when he is dealing with the mass phenomena of modern social life. But sociology consists of statistics as little as philology consists of conjugating irregular verbs or chemistry of making nasty smells in test tubes.

Sociology has, from its beginnings, understood itself as a science.... [T]he allegiance of sociologists to the scientific ethos has meant everywhere a willingness to be bound by certain scientific canons of procedure. If the sociologist remains faithful to his calling, his statements must be arrived at through the observation of certain rules of evidence that allow others to check on or to repeat or to develop his findings further. It is this scientific discipline that often supplies the motive for reading a sociological work as against, say, a novel on the same topic that might describe matters in much more impressive and convincing language....

The charge that many sociologists write in a barbaric dialect must...be admitted.... Any scientific discipline must develop a terminology. This is self-evident for a discipline such as, say, nuclear physics that deals with matters unknown to most people and for which no words exist in common speech. However, terminology is possibly even more important for the social sciences, just because their subject matter *is* familiar and just because words *do* exist to denote it. Because we are well acquainted with the social institutions that surround us, our perception of them is imprecise and often erroneous. In very much the same way most of us will have considerable difficulty giving an accurate description of our parents, husbands or wives, children or close friends. Also, our language is often (and perhaps blessedly) vague and confusing in its references to social reality. Take for an example the concept of *class*, a very important one in sociology: There must be dozens of meanings that this term may have in common speech—income brackets, races, ethnic groups, power cliques, intelligence ratings, and many others. It is obvious that the sociologist must have a precise, unambiguous definition of the concept if his work is to proceed with any degree of scientific rigor. In view of these facts, one can understand that some sociologists have been tempted to invent altogether new words to avoid the semantic traps of the vernacular usage.

Finally, we would look at an image of the sociologist not so much in his professional role as in his being, supposedly, a certain kind of person. This is the image of the sociologist as a detached, sardonic observer, and a cold manipulator of men. Where this image prevails, it may represent an ironic triumph of the sociologist's own efforts to be accepted as a genuine scientist. The sociologist here becomes the self-appointed superior man, standing off from the warm vitality of common existence, finding his satisfactions not in living but in coolly appraising the lives of others, filing them away in little categories, and thus presumably missing the real significance of what he is observing. Further, there is the notion that, when he involves himself in social processes at all, the sociologist does so as an uncommitted technician, putting his manipulative skills at the disposal of the powers that be.

This last image is probably not very widely held.... The problem of the political role of the social scientist is, nevertheless, a very genuine one. For instance, the employment of sociologists by certain branches of industry and government raises moral questions that ought to be faced more widely than they have been so far. These are, however, moral questions that concern all men in positions of responsibility....

How then are we to conceive of the sociologist? The sociologist is someone concerned with understanding society in a disciplined way. The nature of this discipline is scientific. This means that what the sociologist finds and says about the social phenomena he studies occurs within a certain rather strictly defined frame of reference. One of the main characteristics of this scientific frame of reference is that operations are bound by certain rules of evidence. As a scientist, the sociologist tries to be objective, to control his personal preferences and prejudices, to perceive clearly rather than to judge normatively. This restraint, of course, does not embrace the totality of the sociologist's existence as a human being, but is limited to his operations *qua* sociologist. Nor does the sociologist claim that his frame of reference is the only one within which society can be looked at. For that matter, very few scientists in any field would claim today that one should look at the world only scientifically. The botanist looking at a daffodil has no reason to dispute the right of the poet to look at the same object in a very different manner. There are many ways of playing. The point is not that one denies other people's games but that one is clear about the rules of one's own. The game of the sociologist, then, uses scientific rules. As a result, the sociologist must be clear in his own mind as to the meaning of these rules. That is, he must concern himself with methodological questions. Methodology does not constitute his goal. The latter, let us recall once more, is the attempt to understand society. Methodology helps in reaching this goal. In order to understand society, or that segment of it that he is studying at the moment, the sociologist will use a variety of means. Among these are statistical techniques. Statistics can be very useful in answering certain sociological questions. But statistics does not constitute sociology. As a scientist, the sociologist will have to be concerned with the exact significance of the terms he is using. That is, he will have to be careful about terminology. This does not have to mean that he must invent a new language of his own, but it does mean that he cannot naively use the language of everyday discourse. Finally, the interest of the sociologist is primarily theoretical. That is, he is interested in understanding for its own sake. He may be aware of or even concerned with the practical applicability and consequences of his findings, but at that point he leaves the sociological frame of reference as such and moves into realms of values, beliefs and ideas that he shares with other men who are not sociologists....

[W]e would like to go a little bit further here and ask a somewhat more personal (and therefore, no doubt, more controversial) question. We would like to ask not only what it is that the sociologist is doing but also what it is that drives him to it. Or, to use the phrase Max Weber used in a similar connection, we want to inquire a little into the nature of the sociologist's demon. In doing so, we shall evoke an image that is not so much ideal-typical in the above sense but more confessional in the sense of personal commitment. Again, we are not interested in excommunicating anyone. The game of sociology goes on in a spacious playground. We are just describing a little more closely those we would like to tempt to join our game.

We would say then that the sociologist (that is, the one we would really like to invite to our game) is a person intensively, endlessly, shamelessly interested in the doings of men. His natural habitat is all the human gathering places of the world, wherever men come together. The sociologist may be interested in many other things. But his consuming interest remains in the world of men, their institutions, their history, their passions. And since he is interested in men, nothing that men do can be altogether tedious for him. He will naturally be interested in the events that engage men's ultimate beliefs, their moments of tragedy and grandeur and ecstasy. But he will also be fascinated by the common place, the everyday. He will know reverence, but this reverence will not prevent him from wanting to see and to understand. He may sometimes feel revulsion or contempt. But this also will not deter him from wanting to have his questions answered. The sociologist, in his quest for understanding, moves through the world of men without respect for the usual lines of demarcation. Nobility and degradation, power and obscurity, intelligence and folly—these are equally *interesting* to him, however unequal they may be in his personal values or tastes. Thus his questions may lead him to all possible levels of society, the best and the least known places, the most respected and the most despised. And, if he is a good sociologist, he will find himself in all these places because his own questions have so taken possession of him that he has little choice but to seek for answers.

It would be possible to say the same things in a lower key. We could say that the sociologist, but for the grace of his academic title, is the man who must listen to gossip despite himself, who is tempted to look through keyholes, to read other people's mail, to open closed cabinets. Before some otherwise unoccupied psychologist sets out now to construct an aptitude test for sociologists on the basis of sublimated voyeurism, let us quickly say that we are speaking merely by way of analogy. Perhaps some little boys consumed with curiosity to watch their maiden aunts in the bathroom later become inveterate sociologists. This is quite uninteresting. What interests us is the curiosity that grips any sociologist in front of a closed door behind which there are human voices. If he is a good sociologist, he will want to open that door, to understand these voices. Behind each closed door he will anticipate some new facet of human life not yet perceived and understood.

The sociologist will occupy himself with matters that others regard as too sacred or as too distasteful for dispassionate investigation. He will find rewarding the company of priests or of prostitutes, depending not on his personal preferences but on the questions he happens to be asking at the moment. He will also concern himself with matters that others may find much too boring. He will be interested in the human interaction that goes with warfare or with great intellectual discoveries, but also in the relations between people employed in a restaurant or between a group of little girls playing with their dolls. His main focus of attention is not the ultimate significance of what men do, but the action in itself, as another example of the infinite richness of human conduct. So much for the image of our playmate.

In these journeys through the world of men the sociologist will inevitably encounter other professional Peeping Toms. Sometimes these will resent his presence, feeling that he is poaching on their preserves. In some places the sociologist will meet up with the economist, in others with the political scientist, in yet others with the psychologist or the ethnologist. Yet chances are that the questions that have brought him to these same places are different from the ones that propelled his fellow-trespassers. The sociologist's questions always remain essentially the same: "What are people doing with each other here?" "What are their relationships to each other?" "How are these relationships organized in institutions?" "What are the collective ideas that move men and institutions?" In trying to answer these questions in specific instances, the sociologist will, of course, have to deal with economic or political matters, but he will do so in a way rather different from that of the economist or the political scientist. The scene that he contemplates is the same human scene that these other scientists concern themselves with. But the sociologist's angle of vision is different. When this is understood, it becomes clear that it makes little sense to try to stake out a special enclave within which the sociologist will carry on business in his own right. There is, however, one traveler whose path the sociologist will cross more often than anyone else's on his journeys. This is the historian. Indeed, as soon as the sociologist turns from the present to the past, his preoccupations are very hard indeed to distinguish from those of the historian. However, we shall leave this relationship to a later part of our considerations. Suffice it to say here that the sociological journey will be much impoverished unless it is punctuated frequently by conversation with that other particular traveler.

Any intellectual activity derives excitement from the moment it becomes a trail of discovery. In some fields of learning this is the discovery of worlds previously unthought and unthinkable. This is the excitement of the astronomer or of the nuclear physicist on the antipodal boundaries of the realities that man is capable of conceiving. But it can also be the excitement of bacteriology or geology. In a different way it can be the excitement of the linguist discovering new realms of human expression or of the anthropologist exploring human customs in faraway countries. In such discovery, when undertaken with passion, a widening of awareness, sometimes a veritable transformation of consciousness, occurs. The universe turns out to be much more wonder-full than one had ever dreamed. The excitement of sociology is usually of a different sort. Sometimes, it is true, the sociologist penetrates into worlds that had previously been quite unknown to him—for instance, the world of crime, or the world of some bizarre religious sect, or the world fashioned by the exclusive concerns of some group such as medical specialists or military leaders or advertising executives. However, much of the time the sociologist moves in sectors of experience

that are familiar to him and to most people in his society. He investigates communities, institutions and activities that one can read about every day in the newspapers.
Yet there is another excitement of discovery beckoning in his investigations. It is not
the excitement of coming upon the totally unfamiliar, but rather the excitement of
finding the familiar becoming transformed in its meaning. The fascination of sociology lies in the fact that its perspective makes us see in a new light the very world in
which we have lived all our lives. This also constitutes a transformation of consciousness. Moreover, this transformation is more relevant existentially than that of
many other intellectual disciplines, because it is more difficult to segregate in some
special compartment of the mind. The astronomer does not live in the remote galax-
ies, and the nuclear physicist can, outside his laboratory, eat and laugh and marry
and vote without thinking about the insides of the atom. The geologist looks at
rocks only at appropriate times, and the linguist speaks English with his wife. The
sociologist lives in society, on the job and off it. His own life, inevitably, is part of his
subject matter. Men being what they are, sociologists too manage to segregate their
professional insights from their everyday affairs. But it is a rather difficult feat to
perform in good faith.

The sociologist moves in the common world of men, close to what most of them
would call real. The categories he employs in his analyses are only refinements of the
categories by which other men live—power, class, status, race, ethnicity. As a result,
there is a deceptive simplicity and obviousness about some sociological investigations.
One reads them, nods at the familiar scene, remarks that one has heard all this before
and don't people have better things to do than to waste their time on truisms—until
one is suddenly brought up against an insight that radically questions everything one
had previously assumed about this familiar scene. This is the point at which one begins to sense the excitement of sociology.

Let us take a specific example. Imagine a sociology class in a Southern college
where almost all the students are white Southerners. Imagine a lecture on the subject
of the racial system of the South. The lecturer is talking here of matters that have
been familiar to his students from the time of their infancy. Indeed, it may be that
they are much more familiar with the minutiae of this system than he is. They are
quite bored as a result. It seems to them that he is only using more pretentious words
to describe what they already know. Thus he may use the term "caste," one commonly used now by American sociologists to describe the Southern racial system.
But in explaining the term he shifts to traditional Hindu society, to make it clearer.
He then goes on to analyze the magical beliefs inherent in caste tabus, the social dynamics of commensalism and connubium, the economic interests concealed within
the system, the way in which religious beliefs relate to the tabus, the effects of the
caste system upon the industrial development of the society and vice versa—all in India. But suddenly India is not very far away at all. The lecture then goes back to its
Southern theme. The familiar now seems not quite so familiar any more. Questions
are raised that are new, perhaps raised angrily, but raised all the same. And at least
some of the students have begun to understand that there are functions involved in

this business of race that they have not read about in the newspapers (at least not those in their hometowns) and that their parents have not told them—partly, at least, because neither the newspapers nor the parents knew about them.

It can be said that the first wisdom of sociology is this—things are not what they seem. This too is a deceptively simple statement. It ceases to be simple after a while. Social reality turns out to have many layers of meaning. The discovery of each new layer changes the perception of the whole.

Anthropologists use the term "culture shock" to describe the impact of a totally new culture upon a newcomer. In an extreme instance such shock will be experienced by the Western explorer who is told, halfway through dinner, that he is eating the nice old lady he had been chatting with the previous day—a shock with predictable physiological if not moral consequences. Most explorers no longer encounter cannibalism in their travels today. However, the first encounters with polygamy or with puberty rites or even with the way some nations drive their automobiles can be quite a shock to an American visitor. With the shock may go not only disapproval or disgust but a sense of excitement that things can *really* be that different from what they are at home. To some extent, at least, this is the excitement of any first travel abroad. The experience of sociological discovery could be described as "culture shock" minus geographical displacement. In other words, the sociologist travels at home—with shocking results. He is unlikely to find that he is eating a nice old lady for dinner. But the discovery, for instance, that his own church has considerable money invested in the missile industry or that a few blocks from his home there are people who engage in cultic orgies may not be drastically different in emotional impact. Yet we would not want to imply that sociological discoveries are always or even usually outrageous to moral sentiment. Not at all. What they have in common with exploration in distant lands, however, is the sudden illumination of new and unsuspected facets of human existence in society. This is the excitement and, as we shall try to show later, the humanistic justification of sociology.

People who like to avoid shocking discoveries, who prefer to believe that society is just what they were taught in Sunday School, who like the safety of the rules and the maxims of what Alfred Schuetz has called the "world-taken-for-granted," should stay away from sociology. People who feel no temptation before closed doors, who have no curiosity about human beings, who are content to admire scenery without wondering about the people who live in those houses on the other side of that river, should probably also stay away from sociology. They will find it unpleasant or, at any rate, unrewarding. People who are interested in human beings only if they can change, convert or reform them should also be warned, for they will find sociology much less useful than they hoped. And people whose interest is mainly in their own conceptual constructions will do just as well to turn to the study of little white mice. Sociology will be satisfying, in the long run, only to those who can think of nothing more entrancing than to watch men and to understand things human....

To be sure, sociology is an individual pastime in the sense that it interests some men and bores others. Some like to observe human beings, others to experiment with mice. The world is big enough to hold all kinds and there is no logical priority for one interest as against another. But the word "pastime" is weak in describing what we mean. Sociology is more like a passion. The sociological perspective is more like a demon that possesses one, that drives one compellingly, again and again, to the questions that are its own. An introduction to sociology is, therefore, an invitation to a very special kind of passion.

The Lives of Homeless Women

Elliot Liebow

introduction ■ ■ ■ ■ ■

One of the main topics in Chapter 1 of *Core Concepts* is the methods that sociologists use to do their research. A common method is participant observation combined with interviewing. When I was doing research on the homeless, I used this combination. I slept in homeless shelters across the nation—in about a dozen U.S. cities and one in Canada. There and on the streets and in the alleys of these many skid rows, and even on a streetcar and in cafes, I conducted what seemed to be endless interviews. The research was emotionally draining. On dark streets and in back alleys, I had to continuously watch out for danger that appeared to lurk around every corner. One afternoon, as sirens screamed, I squatted next to a building, dictating into my tape recorder. I described the arrival of the police and medics to aid a homeless man who was lying bleeding on the sidewalk. He had been attacked by another homeless man.

Thousands of people live on our city streets. These discards of the advanced technological society have been left behind in our culturally mandated frenetic pursuit after material wealth. Like others, Elliot Liebow, a researcher with the National Institute of Mental Health, had seen these disheveled, unwelcome people sitting in parks and on stoops, sleeping next to shopping carts, sorting through trash bins, and begging on the city streets. Like others, he wondered what their life was like. And like a few of us—very few—he decided to find out firsthand—by experiencing their world. He, too, left his comfortable, upper-middle-class home and joined the street people. This is his engrossing account of that experience.

Thinking Critically

As you read this selection, ask yourself:

1. Liebow is reluctant to say that any of the homeless women he studied were mentally ill. Why does he have this reluctance? Based on what he says in this article, do you think any of these women were mentally ill? Why or why not?

2. How do you think that the problem of homelessness can be solved? You must be practical; that is, try to come up with workable solutions.

3. Assume that we will continue to have homeless people. How can we improve the way they are treated? Cite specific instances from the reading that you would try to solve.

This is a participant observer study of single, homeless women in emergency shelters in a small city just outside Washington, D.C. In participant observation, the researcher tries to participate as fully as possible in the lives of the people being studied. Of course, there are obvious and severe limits to how well a man with a home and family can put himself in the place of homeless women. One simply goes where they go, gets to know them over time as best one can, and tries very hard to see the world from their perspective.

It is often said that, in participant observation studies, the researcher is the research instrument. So is it here. Everything reported about the women in this study has been selected by me and filtered through me, so it is important that I tell you something about myself and my prejudices as well as how this study came about. Indeed, I feel obliged to tell you more than is seemly and more than you may want to know, but these are things that the women themselves knew about me and that had an important if unknown influence on my relationship with them.

In a real sense, I backed into this study, which took shape, more or less, as I went along. In 1984, I learned that I had cancer and a very limited life expectancy. I did not want to spend my last months on the 12th floor of a government office building, so at 58 I retired on disability from my job of 20 some years as an anthropologist with the National Institute of Mental Health.

I looked well, felt well, and had a lot of time on my hands, so I became a volunteer at a soup kitchen that had recently opened. I worked there one night a week. In the early part of the evening, I helped serve food or just sat around with the men and women who had come there, usually eating with them. In case of trouble, I tried to keep the peace. Later I went upstairs to "the counselor's office," where I met with people who needed assistance in getting shelter for the night. For the next hour or so, I called around to the various shelters in the county or in downtown Washington, D.C., trying to locate and reserve sleeping space for the men and women who needed it.

I enjoyed the work and the people at the soup kitchen, but this was only one night a week, so I became a volunteer at The Refuge, an emergency shelter for homeless women. This, too, was one night a week, from 6:30 to 10:00, and involved sleeping overnight twice a month. I picked this shelter because I had visited there briefly the year before and liked the feel of it. Here, along with three other volunteers, my job was to help prepare the food (usually just heat the main dishes and make a salad); help serve the food; distribute towels, soap, and other sundries on request; socialize with the women; keep order; and keep a daily log that included the names of all the women present and their time of arrival.

Almost immediately, I found myself enjoying the company of the women. I was awed by the enormous effort that most of them made to secure the most elementary necessities and decencies of life that the rest of us take for granted. And I was especially struck by their sense of humor, so at odds with any self-pity—the ability to step back and laugh at oneself, however wryly. One evening, soon after I started working at the shelter, several of us remained at the table to talk after finishing dinner. Pauline turned to me and said, in a stage whisper, making sure that Hilda would hear her, "Hilda has a Ph.D."

Hilda laughed. "No," she said, "I don't have a Ph.D., but I do have a bachelor's degree in biology." She paused, then began again. "You know," she said, "all my life I wanted to be an MD and now, at the age of 54, I finally made it. I'm a Manic Depressive."

Seduced by the courage and the humor of the women, and by the pleasure of their company, I started going to the shelter four and sometimes five days a week. (For the first two years, I also kept my one-night-a-week job with the soup kitchen.) Probably because it was something I was trained to do, or perhaps our of plain habit, I decided to take notes.

"Listen," I said at the dinner table one evening, after getting permission to do a study from the shelter director. "I want your permission to take notes. I want to go home at night and write down what I can remember about the things you say and do. Maybe I'll write a book about homeless women."

Most of the dozen or so women there nodded their heads or simply shrugged. All except Regina. Her acceptance was conditional. "Only if you promise not to publish before I do," she said. Believing that neither one of us, for different reasons, would ever publish anything in the future, I readily agreed.[1]

It is difficult to be precise about how I was perceived by the women. I am 6'1" and weigh about 175 pounds. I had a lot of white hair but was otherwise nondescript. I dressed casually, often in corduroy pants, shirt, and cardigan. The fact that I was Jewish did not seem to matter much one way or another so far as I could tell.

Most of the women probably liked having me around. Male companionship was generally in short supply and the women often made a fuss about the few male volunteers. I would guess that there were as many women who actively sought me out as there were women who avoided me. The fact that I had written a book that was available at the library (three or four women took the trouble to read it) enhanced my legitimacy in their eyes.[2]

Principally, I think, the women saw me as an important resource. I had money and a car, and by undertaking to write a book, I had made it my business to be with them. I routinely lent out $2, $5, $10, or even $20 on request to the handful who asked: I told them I had set aside a certain amount as a revolving fund and I could only keep lending money if they kept returning it. This worked fairly well.

There were a few women, of course, who would never be in a position to return the money, and this made for a problem. It would have been patronizing simply to make a gift of the money; they wanted to be borrowers, not beggars, and I was just as eager as they to avoid a demeaning panhandler/donor relationship. But I did not want them to be embarrassed or to avoid me simply because they couldn't repay a loan, nor did I want to shut them off from borrowing more. My solution was to reassure these women I had no immediate need for the money and could wait indefinitely for repayment.

Some of the women would perhaps characterize me as a friend, but I am not certain how deep or steadfast this sense of friendship might be. One day, Regina and I were talking about her upcoming trial about two months away. I had already agreed to accompany her to the courtroom and serve as an advisor, but Regina wanted further reassurance.

"You will be there, won't you?" she said.

As a way of noting the profundity that nothing in life is certain, I said, jokingly, "It's not up to me, it's up to The Man Upstairs."

"Well," she said, "if you die before the trial, you will ask one of your friends to help me, won't you?" I looked hard at her to see if she was joking, too. She wasn't. She was simply putting first things first.

One or two of the women did say something like "If you weren't married, would you give me a run for my money?" Neither "yes" nor "no" was a suitable response, but it usually sufficed for me to say (and mean), "I think you are a very nice person."

I tried to make myself available for driving people to Social Services, a job interview, a clinic or hospital, a cemetery, to someone's house, to another shelter, to help them move their belongings, or on other personal errands. With my consent, several women used my name as a personal reference for jobs or housing, and a few used my home as a mailing address for income tax refunds or other business.

Several of the women got to know my two daughters, both of whom came to The Refuge a few evenings each during the winters. One daughter was engaged to be married and her fiancé also came a few times. These visits helped strengthen my ties to those women who knew my daughters by face and name. They could ask me how my wife, Harriet, or Elisabeth and Jessica and Eric were doing, and my subsequent participation in discussions about family or child-rearing was much more personal and immediate as a result.

My association with the women was most intense during the winter of 1984–85, all of 1986, much of 1987, and the winter of 1987–88. Thereafter, I slackened off, partly for health reasons and partly because I had already collected more notes than I knew what to do with.[3] I continued to go to the shelters intermittently, and several of the women called me regularly at home. It was also at this time that I started playing around with the notes to see how I might eventually make sense of them.

In general, I have tried to avoid labeling any of the women as "mentally ill," "alcoholic," "drug addicted," or any other characterization that is commonly used to describe—or, worse, to explain—the homeless person. Judgments such as these are almost always made against a background of homelessness. If the same person were seen in another setting, the judgment might be altogether different. Like you, I know people who drink, people who do drugs, and bosses who have tantrums and treat their subordinates like dirt. They all have good jobs. Were they to become homeless, some of them would surely also become "alcoholics," "addicts," or "mentally ill." Similarly, if some of the homeless women who are now so labeled were to be magically transported to a more usual and acceptable setting, some of them—not all, of course—would shed their labels and take their places with the rest of us somewhere on the spectrum of normality.

The reader may be puzzled by the short shrift given here to mental illness. This was no oversight. I have no training as a mental health professional so it is not always clear to me who is mentally ill and who is not. There were always some women who acted crazy or whom most considered crazy, and the women themselves often agreed with the public at large that many homeless people are mentally ill.

From the beginning, however, I paid little attention to mental illness, partly because I had difficulty recognizing it, and partly for other reasons. Sometimes mental illness seemed to be "now-you-see-it, now-you-don't" phenomenon; some of the women were fine when their public assistance checks arrived, but became increasingly "symptomatic" as the month progressed and their money (security?) diminished, coming full circle when the next check arrived.[4] Others had good or bad days or weeks but with no obvious pattern or periodicity, although one woman linked her down period to her menstrual cycle. With a little patience on my part, almost all the women with mental or emotional problems were eventually and repeatedly accessible. Even on "bad" days, perhaps especially on "bad" days, these women sometimes said things that seemed to come, uncensored, from the depths of their emotional lives.

It seems to me that those women who may have been mentally ill (or alcoholic or drug addicted) by one or another standard were homeless for exactly the same proximal reason that everyone else was homeless: they had no place to live. Similarly, their greatest need of the moment was the same as everyone else's: to be assured of a safe, warm place to sleep at night, one or more hot meals a day, and the presence, if not the companionship, of fellow human beings. Given this perspective and my purposes, which and how many of the women were mentally ill was not a critical issue.

Whatever one's view of mental illness, it is probably true that the more one gets to know about a person, the easier it is to put oneself in that person's place or to understand his or her viewpoint, and the less reason one has for thinking of that person or treating that person as mentally ill.

This perspective—indeed, participant observation itself—raises the age-old problem of whether anyone can understand another or put oneself in another's place. Many thoughtful people believe that a sane person cannot know what it is to be crazy, that a white man cannot understand a black man, a Jew cannot see through the eyes of a Christian, a man through the eyes of a woman, and so forth in both directions. In an important sense, of course, and to a degree, this is certainly true; in another sense, and to a degree, it is surely false, because the logical extension of such a view is that no one can know another, that only John Jones can know John Jones, in which case social life would be impossible.

I do not mean that a man with a home and family can see and feel the world as homeless women see and feel it. I do mean, however, that it is reasonable and useful to try to do so. Trying to put oneself in the place of the other lies at the heart of the social contract and of social life itself...

In the early months, I sometimes tried to get Betty or one of the other women to see things as I saw them. One night Betty waited half an hour in back of the library for a bus that never came. She was convinced this was deliberate and personal abuse on the part of the Metro system, Metro was out to get her, she said. "But how did Metro know you were waiting for a bus at that time?" I asked. Betty shook her head in pity of me. "Well, Elliot, I was there on the street, right there in public, in the open! How could they not see me waiting for that damn bus?"

Fairly quickly, I learned not to argue with Betty but simply to relax and marvel at her end-of-the-month ingenuity. ("End-of-the-month" because that's when her public assistance money ran out and when she was most bitter at the way the world was treating her. At that time, a $10 or $20 loan could dramatically reduce or even eliminate her paranoid thoughts.) Once, when her food stamps had not come, even two days after Judy had received hers, Betty dryly observed that this was further proof that Richman County was trying to rid itself of homeless women. "They give Judy Tootie her food stamps so she'll eat herself to death [Judy weighed 300 pounds]. They won't give me mine so I'll starve to death." She got no argument from me. I had learned to go with the flow.

Sometimes I annoyed or even angered some of the women. When Louise told me that some of the women were following her around all day and harassing her, I asked her why they did these things. "You're just like the state's attorney," she said, "always asking for reasons. Whenever I tell him that someone assaulted me, he always asks me why they did it. People with criminal minds don't need a reason to do something. That's what makes them criminals."

…I think of Betty and Louise and many of the other women as friends. As a friend, I owe them friendship. Perhaps I also owe them something because I have so much and they have so little, but I do not feel under any special obligation to them as research subjects. Indeed, I do not think of them as "research subjects." Since they knew what I was trying to do and allowed me to do it, they could just as well be considered collaborators in what might fairly be seen as a cooperative enterprise.

NOTES

1. Let the record show that now, some seven-plus years later, I have her permission to go ahead.

2. *Tally's Corner: A Study of Negro Streetcorner Men.*

3. For the same reason, I stopped taking life histories. After the women had known me for a few months, I took about 20 life histories on tape, often at the request of the women themselves and over a period of two years or so. Some of these lasted several hours over two or three sessions and I found myself accumulating more information than I could handle.

4. Many schizophrenics are completely lucid for long periods of time, and their thoughts and behavior are completely indistinguishable from those of normals. Even Bleuler…asserted that there were certain very important cognitive processes…that were frequently identical among schizophrenics and normals. *"In many important respects, then, an insane person may be completely sane"* (emphasis added). Morris Rosenberg, "A Symbolic Interactionist View of Psychosis," *Journal of Health and Social Behavior*, 25, no. 3 (September 1984), p. 291.

The Fierce People

Napoleon Chagnon

introduction ■ ■ ■ ■

The many cultures of humans are fascinating. Each human group has its own culture, whether the group be an urban gang in the United States or a tribe in the jungles of South America. Like an envelope, our culture encloses us into a particular area. It sets boundaries and dictates what is significant and insignificant. It provides the rules for how we should interact with one another. Culture also provides the framework from which we view life. Understand a people's culture, and you come a long way to understanding why they think, feel, and act as they do.

Understanding and appreciation are two different things. To understand a group does not necessarily mean that you appreciate it. It might help, but not necessarily. In this selection, Napoleon Chagnon recounts his harrowing stay with the Yąnomamö, a tribe in South America. As you read this selection, you will see how uncomfortable he was during his lengthy fieldwork.

Thinking Critically

As you read this selection, ask yourself:

1. Why didn't Chagnon develop an appreciation for the way of life of the Yąnomamö?

2. Why was Chagnon so stingy with his food—and so reluctant to accept food from others?

3. How does the culture of the Yąnomamö compare with your own culture? Be sure to compare gender relations (relationships among men and women).

The Yąnomamö Indians live in southern Venezuela and the adjacent portions of northern Brazil. Some 125 widely scattered villages have populations ranging from 40 to 250 inhabitants, with 75 to 80 people the most usual number. In total numbers their population probably approaches 10,000 people, but this is merely a guess. Many of the villages have not yet been contacted by outsiders, and nobody knows for sure exactly how many uncontacted villages there are, or how many people live in them. By comparison to African or Melanesian tribes, the Yąnomamö population is small. Still, they are one of the largest unacculturated tribes left in all of South America.

But they have a significance apart from tribal size and cultural purity: The Yąnomamö are still actively conducting warfare. It is in the nature of man to fight, according to one of their myths, because the blood of "Moon" spilled on this layer of the cosmos, causing men to become fierce. I describe the Yąnomamö as "the fierce people" because that is the most accurate single phrase that describes them. That is how they conceive themselves to be, and that is how they would like others to think of them.

I spent nineteen months with the Yąnomamö during which time I acquired some proficiency in their language and, up to a point, submerged myself in their culture and way of life. The thing that impressed me most was the importance of aggression in their culture. I had the opportunity to witness a good many incidents that expressed individual vindictiveness on the one hand and collective bellicosity on the other. These ranged in seriousness from the ordinary incidents of wife beating and chest pounding to dueling and organized raiding by parties that set out with the intention of ambushing and killing men from enemy villages. One of the villages was raided approximately twenty-five times while I conducted the fieldwork, six times by the group I lived among....

This is not to state that primitive man everywhere is unpleasant. By way of contrast, I have also done limited fieldwork among the Yąnomamö's northern neighbors, the Carib-speaking Makiritare Indians. This group was very pleasant and charming, all of them anxious to help me and honor bound to show any visitor the numerous courtesies of their system of etiquette. In short, they approached the image of primitive man that I had conjured up, and it was sheer pleasure to work with them....

My first day in the field illustrated to me what my teachers meant when they spoke of "culture shock." I had traveled in a small, aluminum rowboat propelled by a large outboard motor for two and a half days. This took me from the Territorial capital, a small town on the Orinoco River, deep into Yąnomamö country. On the morning of the third day we reached a small mission settlement, the field "headquarters" of a group of Americans who were working in two Yąnomamö villages. The missionaries had come out of these villages to hold their annual conference on the progress of their mission work, and were conducting their meetings when I arrived. We picked up a passenger at the mission station, James P. Barker, the first non-Yąnomamö to make a sustained, permanent contact with the tribe (in 1950). He had just returned from a year's furlough in the United States, where I had earlier visited him before leaving for Venezuela. He agreed to accompany me to the village I had selected for my base of operations to introduce me to the Indians. This village was also his own home base, but he had not been there for over a year and did not plan to join me for another three months. Mr. Barker had been living with this particular group about five years.

We arrived at the village, Bisaasi-teri, about 2:00 P.M. and docked the boat along the muddy bank at the terminus of the path used by the Indians to fetch their drinking water. It was hot and muggy, and my clothing was soaked with perspiration.

It clung uncomfortably to my body, as it did thereafter for the remainder of the work. The small, biting gnats were out in astronomical numbers, for it was the beginning of the dry season. My face and hands were swollen from the venom of their numerous stings. In just a few moments I was to meet my first Yąnomamö, my first primitive man. What would it be like? I had visions of entering the village and seeing 125 social facts running about calling each other kinship terms and sharing food, each waiting and anxious to have me collect his genealogy. I would hear them out in turn. Would they like me? This was important to me; I wanted them to be so fond of me that they would adopt me into their kinship system and way of life, because I had heard that successful anthropologists always get adopted by their people. I had learned during my seven years of anthropological training at the University of Michigan that kinship was equivalent to society in primitive tribes and that it was a moral way of life, "moral" being something "good" and "desirable." I was determined to work my way into their moral system of kinship and become a member of their society.

My heart began to pound as we approached the village and heard the buzz of activity within the circular compound. Mr. Barker commented that he was anxious to see if any changes had taken place while he was away and wondered how many of them had died during his absence. I felt into my back pocket to make sure that my notebook was there and felt personally more secure when I touched it. Otherwise, I would not have known what to do with my hands.

I looked up and gasped when I saw a dozen burly, naked, filthy, hideous men staring at us down the shafts of their drawn arrows! Immense wads of green tobacco were stuck between their lower teeth and lips making them look even more hideous, and strands of dark-green slime dripped or hung from their noses. We arrived at the village while the men were blowing a hallucinogenic drug up their noses. One of the side effects of the drug is a runny nose. The mucus is always saturated with the green powder and the Indians usually let it run freely from their nostrils. My next discovery was that there were a dozen or so vicious, underfed dogs snapping at my legs, circling me as if I were going to be their next meal. I just stood there holding my notebook, helpless and pathetic. Then the stench of the decaying vegetation and filth struck me and I almost got sick. I was horrified. What sort of a welcome was this for the person who came here to live with you and learn your way of life, to become friends with you? They put their weapons down when they recognized Barker and returned to their chanting, keeping a nervous eye on the village entrances.

We had arrived just after a serious fight. Seven women had been abducted the day before by a neighboring group, and the local men and their guests had just that morning recovered five of them in a brutal club fight that nearly ended in a shooting war. The abductors, angry because they lost five of the seven captives, vowed to raid the Bisaasi-teri. When we arrived and entered the village unexpectedly, the Indians feared that we were the raiders. On several occasions during the next two hours the men in the village jumped to their feet, armed themselves, and waited nervously for the noise outside the village to be identified. My enthusiasm for collecting ethnographic curiosities diminished in proportion to the number of times such an alarm was raised. In fact, I was relieved when Mr. Barker suggested that we sleep across the river for the evening. It would be safer over there.

As we walked down the path to the boat, I pondered the wisdom of having decided to spend a year and a half with this tribe before I had even seen what they were like. I am not ashamed to admit, either, that had there been a diplomatic way out, I would have ended my fieldwork then and there. I did not look forward to the next day when I would be left alone with the Indians; I did not speak a word of their language, and they were decidedly different from what I had imagined them to be. The whole situation was depressing, and I wondered why I ever decided to switch from civil engineering to anthropology in the first place. I had not eaten all day, I was soaking wet from perspiration, the gnats were biting me, and I was covered with red pigment, the result of a dozen or so complete examinations I had been given by as many burly Indians. These examinations capped an otherwise grim day. The Indians would blow their noses into their hands, flick as much of the mucus off that would separate in a snap of the wrist, wipe the residue into their hair, and then carefully examine my face, arms, legs, hair, and the contents of my pockets. I asked Mr. Barker how to say "Your hands are dirty"; my comments were met by the Indians in the following way: They would "clean" their hands by spitting a quantity of slimy tobacco juice into them, rub them together, and then proceed with the examination.

Mr. Barker and I crossed the river and slung our hammocks. When he pulled his hammock out of a rubber bag, a heavy, disagreeable odor of mildewed cotton came with it. "Even the missionaries are filthy," I thought to myself. Within two weeks everything I owned smelled the same way, and I lived with the odor for the remainder of the fieldwork. My own habits of personal cleanliness reached such levels that I didn't even mind being examined by the Indians, as I was not much cleaner than they were after I had adjusted to the circumstances.

So much for my discovery that primitive man is not the picture of nobility and sanitation I had conceived him to be. I soon discovered that it was an enormously time-consuming task to maintain my own body in the manner to which it had grown accustomed in the relatively antiseptic environment of the northern United States. Either I could be relatively well fed and relatively comfortable in a fresh change of clothes and do very little fieldwork, or, I could do considerably more fieldwork and be less well fed and less comfortable.

It is appalling how complicated it can be to make oatmeal in the jungle. First, I had to make two trips to the river to haul the water. Next, I had to prime my kerosene stove with alcohol and get it burning, a tricky procedure when you are trying to mix powdered milk and fill a coffee pot at the same time: the alcohol prime always burned out before I could turn the kerosene on, and I would have to start all over. Or, I would turn the kerosene on, hoping that the element was still hot enough to vaporize the fuel, and not start a small fire in my palm-thatched hut as the liquid kerosene squirted all over the table and walls and ignited. It was safer to start over with the alcohol. Then I had to boil the oatmeal and pick the bugs out of it. All my supplies, of course, were carefully stored in Indian-proof, ratproof, moisture-proof, and insect-proof containers, not one of which ever served its purpose adequately. Just taking things out of the multiplicity of containers and repacking them afterward was a minor project in itself. By the time I had hauled the water to cook with, unpacked my food, prepared the oatmeal, milk, and coffee, heated water for dishes, washed and dried the dishes, repacked the food in the containers, stored the containers in locked trunks and cleaned up my mess, the ceremony of preparing breakfast had brought me almost up to lunch time.

Eating three meals a day was out of the question. I solved the problem by eating a single meal that could be prepared in a single container, or, at most, in two containers, washed my dishes only when there were no clean ones left, using cold river water, and wore each change of clothing at least a week to cut down on my laundry problem, a courageous undertaking in the tropics. I was also less concerned about sharing my provisions with the rats, insects, Indians, and the elements, thereby eliminating the need for my complicated storage process. I was able to last most of the day on *café con leche*, heavily sugared espresso coffee diluted about five to one with hot milk. I would prepare this in the evening and store it in a thermos. Frequently, my single meal was no more complicated than a can of sardines and a package of crackers. But at least two or three times a week I would do something sophisticated, like make oatmeal or boil rice and add a can of tuna fish or tomato paste to it. I even saved time by devising a water system that obviated the trips to the river. I had a few sheets of zinc roofing brought in and made a rain-water trap. I caught the water on the zinc surface, funneled it into an empty gasoline drum, and then ran a plastic hose from the drum to my hut. When the drum was exhausted in the dry season, I hired the Indians to fill it with water from the river.

I ate much less when I traveled with the Indians to visit other villages. Most of the time my travel diet consisted of roasted or boiled green plantains that I obtained from the Indians, but I always carried a few cans of sardines with me in case I got lost or stayed away longer than I had planned. I found peanut butter and crackers a very nourishing food, and a simple one to prepare on trips. It was nutritious and portable, and only one tool was required to prepare the meal, a hunting knife that could be cleaned by wiping the blade on a leaf. More importantly, it was one of the few foods the Indians would let me eat in relative peace. It looked too much like animal feces to them to excite their appetites.

I once referred to the peanut butter as the dung of cattle. They found this quite repugnant. They did not know what "cattle" were, but were generally aware that I ate several canned products of such an animal. I perpetrated this myth, if for no other reason than to have some peace of mind while I ate. Fieldworkers develop strange defense mechanisms, and this was one of my own forms of adaptation. On another occasion I was eating a can of frankfurters and growing very weary of the demands of one of my guests for a share in my meal. When he asked me what I was eating, I replied: "Beef." He then asked, "What part of the animal are you eating?" to which I replied, "Guess!" He stopped asking for a share.

Meals were a problem in another way. Food sharing is important to the Yąnomamö in the context of displaying friendship. "I am hungry," is almost a form of greeting with them. I could not possibly have brought enough food with me to feed the entire village, yet they seemed not to understand this. All they could see was that I did not share my food with them at each and every meal. Nor could I enter into their system of reciprocities with respect to food; every time one of them gave me something "freely," he would dog me for months to pay him back, not with food, but with steel tools. Thus, if I accepted a plantain from someone in a different village while I was on a visit, he would most likely visit me in the future and demand a machete as payment for the time that he "fed" me. I usually reacted to these kinds of demands by giving a banana, the customary reciprocity in their culture—food for food—but this would be a disappointment for the individual who had visions of that single plantain growing into a machete over time.

Despite the fact that most of them knew I would not share my food with them at their request, some of them always showed up at my hut during mealtime. I gradually became accustomed to this and learned to ignore their persistent demands while I ate. Some of them would get angry because I failed to give in, but most of them accepted it as just a peculiarity of the subhuman foreigner. When I did give in, my hut quickly filled with Indians, each demanding a sample of the food that I had given one of them. If I did not give all a share, I was that much more despicable in their eyes.

A few of them went out of their way to make my meals unpleasant, to spite me for not sharing; for example, one man arrived and watched me eat a cracker with honey on it. He immediately recognized the honey, a particularly esteemed Yąnomamö food. He knew that I would not share my tiny bottle and that it would be futile to ask. Instead, he glared at me and queried icily, "Shaki![1] What kind of animal semen are you eating on that cracker?" His question had the desired effect, and my meal ended.

Finally, there was the problem of being lonely and separated from your own kind, especially your family. I tried to overcome this by seeking personal friendships among the Indians. This only complicated the matter because all my friends simply used my confidence to gain privileged access to my cache of steel tools and trade goods, and looted me. I would be bitterly disappointed that my "friend" thought no more of me than to finesse our relationship exclusively with the intention of getting at any locked up possessions, and my depression would hit new lows every time I discovered this. The loss of the possession bothered me much less than the shock that I was, as far as most of them were concerned, nothing more than a source of desirable items; no holds were barred in relieving me of these, since I was considered something sub-human, a non-Yąnomamö.

The thing that bothered me most was the incessant, passioned, and aggressive demands the Indians made. It would become so unbearable that I would have to lock myself in my mud hut every once in a while just to escape from it: Privacy is one of Western culture's greatest achievements. But I did not want privacy for its own sake; rather, I simply had to get away from the begging. Day and night for the entire time I lived with the Yąnomamö I was plagued by such demands as: "Give me a knife, I am poor!"; "If you don't take me with you on your next trip to Widokaiya-teri, I'll chop a hole in your canoe!"; "Don't point your camera at me or I'll hit you!"; "Share your food with me!"; "Take me across the river in your canoe and be quick about it!"; "Give me a cooking pot!"; "Loan me your flashlight so I can go hunting tonight!"; "Give me medicine…I itch all over!"; "Take us on a week-long hunting trip with your shotgun!"; and "Give me an axe, or I'll break into your hut when you are away visiting and steal one!" And so I was bombarded by such demands day after day, months on end, until I could not bear to see an Indian.

It was not as difficult to become calloused to the incessant begging as it was to ignore the sense of urgency, the impassioned tone of voice, or the intimidation and aggression with which the demands were made. It was likewise difficult to adjust to the fact that the Yąnomamö refused to accept "no" for an answer until or unless it seethed with passion and intimidation—which it did after six months. Giving in to a demand always established a new threshold; the next demand would be for a bigger item or favor, and the anger of the Indians even greater if the demand was not met. I soon learned that I had to become very much like the Yąnomamö to be able to get along with them on their terms: sly, aggressive, and intimidating.

Had I failed to adjust in this fashion I would have lost six months of supplies to them in a single day or would have spent most of my time ferrying them around in my canoe or hunting for them. As it was, I did spend a considerable amount of time doing these things and did succumb to their outrageous demands for axes and machetes, at least at first. More importantly, had I failed to demonstrate that I could not be pushed around beyond a certain point, I would have been the subject of far more ridicule, theft, and practical jokes than was the actual case. In short, I had to acquire a certain proficiency in their kind of interpersonal politics and to learn how to imply subtly that certain potentially undesirable consequences might follow if they did such and such to me. They do this to each other in order to establish precisely the point at which they cannot goad an individual any further without precipitating retaliation. As soon as I caught on to this and realized that much of their aggression was stimulated by their desire to discover my flash point, I got along much better with them and regained some lost ground. It was sort of like a political game that everyone played, but one in which each individual sooner or later had to display some sign that his bluffs and implied threats could be backed up. I suspect that the frequency of wife beating is a component of this syndrome, since men can display their ferocity and show others that they are capable of violence. Beating a wife with a club is considered to be an acceptable way of displaying ferocity and one that does not expose the male to much danger. The important thing is that the man has displayed his potential for violence and the implication is that other men better treat him with respect and caution.

After six months, the level of demand was tolerable in the village I used for my headquarters. The Indians and I adjusted to each other and knew what to expect with regard to demands on their part for goods, favors, and services. Had I confined my fieldwork to just that village alone, the field experience would have been far more enjoyable. But, as I was interested in the demographic pattern and social organization of a much larger area, I made regular trips to some dozen different villages in order to collect genealogies or to recheck those I already had. Hence, the intensity of begging and intimidation was fairly constant for the duration of the fieldwork. I had to establish my position in some sort of pecking order of ferocity at each and every village.

For the most part, my own "fierceness" took the form of shouting back at the Yąnomamö as loudly and as passionately as they shouted at me, especially at first, when I did not know much of their language. As I became more proficient in their language and learned more about their political tactics, I became more sophisticated in the art of bluffing. For example, I paid one young man a machete to cut palm trees and make boards from the wood. I used these to fashion a platform in the bottom of my dugout canoe to keep my possessions dry when I traveled by river. That afternoon I was doing informant work in the village; the long-awaited mission supply boat arrived, and most of the Indians ran out of the village to beg goods from the crew. I continued to work in the village for another hour or so and went down to the river to say "hello" to the men on the supply boat. I was angry when I discovered that the Indians had chopped up all my palm boards and used them to paddle their own canoes across the river. I knew that if I overlooked this incident I would have invited them to take even greater liberties with my goods in the future. I crossed the river, docked amidst their dugouts, and shouted for the Indians to come out and see me. A few of the culprits appeared, mischievous grins on their faces. I gave a spirited lecture about how hard I had worked to put those boards in my canoe, how I had paid a machete for the wood, and how angry I was that they destroyed my work in their haste to cross the river. I then pulled out my hunting knife and, while their grins disappeared, cut each of their canoes loose, set them into the current, and let them float away. I left without further ado and without looking back.

They managed to borrow another canoe and, after some effort, recovered their dugouts. The headman of the village later told me with an approving chuckle that I had done the correct thing. Everyone in the village, except, of course, the culprits, supported and defended my action. This raised my status.

Whenever I took such action and defended my rights, I got along much better with the Yąnomamö. A good deal of their behavior toward me was directed with the forethought of establishing the point at which I would react defensively. Many of them later reminisced about the early days of my work when I was "timid" and a little afraid of them, and they could bully me into giving goods away.

Theft was the most persistent situation that required me to take some sort of defensive action. I simply could not keep everything I owned locked in trunks, and the Indians came into my hut and left at will. I developed a very effective means for recovering almost all the stolen items. I would simply ask a child who took the item and then take that person's hammock when he was not around, giving a spirited lecture to the others as I marched away in a faked rage with the thief's hammock. Nobody ever attempted to stop me from doing this, and almost all of them told me that my technique for recovering my possessions was admirable. By nightfall the thief would either appear with the stolen object or send it along with someone else to make an exchange. The others would heckle him for getting caught and being forced to return the item.

With respect to collecting the data I sought, there was a very frustrating problem. Primitive social organization is kinship organization, and to understand the Yąnomamö way of life I had to collect extensive genealogies. I could not have deliberately picked a more difficult group to work with in this regard: They have very stringent name taboos. They attempt to name people in such a way that when the person dies and they can no longer use his name, the loss of the word in the language is not inconvenient. Hence, they name people for specific and minute parts of things, such as "toenail of some rodent," thereby being able to retain the words "toenail" and "(specific) rodent," but not being able to refer directly to the toenail of that rodent. The taboo is maintained even for the living: One mark of prestige is the courtesy others show you by not using your name. The sanctions behind the taboo seem to be an unusual combination of fear and respect.

I tried to use kinship terms to collect genealogies at first, but the kinship terms were so ambiguous that I ultimately had to resort to names. They were quick to grasp that I was bound to learn everybody's name and reacted, without my knowing it, by inventing false names for everybody in the village. After having spent several months collecting names and learning them, this came as a disappointment to me: I could not cross-check the genealogies with other informants from distant villages.

They enjoyed watching me learn these names. I assumed, wrongly, that I would get the truth to each question and that I would get the best information by working in public. This set the stage for converting a serious project into a farce. Each informant tried to outdo his peers by inventing a name even more ridiculous than what I had been given earlier, or by asserting that the individual about whom I inquired was married to his mother or daughter, and the like. I would have the informant whisper the name of the individual in my ear, noting that he was the father of such and such a child. Everybody would then insist that I repeat the name aloud, roaring in hysterics as I clumsily pronounced the name. I assumed that the laughter was in response to the violation of the name taboo or to my pronunciation. This was a reasonable interpretation, since the individual whose name I said aloud invariably became angry. After I learned what some of the names meant, I began to understand what the laughter was all about. A few of the more colorful examples are: "hairy vagina," "long penis," "feces of the harpy eagle," and "dirty rectum." No wonder the victims were angry.

I was forced to do my genealogy work in private because of the horseplay and nonsense. Once I did so, my informants began to agree with each other and I managed to learn a few new names, real names. I could then test any new informant by collecting a genealogy from him that I knew to be accurate. I was able to weed out the more mischievous informants this way. Little by little I extended the genealogies and learned the real names. Still, I was unable to get the names of the dead and extend the genealogies back in time, and even my best informants continued to deceive me about their own close relatives. Most of them gave me the name of a living man as the father of some individual in order to avoid mentioning that the actual father was dead.

The quality of a genealogy depends in part on the number of generations it embraces, and the name taboo prevented me from getting any substantial information about deceased ancestors. Without this information, I could not detect marriage patterns through time. I had to rely on older informants for this information, but these were the most reluctant of all. As I became more proficient in the language and more skilled at detecting lies, my informants became better at lying. One of them in particular was so cunning and persuasive that I was shocked to discover that he had been inventing his information. He specialized in making a ceremony out of telling me false names. He would look around to make sure nobody was listening outside my hut, enjoin me to never mention the name again, act very nervous and spooky, and then grab me by the head to whisper the name very softly into my ear. I was always elated after an informant session with him, because I had several generations of dead ancestors for the living people. The others refused to give me this information. To show my gratitude, I paid him quadruple the rate I had given the others. When word got around that I had increased the pay, volunteers began pouring in to give me genealogies.

I discovered that the old man was lying quite by accident. A club fight broke out in the village one day, the result of a dispute over the possession of a woman. She had been promised to Rerebawa, a particularly aggressive young man who had married into the village. Rerebawa had already been given her older sister and was enraged when the younger girl began having an affair with another man in the village, making no attempt to conceal it from him. He challenged the young man to a club fight, but was so abusive in his challenge that the opponent's father took offense and entered the village circle with his son, wielding a long club. Rerebawa swaggered out to the duel and hurled insults at both of them, trying to goad them into striking him on the head with their clubs. This would have given him the opportunity to strike them on the head. His opponents refused to hit him, and the fight ended. Rerebawa had won a moral victory because his opponents were afraid to hit him. Thereafter, he swaggered around and insulted the two men behind their backs. He was genuinely angry with them, to the point of calling the older man by the name of his dead father. I quickly seized on this as an opportunity to collect an accurate genealogy and pumped him about his adversary's ancestors. Rerebawa had been particularly nasty to me up to this point, but we became staunch allies: We were both outsiders in the local village. I then asked about other dead ancestors and got immediate replies. He was angry with the whole group and not afraid to tell me the names of the dead. When I compared his version of the genealogies to that of the old man, it was obvious that one of them was lying. I challenged his information, and he explained that everybody knew that the old man was deceiving me and bragging about it in the village. The names the old man had given me were the dead ancestors of the members of a village so far away that he thought I would never have occasion to inquire about them. As it turned out, Rerebawa knew most of the people in that village and recognized the names.

I then went over the complete genealogical records with Rerebawa, genealogies I had presumed to be in final form. I had to revise them all because of the numerous lies and falsifications they contained. Thus, after five months of almost constant work on the genealogies of just one group, I had to begin almost from scratch!

Discouraging as it was to start over, it was still the first real turning point in my fieldwork. Thereafter, I began taking advantage of local arguments and animosities in selecting my informants, and used more extensively individuals who had married into the group. I began traveling to other villages to check the genealogies, picking villages that were on strained terms with the people about whom I wanted information. I would then return to my base camp and check with local informants the accuracy of the new information. If the informants became angry when I mentioned the new names I acquired from the unfriendly group, I was almost certain that the information was accurate. For this kind of checking I had to use informants whose genealogies I knew rather well: They had to be distantly enough related to the dead person that they would not go into a rage when I mentioned the name, but not so remotely related that they would be uncertain of the accuracy of the information. Thus, I had to make a list of names that I dared not use in the presence of each and every informant. Despite the precautions, I occasionally hit a name that put the informant into a rage, such as that of a dead brother or sister that other informants had not reported. This always terminated the day's work with that informant, for he would be too touchy to continue any further, and I would be reluctant to take a chance on accidentally discovering another dead kinsman so soon after the first.

These were always unpleasant experiences, and occasionally dangerous ones, depending on the temperament of the informant. On one occasion I was planning to visit a village that had been raided about a week earlier. A woman whose name I had on my list had been killed by the raiders. I planned to check each individual on the list one by one to estimate ages, and I wanted to remove her name so that I would not say it aloud in the village. I knew that I would be in considerable difficulty if I said this name aloud so soon after her death. I called on my original informant and asked him to tell me the name of the woman who had been killed. He refused, explaining that she was a close relative of his. I then asked him if he would become angry if I read off all the names on the list. This way he did not have to say her name and could merely nod when I mentioned the right one. He was a fairly good friend of mine, and I thought I could predict his reaction. He assured me that this would be a good way of doing it. We were alone in my hut so that nobody could overhear us. I read the names softly, continuing to the next when he gave a negative reply. When I finally spoke the name of the dead woman he flew out of his chair, raised his arm to strike me, and shouted: "You son-of-a-bitch![2] If you ever say that name again, I'll kill you!" He was shaking with rage, but left my hut quietly. I shudder to think what might have happened if I had said the name unknowingly in the woman's village. I had other, similar experiences in different villages, but luckily the dead person had been dead for some time and was not closely related to the individual into whose ear I whispered the name. I was merely cautioned to desist from saying any more names, lest I get people angry with me.

I had been working on the genealogies for nearly a year when another individual came to my aid. It was Kaobawa, the headman of Upper Bisaasi-teri, the group in which I spent most of my time. He visited me one day after the others had left the hut and volunteered to help me on the genealogies. He was poor, he explained, and needed a machete. He would work only on the condition that I did not ask him about his own parents and other very close kinsmen who were dead. He also added that he would not lie to me as the others had done in the past. This was perhaps the most important single event in my fieldwork, for out of this meeting evolved a very warm friendship and a very profitable informant-fieldworker relationship.

Kaobawa's familiarity with his group's history and his candidness were remarkable. His knowledge of details was almost encyclopedic. More than that, he was enthusiastic and encouraged me to learn details that I might otherwise have ignored. If there were things he did not know intimately, he would advise me to wait until he could check things out with someone in the village. This he would do clandestinely, giving me a report the next day. As I was constrained by my part of the bargain to avoid discussing his close dead kinsmen, I had to rely on Rerebawa for this information. I got Rerebawa's genealogy from Kaobawa.

Once again I went over the genealogies with Kaobawa to recheck them, a considerable task by this time: they included about two thousand names, representing several generations of individuals from four different villages. Rerebawa's information was very accurate, and Kaobawa's contribution enabled me to trace the genealogies further back in time. Thus, after nearly a year of constant work on genealogies, Yąnomamö demography and social organization began to fall into a pattern. Only then could I see how kin groups formed and exchanged women with each other over time, and only then did the fissioning of larger villages into smaller ones show a distinct pattern. At this point I was able to begin formulating more intelligent questions because there was now some sort of pattern to work with. Without the help of Rerebawa and Kaobawa, I could not have made very much sense of the plethora of details I had collected from dozens of other informants.

Kaobawa is about 40 years old. I say "about" because the Yąnomamö numeration system has only three numbers: one, two, and more-than-two. He is the headman of Upper Bisaasi-teri. He has had five or six wives so far and temporary affairs with as many more women, one of which resulted in a child. At the present time he has just two wives, Bahimi and Koamashima. He has had a daughter and a son by Bahimi, his eldest and favorite wife. Koamashima, about 20 years old, recently had her first child, a boy. Kaobawa may give Koamashima to his youngest brother. Even now the brother shares in her sexual services. Kaobawa recently gave his third wife to another of his brothers because she was beshi: "horny." In fact, this girl had been married to two other men, both of whom discarded her because of her infidelity. Kaobawa had one daughter by her; she is being raised by his brother.

Kaobawa's eldest wife, Bahimi, is about thirty-five years old. She is his first cross-cousin. Bahimi was pregnant when I began my fieldwork, but she killed the new baby, a boy, at birth, explaining tearfully that it would have competed with Ariwari, her nursing son, for milk. Rather than expose Ariwari to the dangers and uncertainty of an early weaning, she killed the new child instead. By Yąnomamö standards, she and Kaobawa have a very tranquil household. He only beats her once in a while, and never very hard. She never has affairs with other men.

Kaobawa is quiet, intense, wise, and unobtrusive. He leads more by example than by threats and coercion. He can afford to be this way as he established his reputation for being fierce long ago, and other men respect him. He also has five mature brothers who support him, and he has given a number of his sisters to other men in the village, thereby putting them under some obligation to him. In short, his "natural" following (kinsmen) is large, and he does not have to constantly display his ferocity. People already respect him and take his suggestions seriously.

Rerebawa is much younger, only about twenty-two years old. He has just one wife by whom he has had three children. He is from Karohi-teri, one of the villages to which Kaobawa is allied. Rerebawa left his village to seek a wife in Kaobawa's group because there were no eligible women there for him to marry.

Rerebawa is perhaps more typical than Kaobawa in the sense that he is concerned about his reputation for ferocity and goes out of his way to act tough. He is, however, much braver than the other men his age and backs up his threats with action. Moreover, he is concerned about politics and knows the details of intervillage relationships over a large area. In this respect he shows all the attributes of a headman, although he is still too young and has too many competent older brothers in his own village to expect to move easily into the position of leadership there.

He does not intend to stay in Kaobawa's group and has not made a garden. He feels that he has adequately discharged his obligations to his wife's parents by providing them with fresh game for three years. They should let him take the wife and return to his own village with her, but they refuse and try to entice him to remain permanently in Bisaasi-teri to provide them with game when they are old. They have even promised to give him their second daughter if he will stay permanently.

Although he has displayed his ferocity in many ways, one incident in particular shows what his character is like. Before he left his own village to seek a wife, he had an affair with the wife of an older brother. When he was discovered, his brother attacked him with a club. Rerebawa was infuriated so he grabbed an axe and drove his brother out of the village after soundly beating him with the flat of the blade. The brother was so afraid that he did not return to the village for several days. I recently visited his village with him. He made a point to introduce me to this brother. Rerebawa dragged him out of his hammock by the arm and told me, "This is the brother whose wife I had an affair with," a deadly insult. His brother did nothing and slunk back into his hammock, shamed, but relieved to have Rerebawa release the vise-grip on his arm.

Despite the fact that he admires Kaobawa, he has a low opinion of the others in Bisaasi-teri. He admitted confidentially that he thought Bisaasi-teri was an abominable group: "This is a terrible neighborhood! All the young men are lazy and cowards and everybody is committing incest! I'll be glad to get back home." He also admired Kaobawa's brother, the headman of Monou-teri. This man was killed by raiders while I was doing my fieldwork. Rerebawa was disgusted that the others did not chase the raiders when they discovered the shooting: "He was the only fierce one in the whole group; he was my close friend. The cowardly Monou-teri hid like women in the jungle and didn't even chase the raiders!"

Even though Rerebawa is fierce and capable of being quite nasty, he has a good side as well. He has a very biting sense of humor and can entertain the group for hours on end with jokes and witty comments. And, he is one of few Yąnomamö that I feel I can trust. When I returned to Bisaasi-teri after having been away for a year, Rerebawa was in his own village visiting his kinsmen. Word reached him that I had returned, and he immediately came to see me. He greeted me with an immense bear hug and exclaimed, "Shaki! Why did you stay away so long? Did you know that my will was so cold while you were gone that at times I could not eat for want of seeing you?" I had to admit that I missed him, too.

Of all the Yąnomamö I know, he is the most genuine and the most devoted to his culture's ways and values. I admire him for that, although I can't say that I subscribe to or endorse these same values. By contrast, Kaobawa is older and wiser. He sees his own culture in a different light and criticizes aspects of it he does not like. While many of his peers accept some of the superstitions and explanatory myths as truth and as the way things ought to be, Kaobawa questions them and privately pokes fun at some of them. Probably, more of the Yąnomamö are like Rerebawa, or at least try to be.

NOTES

1. "Shaki," or, rather, "Shakiwa," is the name they gave me because they could not pronounce "Chagnon." They like to name people for some distinctive feature when possible. *Shaki* is the name of a species of noisome bees; they accumulate in large numbers around ripening bananas and make pests of themselves by eating into the fruit, showering the people below with the debris. They probably adopted this name for me because I was also a nuisance, continuously prying into their business, taking pictures of them, and, in general, being where they did not want me.

2. This is the closest English translation of his actual statement, the literal translation of which would be nonsensical in our language.

Diary of a Homeless Man

John R. Coleman

introduction ■ ■ ■ ■

As I said in the introduction to the second reading, when I was doing research on the homeless, I slept in homeless shelters across the nation—in about a dozen U.S. cities and one in Canada. The research was emotionally draining, not only because I was immersed into the misery of the homeless, but also because of the jarringly abrupt endings and beginnings thrust upon me as I entered and left two worlds. The world of middle class people in airports and on planes is far removed from the world of the homeless on the streets and in the shelters. Bridging these worlds, usually within a single day, required mental adjustments that I had not anticipated.

Fortuitously, I had built in a break with my brother and his family in California. When he and his wife went to work the day after I arrived, I was left alone in the house. It was at this point that I realized what a marvelous luxury a living room is. I could lie on the couch and flip TV channels to my heart's content. I had always taken the living room for granted, and only by being with the homeless who had no living rooms did the significance of "living room" hit me. The room actually took on a different meaning.

For thousands of people, the city street is their living room. These discards of the advanced technological society have been left behind in our culturally mandated frenetic pursuit for material wealth. Like others, John Coleman, the president of a small, private college, had seen these strange people on the streets of the city. Like others, he wondered what their life was like. And like a few of us—very few—he decided to find out first hand, by experiencing their world. He, too, left his comfortable, upper-middle-class home and joined the street people. This is his engrossing account of that experience.

Thinking Critically

As you read this article, ask yourself:

1. What does this selection on the homeless add to what you learned in the second reading?

2. Why do you think that the homeless are treated with such disdain (lack of respect)?

3. How can we improve the way that agencies treat the homeless? Cite specific instances from the reading that you would try to solve.

■ ■ ■   **WEDNESDAY, 1/19**

Somehow, 12 degrees at 6 A.M. was colder than I had counted on. I think of myself as relatively immune to cold, but standing on a deserted sidewalk outside Penn Station with the thought of ten days ahead of me as a homeless man, the immunity vanished. When I pulled my collar closer and my watch cap lower, it wasn't to look the part of a street person; it was to keep the wind out.

My wardrobe wasn't much help. I had bought my "new" clothes—flannel shirt, baggy sweater, torn trousers, the cap and the coat—the day before on Houston Street for $19. "You don't need to buy shoes," the shop-keeper had said. "The ones you have on will pass for a bum's." I was hurt; they were shoes I often wore to the office.

Having changed out of my normal clothes in the Penn Station men's room and stowed them in a locker, I was ready for the street. Or thought so.

Was I imagining it, or were people looking at me in a completely different way? I felt that men, especially the successful-looking ones in their forties and over, saw me and wondered. For the rest, I wasn't there.

At Seventh Avenue and 35th Street, I went into a coffee shop. The counterman looked me over carefully. When I ordered the breakfast special—99 cents plus tax— he told me I'd have to pay in advance. I did (I'd brought $40 to see me through the ten days), but I noticed that the other customers were given checks, and paid only when they left.

By 9:30, I had read a copy of the *Times* retrieved from a trash basket; I had walked most of the streets around the station; I had watched the construction at the new convention center. There was little else to do.

Later, I sat and watched the drug sales going on in Union Square. Then I went into the Income Maintenance Center on 14th Street and watched the people moving through the welfare lines. I counted the trucks on Houston Street.

I vaguely remembered a quote to the effect that "idleness is only enjoyable when you have a lot to do." It would help to be warm, too.

There was ample time and incentive to stare at the other homeless folk on the street. For the most part, they weren't more interesting than the typical faces on Wall Street or upper Madison Avenue. But the extreme cases caught and held the eye. On Ninth Avenue, there was a man on the sidewalk directing an imaginary (to me) flow of traffic. And another, two blocks away, tracing the flight of planes or birds—or spirits— in the winter sky. And there was a woman with gloves tied to her otherwise bare feet.

Standing outside the Port Authority Bus Terminal was a man named Howard. He was perhaps my age, but the seasons had left deeper marks on his face. "Come summertime, it's all going to be different," he told me. "I'm going to have a car to go to the beach. And I'm going to get six lemons and make me a jug of ice-cold lemonade to go with the car.

"This whole country's gone too far with the idea of one person being at the top. It starts with birthday parties. Who gets to blow out the candle? One person.

And it takes off from there. If we're ever going to make things better, we gotta start with those candles."

Was there any chance of people like us finding work?

"Jobs are still out there for the young guys who want them," Howard said. "But there's nothing for us. Never again. No, I stopped dreaming about jobs a long time ago. Now I dream about cars. And lemonade."

Drugs and alcohol are common among the homeless. The damage done by them was evident in almost every street person I saw. But which was cause, and which was effect? Does it matter, once this much harm has been done?

My wanderings were all aimless. There was no plan, no goal, no reason to be anywhere at any time. Only hours into this role, I felt a useless part of the city streets. I wasn't even sure why I was doing this....

A weathered drifter told me about a hideaway down in the bowels of the station, where it was warm and quiet. I found my way there and lay down on some old newspapers to sleep.

How long did I sleep? It didn't seem long at all. I was awakened by a flashlight shining in my eyes, and a voice, not an unkind one, saying, "You can't sleep here. Sorry, but you have to go outside."

I hadn't expected to hear that word "sorry." It was touching.

I left and walked up to 47th Street, between Fifth and Madison Avenues, where I knew there was a warm grate in the sidewalk. (I've been passing it every morning for over five years on my way to work.) One man was asleep there already. But there was room for two, and he moved over.

■ ■ ■ THURSDAY, 1/20

When you're spending the night on the street, you learn to know morning is coming by the kinds of trucks that roll by. As soon as there are other than garbage trucks— say, milk or bread trucks—you know the night will soon be over.

I went back to Penn Station to clean up in the washroom. The care with which some of the other men with me bathed themselves at the basins would have impressed any public-health officer. And I couldn't guess from the appearance of their clothes who would be the most fastidious.

I bought coffee and settled back to enjoy it out of the main traffic paths in the station. No luck. A cop found me and told me to take it to the street.

After breakfast ($1.31 at Blimpie), I walked around to keep warm until the public library opened. I saw in a salvaged copy of the *Times* that we had just had our coldest night of the year, well below zero with the windchill factor, and that a record 4,635 people had sought shelter in the city's hostels.

The library was a joy. The people there treated me the same as they might have had I been wearing my business suit. To pass the time, I got out the city's welfare reports for 50 years ago. In the winter of 1933, the city had 4,524 beds available for the homeless, and all were said to be filled every night. The parallel to 1983 was uncanny. But, according to the reports, the man in charge of the homeless program in 1933, one Joseph A. Manning, wasn't worried about the future. True, the country was in the midst of a depression. But there had been a slight downturn in the numbers served in the shelters in the two months immediately preceding his report. This meant, wrote Manning, that "the depression, in the parlance of the ring, is K.O.'d."

Already, I notice changes in me. I walk much more slowly. I no longer see a need to beat a traffic light or to be the first through a revolving door. Force of habit still makes me look at my wrist every once in a while. But there's no watch there, and it wouldn't make any difference if there were. The thermometer has become much more important to me now than any timepiece could be....

The temperature rose during the day. Just as the newspaper headlines seem to change more slowly when you're on the streets all day long, so the temperature seems to change more rapidly and tellingly.

At about 9 P.M., I went back to the heated grate on 47th Street. The man who had been there last night was already in place. He made it clear that there was again room for me:

I asked him how long he had been on the streets.

"Eleven years, going on twelve," he said.

"This is only my second night."

"You may not stick it out. This isn't for every man."

"Do you ever go into the shelters?"

"I couldn't take that. I prefer this anytime."

■ ■ ■ FRIDAY, 1/21

When I left my grate mate—long before dawn—he wished me a good day. I returned the gesture: He meant his, and I meant mine.

In Manhattan's earliest hours, you get the feeling that the manufacture and removal of garbage is the city's main industry. So far, I haven't been lucky or observant enough to rescue much of use from the mounds of trash waiting for the trucks and crews. The best find was a canvas bag that will fit nicely over my feet at night.

I'm slipping into a routine: Washing up at the station. Coffee on the street. Breakfast at Blimpie. A search for the *Times* in the trash baskets. And then a leisurely stretch of reading in the park.

Some days bring more luck than others. Today I found 20 cents in a pay-phone slot and heard a young flutist playing the music of C.P.E. Bach on Sixth Avenue between 9th and 10th streets. A lot of people ignored her, even stepped over her flute case as if it were litter on the sidewalk. More often than not, those who put money in the case looked embarrassed. They seemed to be saying, "Don't let anyone see me being appreciative."

By nightfall, the streets were cruelly cold once again....

I headed for the 47th Street grate again but found my mate gone. There was no heat coming up through it. Do they turn it off on Friday nights? Don't we homeless have any rights?

On the northwest corner of Eighth Avenue and 33rd Street, there was a blocked-off subway entrance undergoing repair. I curled up against the wall there under some cardboard sheets. Rain began to fall, but I stayed reasonably dry and was able to get to sleep.

At some point, I was awakened by a man who had pulled back the upper piece of cardboard.

"You see my partner here. You need to give us some money."

I was still half-asleep. "I don't have any."

"You must have something, man."

"Would I be sleeping here in the rain if I did?"

His partner intervened. "C'mon. Leave the old bastard alone. He's not worth it."

"He's got something. Get up and give it to us."

I climbed to my feet and began fumbling in my pocket. Both men were on my left side. That was my chance. Suddenly I took off and ran along 33rd Street toward Ninth Avenue. They gave no chase. And a good thing, too, because I was too stiff with cold to run a good race.

■ ■ ■ SATURDAY, 1/22

A man I squatted next to in a doorway on 29th Street said it all: "The onliest thing is to have a warm place to sleep. That and having somebody care about you. That'd be even onlier."

He had what appeared to be rolls of paper toweling wrapped around one leg and tied with red ribbon. But the paper, wet with rain by now, didn't seem to serve any purpose.

I slept little. The forecast was for more rain tomorrow, so why wish the night away?

The morning paper carried news of Mayor Koch's increased concern about the homeless.

But what can he do? He must worry that the more New York does to help, the greater the numbers will grow. At the moment he's berating the synagogues for not doing anything to take street people in.

Watching people come and go at the Volvo tennis tournament at Madison Square Garden, I sensed how uncomfortable they were at the presence of the homeless. Easy to love in the abstract, not so easy face to face.

It's no wonder that the railway police are under orders to chase us out of sight.

Perhaps a saving factor is that we're not individuals. We're not people anybody knows. So far I've had eye contact with only three people who know me in my other life. None showed a hint of recognition. One was the senior auditor at Arthur Andersen & Company, the accounting firm that handles the Clark Foundation, my employer. One was a fellow lieutenant in the Auxiliary Police Force, a man with whom I had trained for many weeks. And one was an owner in the cooperative apartment where I live....

Early in the evening I fell asleep on the Seventh Avenue steps outside the Garden. Three Amtrak cops shook me awake to ask if two rather good-looking suitcases on the steps were mine. I said that I had never seen them

One cop insisted that I was lying, but then a black man appeared and said they belonged to a friend of his. The rapid-fire questioning from two of the cops soon made that alibi rather unlikely. The third cop was going through the cases and spreading a few of the joints he found inside on the ground.

As suddenly as it had begun, the incident was over. The cops walked away, and the man retrieved the bags. I fell back to sleep. Some hours later when I woke up again, the black man was still there, selling.

■ ■ ■ SUNDAY, 1/23

A new discovery of a warm and dry, even scenic, place to sit on a rainy day: the Staten Island Ferry.

For one 25-cent fare, I had four crossings of the harbor, read all I wanted of the copy of the Sunday *Times* I'd found, and finished the crossword puzzle.

When I got back to the Garden, where the tennis tournament was in its last hours, I found the police were being extra diligent in clearing us away from the departing crowds. One older woman was particularly incensed at being moved. "You're ruining my sex life," she shouted. "That's what you're doing. My sex life. Do you hear?"

A younger woman approached me to ask if I was looking for love. "No, ma'am. I'm just trying to stay out of the rain." ...

So, back to the unused subway entrance, because there was still no heat across town on the 47th Street grate.

The night was very cold. Parts of me ached as I tried to sleep. Turning over was a chore, not only because the partially wet cardboard had to be re-arranged with such care, but also because the stiffer parts of my body seemed to belong to someone else. Whatever magic there was in those lights cutting down through the fog was gone by now. All I wanted was to be warm and dry once more. Magic could wait.

■ ■ ■ MONDAY, 1/24

Early this morning I went to the warren of employment agencies on 14th Street to see if I could get a day's work. There was very little action at most of these last-ditch offices, where minimum wages and sub-minimum conditions are the rule.

But I did get one interview and thought I had a dishwashing job lined up. I'd forgotten one thing. I had no identification with me. No identification, no job.

There was an ageless, shaggy woman in Bryant Park this morning who delivered one of the more interesting monologues I've heard. For a full ten minutes, with no interruption from me beyond an occasional "Uh huh," she analyzed society's ills without missing a beat.

Beginning with a complaint about the women's and men's toilets in the park being locked ("What's a poor body to do?"), she launched into the strengths of the Irish, who, though strong, still need toilets more than others, and the weaknesses of the English and the Jews, the advantages of raising turkeys over other fowl, and the wickedness of Eleanor Roosevelt in letting the now Queen Mother and that stuttering king of hers rave so much about the hot dogs served at Hyde Park that we had no alternative but to enter World War II on their side. The faulty Russian satellite that fell into the Indian Ocean this morning was another example of shenanigans, she said. It turns out the Russians and Lady Diana, "that so-called Princess of Wales," are in cahoots to keep us so alarmed about such things far away from home that we don't get anything done about prayer in schools or the rest of it. But after all, what would those poor Protestant ministers do for a living if the children got some real religion in school, like the kind we got from the nuns, God bless them?

That at least was the gist of what she said. I know I've missed some of the finer points.

At 3:30 P.M., with more cold ahead, I sought out the Men's Shelter at 8 East 3rd Street. This is the principal entry point for men seeking the city's help. It provides meals for 1,300 or so people every day and beds for some few of those. I had been told that while there was no likelihood of getting a bed in this building I'd be given a meal here and a bed in some other shelter.

I've seen plenty of drawings of London's workhouses and asylums in the times of Charles Dickens. Now I've seen the real thing, in the last years of the twentieth century in the world's greatest city.

The lobby, and the adjacent "sitting room" were jammed with men standing, sitting, or stretched out in various positions on the floor. It was as lost a collection of souls as I could have imagined. Old and young, scarred and smooth, stinking and clean, crippled and hale, drunk and sober, ranting and still, parts of another world and parts of this one. The city promises to take in anyone who asks. Those rejected everywhere else find their way to East 3rd Street.

The air was heavy with the odors of Thunderbird wine, urine, sweat, and, above all, nicotine and marijuana. Three or four Human Resources Administration police officers seemed to be keeping the violence down to tolerable levels, but barely so.

After a long delay, I got a meal ticket for dinner and was told to come back later for a lodging ticket.

It was time to get in line to eat. This meant crowding into what I can only compare to a cattle chute in a stockyard. It ran along two walls of the sitting room and was already jammed. A man with a bullhorn kept yelling at us to stand up and stay in line. One very old and decrepit (or drunk?) man couldn't stay on his feet. He was helped to a chair, from which he promptly fell onto the floor. The bullhorn man had some choice obscenities for him, but they didn't seem to have any effect. The old man just lay there; and we turned our thoughts back to the evening meal.

I made a quick, and probably grossly unfair, assessment of the hundreds of men I could see in the room. Judging them solely by appearance, alertness, and body movements, I decided that one-quarter of them were perfectly able to work; they, more likely than not, were among the warriors who helped us win the battle against inflation by the selfless act of joining the jobless ranks. Another quarter might be brought back in time into job-readiness by some counseling and some caring for them as individuals. But the other half seemed so ravaged by illness, addiction, and sheer neglect that I couldn't imagine them being anything but society's wards from here on out to—one hopes—a peaceful end.

At the appointed hour, we were released in groups of twenty or thirty to descend the dark, filthy steps to the basement eating area. The man with the bullhorn was there again, clearly in charge and clearly relishing the extra power given to his voice by electric amplification. He insulted us collectively and separately without pause, but because his vocabulary was limited it tended to be the same four-letter words over and over.

His loudest attack on me came when I didn't move fast enough to pick up my meal from the counter. His analysis of certain flaws in my white ancestry wasn't hard to follow, even for a man in as much of a daze as I was.

The shouting and the obscenities didn't stop once we had our food. Again and again we were told to finish and get out. Eating took perhaps six minutes, but those minutes removed any shred of dignity a man might have brought in with him from the street.

Back upstairs, the people in charge were organizing the people who were to go to a shelter in Brooklyn. Few had volunteered, so there was more haranguing.

In the line next to the one where I was waiting for my lodging ticket a fight suddenly broke out. One man pulled a long knife from his overcoat pocket. The other man ran for cover, and a police officer soon appeared to remove the man with the knife from the scene. The issue, it seems, was one of proper places in the line.

There still weren't enough Brooklyn volunteers to suit the management, so they brought in their big gun: Mr. Bullhorn. "Now, listen up," he barked. "There aren't any buses going to Ft. Washington [another shelter] until 11:30, so if you want to get some sleep; go to Brooklyn. Don't ask me any questions. Just shut up and listen. It's because you don't listen up that you end up in a place like this."

I decided to ask a question anyway, about whether there would still be a chance for me to go Brooklyn once I got my lodging ticket. He turned on me and let me have the full force of the horn: "Don't ask questions, I said. You're not nobody."

The delays at the ticket-issuing window went on and on. Three staff members there seemed reasonably polite and even efficient. The fourth and heaviest one—I have no idea whether it was a man or woman—could not have moved more slowly without coming to a dead halt. The voice of someone who was apparently a supervisor came over the public-address system from time to time to apologize for the delay in going to the Ft. Washington shelter, which was in an armory, but any good he did from behind the scenes was undone by the staff out front and a "see-no-work, hear-no-work, do-no-work" attendant in the office.

As 11:30 approached, we crowded back into the sitting room to get ready to board the buses. A new martinet had appeared on the scene. He got as much attention through his voice, cane, and heavy body as Mr. Bullhorn had with his amplifying equipment. But this new man was more openly vile and excitable; he loved the power that went with bunching us all up close together and then ordering us to stretch out again in a thinner line. We practiced that routine several times....

Long after the scheduled departure, the lines moved. We sped by school buses to the armory at Ft. Washington Avenue and 168th Street. There we were met, just before 2:30 A.M., by military police, social workers, and private guards. They marched us into showers (very welcome), gave us clean underwear, and sent us upstairs to comfortable cots arranged in long rows in a room as big as a football field.

There were 530 of us there for the night, and we were soon quiet.

■ ■ ■ ■ TUESDAY, 1/25

We were awakened at 6 A.M. by whistles and shouting, and ordered to get back onto the buses for the return trip to lower Manhattan as soon as possible.

Back at 8 East 3rd Street, the worst of the martinets were off duty. So I thought breakfast might be a bit quieter than dinner had been. Still, by eight, I had seen three incidents a bit out of the ordinary for me.

A man waiting for breakfast immediately ahead of me in the cattle chute suddenly grabbed a chair from the adjoining area and prepared to break it over his neighbor's head. In my haste to get out of the way, I fell over an older man sleeping against the wall. After some shouts about turf, things cooled off between the fighters, and the old man forgave me.

In the stairwell leading down to the eating area, a young man made a sexual advance to me. When I withdrew from him and stupidly reached for my coat pocket, he thought I was going for a weapon. He at once pinned me against the wall and searched my pockets; there was nothing there.

As I came out of the building onto East 3rd Street, two black Human Resources Administration policemen were bringing two young blacks into the building. One officer had his man by the neck. The other officer had his man's hands cuffed behind his back and repeatedly kicked him hard in the buttocks.

My wanderings were still more aimless today. I couldn't get East 3rd Street out of my mind. What could possibly justify some of that conduct? If I were a staff member there, would I become part of the worst in that pattern? Or would I simply do as little, and think as little, as possible?

At day's end I can't recall much of where I went or why I went there.

Only isolated moments remain with me. Like…staring at the elegant crystal and silver in the shops just north of Madison Square Park and wondering what these windows say to the people I'd spent the night with.

Much too soon it was time to go back to the shelter for dinner and another night. At first I thought I didn't have the guts to do it again. Does one have to do *this* to learn who the needy are? I wanted to say, "Enough! There's only so much I need to see."

But I went back to the shelter anyway, probably because it took more guts to quit than it did to go ahead.

A man beside me in the tense dinner line drove one truth of this place home to me. "I never knew hell came in this color," he said.

I was luckier in my assignment for the night. I drew the Keener Building, on Wards Island, a facility with a capacity of 416 men. The building was old and neglected, and the atmosphere of a mental hospital, which it once was, still hung over it. But the staff was polite, the rooms weren't too crowded (there were only twelve beds in Room 326), the single sheet on each bed was clean, and there was toilet paper in the bathroom.

There were limits and guards and deprivations, but there was also an orderliness about the place. Here, at least, I didn't feel I had surrendered all of my dignity at the door.

■ ■ ■ WEDNESDAY, 1/26

…Back to the shelter on East 3rd Street for dinner.

There is simply no other situation I've seen that is so devoid of any graces at all, so tense at every moment, or so empty of hope. The food isn't bad, and the building is heated; that's all it has going for it.

The only cutlery provided is a frail plastic spoon. With practice you can spread hard oleo onto your bread with the back of one. If there's liver or ham, you don't have to cut it; just put it between the two pieces of bread that go with each meal. Everything else—peas, collard greens, apple pudding, plums—can be managed with the spoon. And talk over dinner or sipping, rather than gulping, coffee isn't all that important.

What is hardest to accept is the inevitable jungle scene during the hour you stand in line waiting to eat. Every minute seems to be one that invites an explosion. You know instinctively that men can't come this often to the brink without someone going over. One person too many is going to try to jump ahead in line. One particular set of toes is going to be stepped on by mistake. And the lid is going to blow.

The most frightening people here are the many young, intensely angry blacks. Hatred pours out in all of their speech and some of their actions. I could spend a lot of time imagining how and why they became so completely angry—but if I were the major, the counselor, or the man with the bullhorn, I wouldn't know how to divert them from that anger any more. Hundreds and hundreds of men here have been destroyed by alcohol or drugs. A smaller, but for me more poignant, number are being destroyed by hate.

Their loudest message—and because their voices are so strong it is very loud indeed—is "Respect me, man." The constant theme is that someone or some group is putting them down, stepping on them, asking them to conform to a code they don't accept, getting in their way, writing them off.

So most of the fights begin over turf. A place in line. A corner to control. The have-nots scrapping with the have-nots….

Tonight, I chose the Brooklyn shelter because I thought the buses going there would leave soonest. The shelter, a converted school, is on Williams Avenue and has about 400 beds.

We left in fairly good time but learned when we got to the shelter that no new beds would be assigned until after 11 P.M. We were to sit in the auditorium until then.

At about ten, a man herded as many of us newcomers as would listen to him into a corner of the auditorium. There he delivered an abusive diatribe outlining the horror that lay ahead for our possessions and our bodies during the night to come. It made the ranting at East 3rd Street seem tame.

It's illustrative of what the experience of homelessness and helplessness does to people that all of us—regardless of age, race, background, or health—listened so passively.

Only at midnight, when some other officials arrived, did we learn that this man had no standing whatsoever. He was just an underling who strutted for his time on the stage before any audience cowed enough to take what he dished out....

■ ■ ■ THURSDAY, 1/27

Back on the street this morning, I became conscious of how little time I had left to live this way. There seemed so much still to do, and so little time in which to do it.

One part of me tells me I have been fully a part of this. I know I walk with slower steps and bent shoulders.... I know I worry a lot more about keeping clean.

But then I recall how foolish that is, I'm acting. This will end tomorrow night. I can quit any time I want to. And unlike my mate from 47th Street, I haven't the slightest idea of what eleven years of sleeping on a grate amount to.

Early this afternoon, I went again to the Pavilion restaurant, where I had eaten five times before. I didn't recognize the man at the cash register.

"Get out," he said.

"But I have money."

"You heard me. Get out." His voice was stronger.

"That man knows me," I said, looking toward the owner in the back of the restaurant.

The owner nodded, and the man at the register said, "Okay, but sit in the back."

If this life in the streets had been real, I'd have gone out the door at the first "Get out." And the assessment of me as not worthy would have been self-fulfilling; I'd have lost so much respect for myself that I wouldn't have been worthy of being served the next time. The downward spiral would have begun.

Until now I haven't understood the extent of nicotine addiction. Dependencies on drugs and alcohol have been around me for a long time, but I thought before that smoking was a bad habit rather easy to overcome.

How many times have I, a nonsmoker, been begged for a cigarette in these days? Surely hundreds. Cigarettes are central. A few folks give them away, a small number sell them for up to 8 cents apiece, and almost all give that last pathetic end of a butt to the first man who asks for what little bit is left. I know addiction now as I didn't before.

Tonight, after a repeat of the totally degrading dinner-line scene at East 3rd Street, I signed up for Keener once again. No more Brooklyn for me.

Sitting upstairs with the other Keener-bound men, I carelessly put my left foot on the rung of the chair in front of me, occupied by a young black.

"Get your foot off, yo."

("Yo" means "Hey, there," "Watch yourself," "Move along," and much more.)

I took it off. "Sorry," I said.

But it was too late. I had broken a cardinal rule. I had violated the man's turf. As we stood in the stairwell waiting for the buses, he told a much bigger, much louder, much angrier friend what I had done.

That man turned on me.

"Wait till we get you tonight, whitey. You stink. Bad. The worst I've ever smelled. And when you put your foot on that chair, you spread your stink around. You better get yourself a shower as soon as we get there, but it won't save you later on.... And don't sit near me or him on the bus. You hear, whitey?"

I didn't reply.

The bombardment went on as we mounted the bus. No one spoke up in my defense. Three people waved me away when I tried to sit next to them. The next person, black and close to my age, made no objection when I sat beside him.

The big man continued to tirade for a while, but he soon got interested in finding out from the driver how to go about getting a bus-driver's license. Perhaps he had come down from a high.

I admit I was scared. I wrote my name, address, and office telephone number on a piece of paper and slipped it into my pocket. At least someone would know where to call if the threats were real. I knew I couldn't and wouldn't defend myself in this setting.

While we stood in line on Wards Island waiting for our bed assignments, there were plenty of gripes about the man who was after me. But no one said anything directly to him. Somehow it didn't seem that this was the night when the meek would inherit the earth.

I slept fitfully. I don't like lying with the sheet hiding my face.

■ ■ ■   **FRIDAY, 1/28**

I was up and out of Keener as early as possible. That meant using some of my little remaining money for a city-bus ride back to Manhattan, but it was worth it to get out of there.

After breakfast on East 3rd Street, I was finished with the public shelters. That was an easy break for me to make, because I had choices and could run.

The day was cold and, for the early hours, clear. I washed the memory of the big man at 3rd Street out of my mind by wandering through the Fulton Fish Market. I walked across the Brooklyn Bridge and even sang as I realized how free I was to relax and enjoy its beauty.

With a cup of coffee and the *Times*, I sat on a cinder block by the river and read. In time, I wandered through the Wall Street district and almost learned the lay of some of the streets.

I walked up to the Quaker Meeting House at Rutherford Place and 15th Street. Standing on the porch outside, I tried hard to think how the doctrine that "there is that of God in every person" applied to that man last night and to some of the others I had encountered in these ten days. I still think it applies, but it isn't always easy to see how....

Darkness came. I got kicked out of both the bus terminal and Grand Central. I got my normal clothes out of the locker at Penn Station, changed in the men's room, and rode the AA train home.

My apartment was warm, and the bed was clean.

That's the onliest thing.

Extreme Isolation

Kingsley Davis

introduction ■ ■ ■ ■

One of the questions that sociologists and other social scientists have wrestled with is the extent to which biology and society (or nature and nurture) contribute to what we become. As stressed in *Core Concepts*, sociologists almost invariably side with society or nurture. The subject of sociology is society (or social groups), and the dominant view in sociology is that, beyond the body itself, nature (biology) contributes little to human behavior.

The contributions of the social group to human behavior certainly reach much farther than most of us realize. Our speech, for example, helps to shape our basic attitudes and orientations to life. The social group may even contribute characteristics that most of us presume are biological, such as our ability to walk. The opening vignette to the chapter on socialization is based on an event that occurred in the 1940s. Here is the original report on this case of extreme isolation. Although it will not present any final answers to this age-old question, it should stir up your sociological imagination.

Thinking Critically

As you read this selection, ask yourself:

1. What is your opinion about the nature vs. nurture question? On what do you base your opinion?

2. What were the differences between Anna and Isabelle?

3. Based only on the cases of Anna and Isabelle, what can we conclude about the role of nature and nurture for the development of humans?

Early in 1940 there appeared…an account of a girl called Anna.[1] She had been deprived of normal contact and had received a minimum of human care for almost the whole of her first six years of life. At this time observations were not complete and the report had a tentative character. Now, however, the girl is dead, and with more

From Kingsley Davis, "Extreme Isolation," *American Journal of Sociology,* Vol. 52, pp. 432–437, 1947.

information available,[2] it is possible to give a fuller and more definitive description of the case from a sociological point of view.

Anna's death, caused by hemorrhagic jaundice, occurred on August 6, 1942. Having been born on March 1 or 6,[3] 1932, she was approximately ten and a half years of age when she died. The previous report covered her development up to the age of almost eight years; the present one recapitulates the earlier period on the basis of new evidence and then covers the last two and a half years of her life.

■ ■ ■ **EARLY HISTORY**

The first few days and weeks of Anna's life were complicated by frequent changes of domicile. It will be recalled that she was an illegitimate child, the second such child born to her mother, and that her grandfather, a widowed farmer in whose house her mother lived, strongly disapproved of this new evidence of the mother's indiscretion. This fact led to the baby's being shifted about.

Two weeks after being born in a nurse's private home, Anna was brought to the family farm, but the grandfather's antagonism was so great that she was shortly taken to the house of one of her mother's friends. At this time a local minister became interested in her and took her to his house with an idea of possible adoption. He decided against adoption, however, when he discovered that she had vaginitis. The infant was then taken to a children's home in the nearest large city. This agency found that at the age of only three weeks she was already in a miserable condition, being "terribly galled and otherwise in very bad shape." It did not regard her as a likely subject for adoption but took her in for a while anyway, hoping to benefit her. After Anna had spent nearly eight weeks in this place, the agency notified her mother to come and get her. The mother responded by sending a man and his wife to the children's home with a view to their adopting Anna, but they made such a poor impression on the agency that permission was refused. Later the mother came herself and took the child out of the home and then gave her to this couple. It was in the home of this pair that a social worker found the girl a short time thereafter. The social worker went to the mother's home and pleaded with Anna's grandfather to allow the mother to bring the child home. In spite of threats, he refused. The child, by then more than four months old, was next taken to another children's home in a near-by town. A medical examination at this time revealed that she had impetigo, vaginitis, umbilical hernia, and a skin rash.

Anna remained in this second children's home for nearly three weeks, at the end of which time she was transferred to a private foster-home. Since, however, the grandfather would not, and the mother could not, pay for the child's care, she was finally taken back as a last resort to the grandfather's house (at the age of five and a half months). There she remained, kept on the second floor in an attic-like room because her mother hesitated to incur the grandfather's wrath by bringing her downstairs.

The mother, a sturdy woman weighing about 180 pounds, did a man's work on the farm. She engaged in heavy work such as milking cows and tending hogs and had little time for her children. Sometimes she went out at night, in which case Anna was left entirely without attention. Ordinarily, it seems, Anna received only enough care to keep her barely alive. She appears to have been seldom moved from one position to another. Her clothing and bedding were filthy. She apparently had no instruction, no friendly attention.

It is little wonder that, when finally found and removed from the room in the grandfather's house at the age of nearly six years, the child could not talk, walk, or do anything that showed intelligence. She was in an extremely emaciated and undernourished condition, with skeletonlike legs and a bloated abdomen. She had been fed on virtually nothing except cow's milk during the years under her mother's care.

Anna's condition when found, and her subsequent improvement, have been described in the previous report. It now remains to say what happened to her after that.

■ ■ ■ LATER HISTORY

In 1939, nearly two years after being discovered, Anna had progressed, as previously reported, to the point where she could walk, understand simple commands, feed herself, achieve some neatness, remember people, etc. But she still did not speak, and, though she was much more like a normal infant of something over one year of age in mentality, she was far from normal for her age.

On August 30, 1939, she was taken to a private home for retarded children, leaving the county home where she had been for more than a year and a half. In her new setting she made some further progress, but not a great deal. In a report of an examination made November 6 of the same year, the head of the institution pictured the child as follows:

> Anna walks about aimlessly, makes periodic rhythmic motions of her hands, and, at intervals, makes guttural and sucking noises. She regards her hands as if she had seen them for the first time. It was impossible to hold her attention for more than a few seconds at a time—not because of distraction due to external stimuli but because of her inability to concentrate. She ignored the task in hand to gaze vacantly about the room. Speech is entirely lacking. Numerous unsuccessful attempts have been made with her in the hope of developing initial sounds. I do not believe that this failure is due to negativism or deafness but that she is not sufficiently developed to accept speech at this time.... The prognosis is not favorable....

More than five months later, on April 25, 1940, a clinical psychologist, the late Professor Francis N. Maxfield, examined Anna and reported the following: large for her age; hearing "entirely normal"; vision apparently normal; able to climb stairs; speech in the "babbling stage" and "promise for developing intelligible speech later seems to be good." He said further that "on the Merrill-Palmer scale she made a mental score of 19 months. On the Vineland social maturity scale she made a score of 23 months.[4]

Professor Maxfield very sensibly pointed out that prognosis is difficult in such cases of isolation. "It is very difficult to take scores on tests standardized under average conditions of environment and experience," he wrote, "and interpret them in a case where environment and experience have been so unusual." With this warning he gave it as his opinion at that time that Anna would eventually "attain an adult mental level of six or seven years."[5]

The school for retarded children, on July 1, 1941, reported that Anna had reached 46 inches in height and weighed 60 pounds. She could bounce and catch a ball and was said to conform to group socialization, though as a follower rather than a leader. Toilet habits were firmly established. Food habits were normal, except that she still used a spoon as her sole implement. She could dress herself except for fastening her clothes. Most remarkable of all, she had finally begun to develop speech. She was characterized as being at about the two-year level in this regard. She could call attendants by name and bring in one when she was asked to. She had a few complete sentences to express her wants. The report concluded that there was nothing peculiar about her, except that she was feebleminded—"probably congenital in type."[6]

A final report from the school made on June 22, 1942, and evidently the last report before the girl's death, pictured only a slight advance over that given above. It said that Anna could follow directions, string beads, identify a few colors, build with blocks, and differentiate between attractive and unattractive pictures. She had a good sense of rhythm and loved a doll. She talked mainly in phrases but would repeat words and try to carry on a conversation. She was clean about clothing. She habitually washed her hands and brushed her teeth. She would try to help other children. She walked well and could run fairly well, though clumsily. Although easily excited, she had a pleasant disposition.

■ ■ ■ ■ INTERPRETATION

Such was Anna's condition just before her death. It may seem as if she had not made much progress, but one must remember the condition in which she had been found. One must recall that she had no glimmering of speech, absolutely no ability to walk, no sense of gesture, not the least capacity to feed herself even when the food was put in front of her, and no comprehension of cleanliness. She was so apathetic that it was hard to tell whether or not she could hear. And all this at the age of nearly six years. Compared with this condition, her capacities at the time of her death seem striking indeed, though they do not amount to much more than a two-and-a-half-year mental level. One conclusion therefore seems safe, namely, that her isolation prevented a considerable amount of mental development that was undoubtedly part of her capacity. Just what her original capacity was, of course, is hard to say; but her development after her period of confinement (including the ability to walk and run, to play, dress, fit into a social situation, and, above all, to speak) shows that she had at least this capacity—capacity that never could have been realized in her original condition of isolation.

A further question is this: What would she have been like if she had received a normal upbringing from the moment of birth? A definitive answer would have been impossible in any case, but even an approximate answer is made difficult her early death. If one assumes, as was tentatively surmised in the previous report, that it is "almost impossible for any child to learn to speak, drink, and act like a normal person after a long period of early isolation," it seems likely that Anna might have had a normal or near-normal capacity genetically speaking. On the other hand, it was pointed out that Anna represented "a marginal case, [because] she was discovered before she had reached six years of age," an age "young enough to allow for some plasticity."[7] While admitting, then, that Anna's isolation *may* have been the major cause (and was certainly a minor cause) of her lack of rapid mental progress during the four and a half years following her rescue from neglect, it is necessary to entertain the hypothesis that she was congenitally deficient.

In connection with this hypothesis, one suggestive though by no means conclusive circumstance needs consideration, namely, the mentality of Anna's forebears. Information on this subject is easier to obtain, as one might guess, on the mother's than on the father's side. Anna's maternal grandmother, for example, is said to have been college educated and wished to have her children receive a good education, but her husband, Anna's stern grandfather, apparently a shrewd, hard-driving, calculating farmowner, was so penurious that her ambitions in this direction were thwarted. Under the circumstances her daughter (Anna's mother) managed, despite having to do hard work on the farm, to complete the eighth grade in a country school. Even so, however, the daughter was evidently not very smart. "A schoolmate of [Anna's mother] stated that she was retarded in school work; was very gullible at this age; and that her morals even at this time were discussed by other students." Two tests administered to her on March 4, 1938, when she was thirty-two years of age, showed that she was mentally deficient. On the Standard Revision of the Binet-Simon Scale her performance was equivalent to that of a child of eight years, giving her an I.Q. of 50 and indicating mental deficiency of "middle-grade moron type."[8]

As to the identity of Anna's father, the most persistent theory holds that he was an old man about seventy-four years of age at the time of the girl's birth. If he was the one, there is no indication of mental or other biological deficiency, whatever one may think of his morals. However, someone else may actually have been the father.

To sum up: Anna's heredity is the kind that *might* have given rise to innate mental deficiency, though not necessarily.

■ ■ ■ **COMPARISON WITH ANOTHER CASE**

Perhaps more to the point than speculations about Anna's ancestry would be a case for comparison. If a child could be discovered who had been isolated about the same length of time as Anna but had achieved a much quicker recovery and a greater mental development, it would be a stronger indication that Anna was deficient to start with.

Such a case does exist. It is the case of a girl found at about the same time as Anna and under strikingly similar circumstances. A full description of the details of this case has not been published, but in addition to newspaper reports, an excellent preliminary account by a speech specialist, Dr. Marie K. Mason, who played an important role in the handling of the child, has appeared.[9] Also the late Dr. Francis N. Maxfield, clinical psychologist at Ohio State University, as was Dr. Mason, has written an as yet unpublished but penetrating analysis of the case.[10] Some of his observations have been included in Professor Zingg's book on feral man.[11] The following discussion is drawn mainly from these enlightening materials. The writer, through the kindness of Professors Mason and Maxfield, did have a chance to observe the girl in April, 1940, and to discuss the features of her case with them.

Born apparently one month later than Anna, the girl in question, who has been given the pseudonym Isabelle, was discovered in November, 1938, nine months after the discovery of Anna. At the time she was found she was approximately six and a half years of age. Like Anna, she was an illegitimate child and had been kept in seclusion for that reason. Her mother was a deaf-mute, having become so at the age of two, and it appears that she and Isabelle had spent most of their time together in a dark room shut off from the rest of the mother's family. As a result Isabelle had no chance to develop speech; when she communicated with her mother, it was by means of gestures. Lack of sunshine and inadequacy of diet had caused Isabelle to become rachitic. Her legs in particular were affected; they "were so bowed that as she stood erect the soles of her shoes came nearly flat together, and she got about with a skittering gait."[12] Her behavior toward strangers, especially men, was almost that of a wild animal, manifesting much fear and hostility. In lieu of speech she made only a strong croaking sound. In many ways she acted like an infant. "She was apparently utterly unaware of relationships of any kind. When presented with a ball for the first time, she held it in the palm of her hand, then reached out and stroked my face with it. Such behavior is comparable to that of a child of six months."[13] At first it was even hard to tell whether or not she could hear, so unused were her senses. Many of her actions resembled those of deaf children.

It is small wonder that, once it was established that she could hear, specialists working with her believed her to be feeble-minded. Even on nonverbal tests her performance was so low as to promise little for the future. Her first score on the Stanford-Binet was 19 months, practically at the zero point of the scale. On the Vineland social maturity scale her first score was 39, representing an age level of two and a half years.[14] "The general impression was that she was wholly uneducable and that any attempt to teach her to speak, after so long; a period of silence, would meet with failure."[15]

In spite of this interpretation, the individuals in charge of Isabelle launched a systematic and skillful program of training. It seemed hopeless at first. The approach had to be through pantomime and dramatization, suitable to an infant. It required one week of intensive effort before she even made her first attempt at vocalization. Gradually she began to respond, however, and, after the first hurdles had at last been overcome, a curious thing happened. She went through the usual stages of learning characteristic of the years from one to six not only in proper succession but far more rapidly than normal. In a little over two months after her first vocalization she was putting sentences together. Nine months after that she could identify words and sentences on the printed page, could write well, could add to ten, and could retell a story after hearing it. Seven months beyond this point she had a vocabulary of 1,500–2,000 words and was asking complicated questions. Starting from an educational level of between one and three years (depending on what aspect one considers), she had reached a normal level by the time she was eight and a half years old. In short, she covered in two years the stages of learning that ordinarily require six.[16] Or, to put it another way, her I.Q. trebled in a year and a half.[17] The speed with which she reached the normal level of mental development seems analogous to the recovery of body weight in a growing child after an illness, the recovery being achieved by an extra fast rate of growth for a period after the illness until normal weight for the given age is again attained.

When the writer saw Isabelle a year and a half after her discovery, she gave him the impression of being a very bright, cheerful, energetic little girl. She spoke well, walked and ran without trouble, and sang with gusto and accuracy. Today she is over fourteen years old, and has passed the sixth grade in a public school. Her teachers say that she participates in all school activities as normally as other children. Though older than her classmates, she has fortunately not physically matured too far beyond their level.[18]

Clearly the history of Isabelle's development is different from that of Anna's. In both cases there was exceedingly low, or rather blank, intellectual level to begin with. In both cases it seemed that the girl might be congenitally feeble-minded. In both a considerably higher level was reached later on. But the Ohio girl achieved a normal mentality within two years, whereas Anna was still markedly inadequate at the end of four and half years. This difference in achievement may suggest that Anna had less initial capacity. But an alternative hypothesis is possible.

One should remember that Anna never received the prolonged and expert attention that Isabelle received. The result of such attention, in the case of the Ohio girl, was to give her speech at an early stage, and her subsequent rapid development seems to have been a consequence of that. "Until Isabelle's speech and language development, she had all the characteristics of a feeble-minded child." Had Anna, who, from the standpoint of psychometric tests and early history, closely resembled this girl at the start, been given a mastery of speech at an earlier point by intensive training, her subsequent development might have been much more rapid.[19]

The hypothesis that Anna began with a sharply inferior mental capacity is therefore not established. Even if she were deficient to start with, we have no way of knowing how much so. Under ordinary conditions she might have been a dull normal or, like her mother, a moron. Even after the blight of her isolation, if she had lived to maturity, she might have finally reached virtually the full level of her capacity, whatever it may have been. That her isolation did have a profound effect upon her mentality, there can be no doubt. This is proved by the substantial degree of change during the four and a half years following her rescue.

Consideration of Isabelle's case serves to show, as Anna's case does not clearly show, that isolation up to the age of six, with failure to acquire any form of speech and hence failure to grasp nearly the whole world of cultural meaning, does not preclude the subsequent acquisition of these. Indeed, there seems to be a process of accelerated recovery in which the child goes through the mental stages at a more rapid rate than would be the case in normal development. Just what would be the maximum age at which a person could remain isolated and still retain the capacity for full cultural acquisition is hard to say. Almost certainly it would not be as high as age fifteen; it might possibly be as low as age ten. Undoubtedly various individuals would differ considerably as to the exact age.

Anna's is not an ideal case for showing the effects of extreme isolation, partly because she was possibly deficient to begin with, partly because she did not receive the best training available, and partly because she did not live long enough. Nevertheless, her case is instructive when placed in the record with numerous other cases of extreme isolation. This and the previous article about her are meant to place her in the record. It is to be hoped that other cases will be described in the scientific literature as they are discovered (as unfortunately they will be), for only in these rare cases of extreme isolation is it possible "to observe *concretely separated* two factors in the development of human personality which are always otherwise only analytically separated, the biogenic and the sociogenic factors."[20]

NOTES

1. Kingsley Davis, "Extreme Social Isolation of a Child," *American Journal of Sociology*, XLV (January, 1940), 554–65.

2. Sincere appreciation is due to the officials in the Department of Welfare, Commonwealth of Pennsylvania, for the kind cooperation in making available the records concerning Anna and discussing the case frankly with the writer. Helen C. Hubbell, Florentine Hackbusch, and Eleanor Mecklenburg were particularly helpful, as was Fanny L. Matchette. Without their aid neither of the reports on Anna could have been written.

3. The records are not clear as to which day.

4. Letter to one of the state officials in charge of the case.

5. *Ibid.*

6. Progress report of the school.

7. Davis, *op. cit.*, p. 564.

8. The facts set forth here as to Anna's ancestry are taken chiefly from a report of mental tests administered to Anna's mother by psychologists at a state hospital where she was taken for this purpose after the discovery of Anna's seclusion. This excellent report was not available to the writer when the previous paper on Anna was published.

9. Marie K. Mason, "Learning to Speak after Six and One-Half Years of Silence," *Journal of Speech Disorders*, VII (1942), 295–304.

10. Francis N. Maxfield, "What Happens When the Social Environment of a Child Approaches Zero." The writer is greatly indebted to Mrs. Maxfield and to Professor Horace B. English, a colleague of Professor Maxfield, for the privilege of seeing this manuscript and other materials collected on isolated and feral individuals.

11. J. A. L. Singh and Robert M. Zingg, *Wolf-Children and Feral Man* (New York: Harper & Bros., 1941), pp. 248–51.

12. Maxfield, unpublished manuscript cited above.

13. Mason, *op. cit.*, p. 299.

14. Maxfield, unpublished manuscript.

15. Mason, *op. cit.*, p. 299.

16. *Ibid.*, pp. 300–304.

17. Maxfield, unpublished manuscript.

18. Based on a personal letter from Dr. Mason to the writer, May 13, 1946.

19. This point is suggested in a personal letter from Dr. Mason to the writer, October 22, 1946.

20. Singh and Zingg, *op. cit.*, pp. xxi–xxii, in a foreword by the writer.

Anybody's Son Will Do

Gwynne Dyer

introduction ■ ▪ ■ ▪ ▪

To understand the term *socialization*, just substitute the word *learning*. Socialization does not refer only to children. All of us are being socialized all the time. Each time we are exposed to something new, we are being socialized. If we learn how to operate a new computer, play a new (or old) video game, watch a movie, read a book, or listen to a college lecture, we are being socialized. Even when we talk to a friend, socialization occurs. And socialization doesn't stop at a certain age. When we are old, we will still have experiences (even watching televised news) that influence our viewpoints. Socialization, then, is a lifelong process. You could say that in this process we are becoming more and more a part of our culture or of our subculture.

From the examples just given, you can see that socialization is usually gentle and gradual. But there are remarkable exceptions, and in this reading we look at one of them. Gwynne Dyer analyzes the process by which the U.S. Marine Corps turns young men into killers—and how this organization accomplishes such a drastic change in just a few weeks. As you will see, the Marines' techniques are brutal, swift, and effective.

Thinking Critically

As you read this selection, ask yourself:

1. How do the U.S. Marines socialize their recruits?

2. How do the socialization techniques of the Marines compare with the socialization techniques that have been used to bring you to your current place in life?

3. Why are the socialization techniques of the Marines so effective?

You think about it and you know you're going to have to kill but you don't understand the implications of that, because in the society in which you've lived murder is the most heinous of crimes...and you are in a situation in which it's turned the other way round....When you do actually kill someone the experience, my experience, was one of revulsion and disgust....

From *War: Past, Present, and Future*, by Gwynne Dyer. Copyright © 1985 by Media Resources. Reprinted with the permission of Crown Publishers, a division of Random House, Inc.

I was utterly terrified—petrified—but I knew there had to be a Japanese sniper in a small fishing shack near the shore. He was firing in the other direction at Marines in another battalion, but I knew as soon as he picked off the people there—there was a window on our side—that he would start picking us off. And there was nobody else to go...and so I ran towards the shack and broke in and found myself in an empty room....

There was a door which meant there was another room and the sniper was in that—and I just broke that down. I was just absolutely gripped by the fear that this man would expect me and would shoot me. But as it turned out he was in a sniper harness and he couldn't turn around fast enough. He was entangled in the harness so I shot him with a .45, and I felt remorse and shame. I can remember whispering foolishly, "I'm sorry" and then just throwing up....I threw up all over myself. It was a betrayal of what I'd been taught since a child.

—William Manchester

Yet he did kill the Japanese soldier, just as he had been trained to—the revulsion only came afterward. And even after Manchester knew what it was like to kill another human being, a young man like himself, he went on trying to kill his "enemies" until the war was over. Like all the other tens of millions of soldiers who had been taught from infancy that killing was wrong, and had then been sent off to kill for their countries, he was almost helpless to disobey, for he had fallen into the hands of an institution so powerful and so subtle that it could quickly reverse the moral training of a lifetime.

The whole vast edifice of the military institution rests on its ability to obtain obedience from its members even unto death—and the killing of others. It has enormous powers of compulsion at its command, of course, but all authority must be based ultimately on consent. The task of extracting that consent from its members has probably grown harder in recent times, for the gulf between the military and the civilian worlds has undoubtedly widened: Civilians no longer perceive the threat of violent death as an everyday hazard of existence, and the categories of people whom it is not morally permissible to kill have broadened to include (in peacetime) the entire human race. Yet the armed forces of every country can still take almost any young male civilian and turn him into a soldier with all the right reflexes and attitudes in only a few weeks. Their recruits usually have no more than twenty years' experience of the world, most of it as children, while the armies have had all of history to practice and perfect their techniques.

Just think of how the soldier is treated. While still a child he is shut up in the barracks. During his training he is always being knocked about. If he makes the least mistake he is beaten, a burning blow on his body, another on his eye, perhaps his head is laid open with a wound. He is battered and bruised with flogging. On the march...they hang heavy loads round his neck like that of an ass.

—Egyptian, ca. 1500 B.C.

The moment I talk to the new conscripts about the homeland I strike a land mine. So I kept quiet. Instead, I try to make soldiers of them. I give them hell from morning to sunset. They begin to curse me, curse the army, curse the state.

Then they begin to curse together, and become a truly cohesive group, a unit, a fighting unit.

—Israeli, ca. A.D. 1970

All soldiers belong to the same profession, no matter what country they serve, and it makes them different from everybody else. They have to be different, for their job is ultimately about killing and dying, and those things are not a natural vocation for any human being. Yet all soldiers are born civilians. The method for turning young men into soldiers—people who kill other people and expose themselves to death—is basic training. It's essentially the same all over the world, and it always has been, because young men everywhere are pretty much alike.

Human beings are fairly malleable, especially when they are young, and in every young man there are attitudes for any army to work with: the inherited values and postures, more or less dimly recalled, of the tribal warriors who were once the model for every young boy to emulate. Civilization did not involve a sudden clean break in the way people behave, but merely the progressive distortion and redirection of all the ways in which people in the old tribal societies used to behave, and modern definitions of maleness still contain a great deal of the old warrior ethic. The anarchic machismo of the primitive warrior is not what modern armies really need in their soldiers, but it does provide them with promising raw material for the transformation they must work in their recruits.

Just how this transformation is wrought varies from time to time and from country to country. In totally militarized societies—ancient Sparta, the samurai class of medieval Japan, the areas controlled by organizations like the Eritrean People's Liberation Front today—it begins at puberty or before, when the young boy is immersed in a disciplined society in which only the military values are allowed to penetrate. In more sophisticated modern societies, the process is briefer and more concentrated, and the way it works is much more visible. It is, essentially, a conversion process in an almost religious sense—and as in all conversion phenomena, the emotions are far more important than the specific ideas....

Armies know this. It is their business to get men to fight, and they have had a long time to work out the best way of doing it. All of them pay lip service to the symbols and slogans of their political masters, though the amount of time they must devote to this activity varies from country to country.... Nor should it be thought that the armies are hypocritical—most of their members really do believe in their particular national symbols and slogans. But their secret is that they know these are not the things that sustain men in combat.

What really enables men to fight is their own self-respect, and a special kind of love that has nothing to do with sex or idealism. Very few men have died in battle, when the moment actually arrived, for the United States of America or for the sacred cause of Communism, or even for their homes and families; if they had any choice in the matter at all, they chose to die for each other and for their own vision of themselves....

The way armies produce this sense of brotherhood in a peacetime environment is basic training: a feat of psychological manipulation on the grand scale which has been so consistently successful and so universal that we fail to notice it as remarkable.

In countries where the army must extract its recruits in their late teens, whether voluntarily or by conscription, from a civilian environment that does not share the military values, basic training involves a brief but intense period of indoctrination whose purpose is not really to teach the recruits basic military skills, but rather to change their values and their loyalties. "I guess you could say we brainwash them a little bit," admitted a U.S. Marine drill instructor, "but you know they're good people."

The duration and intensity of basic training, and even its major emphases, depend on what kind of society the recruits are coming from, and on what sort of military organization they are going to. It is obviously quicker to train men from a martial culture than from one in which the dominant values are civilian and commercial, and easier to deal with volunteers than with reluctant conscripts. Conscripts are not always unwilling, however; there are many instances in which the army is popular for economic reasons....

It's easier if you catch them young. You can train older men to be soldiers; it's done in every major war. But you can never get them to believe that they like it, which is the major reason armies try to get their recruits before they are 20. There are other reasons too, of course, like the physical fitness, lack of dependents, and economic dispensability of teenagers, that make armies prefer them, but the most important qualities teenagers bring to basic training are enthusiasm and naiveté. Many of them actively want the discipline and the closely structured environment that the armed forces will provide, so there is no need for the recruiters to deceive the kids about what will happen to them after they join.

> There is discipline. There is drill.... When you are relying on your mates and they are relying on you, there's no room for slackness or sloppiness. If you're not prepared to accept the rules, you're better off where you are.
> —British army recruiting advertisement, 1976

> People are not born soldiers, they become soldiers.... And it should not begin at the moment when a new recruit is enlisted into the ranks, but rather much earlier, at the time of the first signs of maturity, during the time of adolescent dreams.
> —Red Star (Soviet army newspaper), 1973

Young civilians who have volunteered and have been accepted by the Marine Corps arrive at Parris Island, the Corps's East Coast facility for basic training, in a state of considerable excitement and apprehension: Most are aware that they are about to undergo an extraordinary and very difficult experience. But they do not make their own way to the base; rather, they trickle in to Charleston airport on various flights throughout the day on which their training platoon is due to form, and are held there, in a state of suppressed but mounting nervous tension, until late in the evening. When the buses finally come to carry them the seventy-six miles to Parris Island, it is often after midnight—and this is not an administrative oversight. The shock treatment they are about to receive will work most efficiently if they are worn out and somewhat disoriented when they arrive.

The basic training organization is a machine, processing several thousand young men every month, and every facet and gear of it has been designed with the sole purpose of turning civilians into Marines as efficiently as possible. Provided it can have total control over their bodies and their environment for approximately three months, it can practically guarantee converts. Parris Island provides that controlled environment, and the recruits do not set foot outside it again until they graduate as Marine privates eleven weeks later.

> *They're allowed to call home, so long as it doesn't get out of hand—every three weeks or so they can call home and make sure everything's all right, if they haven't gotten a letter or there's a particular set of circumstances. If it's a case of an emergency call coming in, then they're allowed to accept that call; if not, one of my staff will take the message....*
>
> *In some cases I'll get calls from parents who haven't quite gotten adjusted to the idea that their son had cut the strings—and in a lot of cases that's what they're doing. The military provides them with an opportunity to leave home but they're still in a rather secure environment.*
>
> —Captain Brassington, USMC

For the young recruits, basic training is the closest thing their society can offer to a formal rite of passage, and the institution probably stands in an unbroken line of descent from the lengthy ordeals by which young males in precivilized groups were initiated into the adult community of warriors. But in civilized societies it is a highly functional institution whose product is not anarchic warriors, but trained soldiers.

Basic training is not really about teaching people skills; it's about changing them, so that they can do things they wouldn't have dreamt of otherwise. It works by applying enormous physical and mental pressure to men who have been isolated from their normal civilian environment and placed in one where the only right way to think and behave is the way the Marine Corps wants them to. The key word the men who run the machine use to describe this process is *motivation*.

> *I can motivate a recruit and in third phase, if I tell him to jump off the third deck, he'll jump off the third deck. Like I said before, it's a captive audience and I can train that guy; I can get him to do anything I want him to do.... They're good kids and they're out to do the right thing. We get some bad kids, but you know, we weed those out. But as far as motivation—here, we can motivate them to do anything you want, in recruit training.*
>
> —USMC drill instructor, Parris Island

The first three days the raw recruits spend at Parris Island are actually relatively easy, though they are hustled and shouted at continuously. It is during this time that they are documented and inoculated, receive uniforms, and learn the basic orders of drill that will enable young Americans (who are not very accustomed to this aspect of life) to do everything simultaneously in large groups. But the most important thing that happens in "forming" is the surrender of the recruits' own clothes, their hair—all the physical evidence of their individual civilian identities.

During a period of only 72 hours, in which they are allowed little sleep, the recruits lay aside their former lives in a series of hasty rituals (like being shaven to the scalp) whose symbolic significance is quite clear to them even though they are quite deliberately given absolutely no time for reflection, or any hint that they might have the option of turning back from their commitment. The men in charge of them know how delicate a tightrope they are walking, though, because at this stage the recruits are still newly caught civilians who have not yet made their ultimate inward submission to the discipline of the Corps.

> *Forming Day One makes me nervous. You've got a whole new mob of recruits, you know, 60 or 70 depending, and they don't know anything. You don't know what kind of a reaction you're going to get from the stress you're going to lay on them, and it just worries me the first day....*
>
> *Things could happen, I'm not going to lie to you. Something might happen. A recruit might decide he doesn't want any part of this stuff and maybe take a poke at you or something like that. In a situation like that it's going to be a spur-of-the-moment thing and that worries me.*
>
> —USMC drill instructor

But it rarely happens. The frantic bustle of forming is designed to give the recruit no time to think about resisting what is happening to him. And so the recruits emerge from their initiation into the system, stripped of their civilian clothes, shorn of their hair, and deprived of whatever confidence in their own identity they may previously have had as 18-year-olds, like so many blanks ready to have the Marine identity impressed upon them.

The first stage in any conversion process is the destruction of an individual's former beliefs and confidence, and his reduction to a position of helplessness and need. It isn't really as drastic as all that, of course, for three days cannot cancel out 18 years; the inner thoughts and the basic character are not erased. But the recruits have already learned that the only acceptable behavior is to repress any unorthodox thoughts and to mimic the character the Marine Corps wants. Nor are they, on the whole, reluctant to do so, for they *want* to be Marines. From the moment they arrive at Parris Island, the vague notion that has been passed down for a thousand generations that masculinity means being a warrior becomes an explicit article of faith, relentlessly preached: To be a man means to be a Marine.

There are very few 18-year-old boys who do not have highly romanticized ideas of what it means to be a man, so the Marine Corps has plenty of buttons to push. And it starts pushing them on the first day of real training: The officer in charge of the formation appears before them for the first time, in full dress uniform with medals, and tells them how to become men.

> *The United States Marine Corps has 205 years of illustrious history to speak for itself. You have made the most important decision in your life...by signing your name, your life, pledge to the Government of the United States, and even more importantly, to the United States Marine Corps—a brotherhood, an elite unit. In 10.3 weeks you are going to become a member of that history, those traditions, this organization—if you have what it takes....*
>
> *All of you want to do that by virtue of your signing your name as a man. The Marine Corps says that we build men. Well, I'll go a little bit further. We develop the tools that you have—and everybody has those tools to a certain extent right*

now. We're going to give you the blueprints, and we are going to show you how to build a Marine. You've got to build a Marine—you understand?

—Captain Pingree, USMC

The recruits, gazing at him with awe and adoration, shout in unison, "Yes, sir!" just as they have been taught. They do it willingly, because they are volunteers—but even conscripts tend to have the romantic fervor of volunteers if they are only 18 years old. Basic training, whatever its hardships, is a quick way to become a man among men, with an undeniable status, and beyond the initial consent to undergo it, it doesn't even require any decisions.

I had just dropped out of high school and I wasn't doing much on the street except hanging out, as most teenagers would be doing. So they gave me an opportunity— a recruiter picked me up, gave me a good line, and said that I could make it in the Marines, that I have a future ahead of me. And since I was living with my parents, I figured that I could start my own life here and grow up a little.

—USMC recruit

I like the hand-to-hand combat and...things like that. It's a little rough going on me, and since I have a small frame I would like to become deadly, as I would put it. I like to have them words, especially the way they've been teaching me here.

—USMC recruit (from Brooklyn), Parris Island

The training, when it starts, seems impossibly demanding physically for most of the recruits—and then it gets harder week by week. There is a constant barrage of abuse and insults aimed at the recruits, with the deliberate purpose of breaking down their pride and so destroying their ability to resist the transformation of values and attitudes that the Corps intends them to undergo. At the same time the demands for constant alertness and for instant obedience are continuously stepped up, and the standards by which the dress and behavior of the recruits are judged become steadily more unforgiving. But it is all carefully calculated by the men who run the machine, who think and talk in terms of the stress they are placing on the recruits: "We take so many c.c.'s of stress and we administer it to each man—they should be a little bit scared and they should be unsure, but they're adjusting." The aim is to keep the training arduous but just within most of the recruits' capability to withstand. One of the most striking achievements of the drill instructors is to create and maintain the illusion that basic training is an extraordinary challenge, one that will set those who graduate apart from others, when in fact almost everyone can succeed.

There has been some preliminary weeding out of potential recruits even before they begin training, to eliminate the obviously unsuitable minority, and some people do "fail" basic training and get sent home, at least in peacetime. The standards of acceptable performance in the U.S. armed forces, for example, tend to rise and fall in inverse proportion to the number and quality of recruits available to fill the forces to the authorized manpower levels. But there are very few young men who cannot be turned into passable soldiers if the forces are willing to invest enough effort in it.

Not even physical violence is necessary to effect the transformation, though it has been used by most armies at most times.

It's not what it was 15 years ago down here. The Marine Corps still occupies the position of a tool which the society uses when it feels like that is a resort that they have to fall to. Our society changes as all societies do, and our society felt that through enlightened training methods we could still produce the same product— and when you examine it, they're right.... Our 100 c.c.'s of stress is really all we need, not two gallons of it, which is what used to be.... In some cases with some of the younger drill instructors it was more an initiation than it was an acute test, and so we introduced extra officers and we select our drill instructors to "fine-tune" it.
—Captain Brassington, USMC

There is, indeed, a good deal of fine-tuning in the roles that the men in charge of training any specific group of recruits assume. At the simplest level, there is a sort of "good cop–bad cop" manipulation of the recruits' attitudes toward those applying the stress. The three younger drill instructors with a particular serial are quite close to them in age and unremittingly harsh in their demands for ever higher performance, but the senior drill instructor, a man almost old enough to be their father, plays a more benevolent and understanding part and is available for individual counseling. And generally offstage, but always looming in the background, is the company commander, an impossibly austere and almost godlike personage.

At least these are the images conveyed to the recruits, although of course all these men cooperate closely with an identical goal in view. It works: In the end they become not just role models and authority figures, but the focus of the recruits' developing loyalty to the organization.

I imagine there's some fear, especially in the beginning, because they don't know what to expect.... I think they hate you at first, at least for a week or two, but it turns to respect.... They're seeking discipline, they're seeking someone to take charge, 'cause at home they never got it.... They're looking to be told what to do and then someone is standing there enforcing what they tell them to do, and it's kind of like the father-and-son game, all the way through. They form a fatherly image of the DI whether they want to or not.
—Sergeant Carrington, USMC

Just the sheer physical exercise, administered in massive doses, soon has the recruits feeling stronger and more competent than ever before. Inspections, often several times daily, quickly build up their ability to wear the uniform and carry themselves like real Marines, which is a considerable source of pride. The inspections also help to set up the pattern in the recruits of unquestioning submission to military authority: Standing stock-still, staring straight ahead, while somebody else examines you closely for faults is about as extreme a ritual act of submission as you can make with your clothes on.

But they are not submitting themselves merely to the abusive sergeant making unpleasant remarks about the hair in their nostrils. All around them are deliberate reminders—the flags and insignia displayed on parade, the military music, the marching formations and drill instructors' cadenced calls—of the idealized organization, the "brotherhood" to which they will be admitted as full members if they submit and conform. Nowhere in the armed forces are the military courtesies so elaborately observed, the staffs' uniforms so immaculate (some DIs change several times a day), and the ritual aspects of military life so highly visible as on a basic training establishment.

Even the seeming inanity of close-order drill has a practical role in the conversion process. It has been over a century since mass formations of men were of any use on the battlefield, but every army in the world still drills its troops, especially during basic training, because marching in formation, with every man moving his body in the same way at the same moment, is a direct physical way of learning two things a soldier must believe: that orders have to be obeyed automatically and instantly, and that you are no longer an individual, but part of a group.

The recruits' total identification with the other members of their unit is the most important lesson of all, and everything possible is done to foster it. They spend almost every waking moment together—a recruit alone is an anomaly to be looked into at once—and during most of that time they are enduring shared hardships. They also undergo collective punishments, often for the misdeed or omission of a single individual (talking in the ranks, a bed not swept under during barracks inspection), which is a highly effective way of suppressing any tendencies toward individualism. And, of course, the DIs place relentless emphasis on competition with other "serials" in training: there may be something infinitely pathetic to outsiders about a marching group of anonymous recruits chanting, "Lift your heads and hold them high, 3313 is a-passin' by," but it doesn't seem like that to the men in the ranks.

Nothing is quite so effective in building up a group's morale and solidarity, though, as a steady diet of small triumphs. Quite early in basic training, the recruits begin to do things that seem, at first sight, quite dangerous: descend by ropes from fifty-foot towers, cross yawning gaps hand-over-hand on high wires (known as the Slide for Life, of course), and the like. The common denominator is that these activities are daunting but not really dangerous: the ropes will prevent anyone from falling to his death off the rappelling tower, and there is a pond of just the right depth—deep enough to cushion a falling man, but not deep enough that he is likely to drown—under the Slide for Life. The goal is not to kill recruits, but to build up their confidence as individuals and as a group by allowing them to overcome apparently frightening obstacles.

> *You have an enemy here at Parris Island. The enemy that you're going to have at Parris Island is in every one of us. It's in the form of cowardice. The most rewarding experience you're going to have in recruit training is standing on line every evening, and you'll be able to look into each other's eyes, and you'll be able to say to each other with your eyes: "By God, we've made it one more day! We've defeated the coward."*
>
> —Captain Pingree

> *Number on deck, sir, 45…highly motivated, truly dedicated, rompin', stompin', bloodthirsty, kill-crazy United States Marine Corps recruits, SIR!*
>
> —Marine chant, Parris Island

If somebody does fail a particular test, he tends to be alone, for the hurdles are deliberately set low enough that most recruits can clear them if they try. In any large group of people there is usually a goat: someone whose intelligence or manner or lack of physical stamina marks him for failure and contempt. The competent drill instructor, without deliberately setting up this unfortunate individual for disgrace, will use his failure to strengthen the solidarity and confidence of the rest. When one hapless young man fell off the Slide for Life into the pond, for example, his drill instructor shouted the usual invective—"Well, get out of the water. Don't contaminate it all day"—and then delivered the payoff line: "Go back and change your clothes. You're useless to your unit now."

"Useless to your unit" is the key phrase, and all the recruits know that what it means is "useless in *battle.*" The Marine drill instructors at Parris Island know exactly what they are doing to the recruits, and why. They are not rear-echelon people filling comfortable jobs, but the most dedicated and intelligent NCOs the Marine Corps can find; even now, many of them have combat experience. The Corps has a clear-eyed understanding of precisely what it is training its recruits for—combat—and it ensures that those who do the training keep that objective constantly in sight.

The DIs "stress" the recruits, feed them their daily ration of synthetic triumphs over apparent obstacles, and bear in mind all the time that the goal is to instill the foundations for the instinctive, selfless reactions and the fierce group loyalty that is what the recruits will need if they ever see combat. They are arch-manipulators, fully conscious of it, and utterly unashamed. These kids have signed up as Marines, and they could well see combat; this is the way they have to think if they want to live.

> *I've seen guys come to Vietnam from all over. They were all sorts of people that had been scared—some of them had been scared all their life and still scared. Some of them had been a country boy, city boys—you know, all different kinds of people—but when they got in combat they all reacted the same—99 percent of them reacted the same.... A lot of it is training here at Parris Island, but the other part of it is survival. They know if they don't conform—conform I call it, but if they don't react in the same way other people are reacting, they won't survive. That's just it. You know, if you don't react together, then nobody survives.*
> —USMC drill instructor, Parris Island

> *When I went to boot camp and did individual combat training they said if you walk into an ambush what you want to do is just do a right face—you just turn right or left, whichever way the fire is coming from, and assault. I said, "Man, that's crazy. I'd never do anything like that. It's stupid."...*
>
> *The first time we came under fire, on Hill 1044 in Operation Beauty Canyon in Laos, we did it automatically. Just like you look at your watch to see what time it is. We done a right face, assaulted the hill—a fortified position with concrete bunkers emplaced, machine guns, automatic weapons—and we took it. And we killed—I'd estimate probably 35 North Vietnamese soldiers in the assault, and we only lost three killed. I think it was about two or three, and about eight or ten wounded....*
>
> *But you know, what they teach you, it doesn't faze you until it comes down to the time to use it, but it's in the back of your head, like, What do you do when you come to a stop sign? It's in the back of your head, and you react automatically.*
> —USMC sergeant

Combat is the ultimate reality that Marines—or any other soldiers, under any flag—have to deal with. Physical fitness, weapons training, battle drills, are all indispensable elements of basic training, and it is absolutely essential that the recruits learn the attitudes of group loyalty and interdependency which will be their sole hope of survival and success in combat. The training inculcates or fosters all of those things, and even by the halfway point in the 11-week course, the recrults are generally responding with enthusiasm to their tasks....

In basic training establishments,...the malleability is all one way: in the direction of submission to military authority and the internalization of military values. What a place like Parris Island produces when it is successful, as it usually is, is a soldier who will kill because that is his job.

Streetwise

Elijah Anderson

introduction ▪ ▪ ▪ ▪ ▪

The city can be a dangerous place, and all of us avoid certain areas of the city. Those areas make us uncomfortable. They seem threatening, foreboding places where we can expect the worst. We help control our lives by sticking to areas with which we are familiar and comfortable. Part of the discomfort that we feel in some areas is because we don't know the norms of interaction. We know that different things are expected there, but we don't know exactly what.

In this reading, Elijah Anderson analyzes interaction on city streets. For 14 years, he did participant observation in a changing neighborhood of Philadelphia that he refers to as the Village-Northton. The Village has undergone *gentrification*, a process by which the relatively affluent move into an urban area inhabited by the poor and renovate the buildings. Next to the Village is a ghetto, from where high crime spills over into the Village. Consequently, for the relatively affluent African Americans and whites who live in the Village, the presence of strangers makes even walking down the street a problem, and the middle class interacts uneasily with the poor. This selection examines public interaction when distrust and the threat of violence enshroud people's relationships.

Thinking Critically

As you read this selection, ask yourself:

1. Are there areas of the city (or entire cities, perhaps) that you avoid? Apply ideas in this article to explain why you avoid those areas.

2. If you lived in the Village-Northton, how would your interactions be different from what they now are? Exactly what behaviors would you change?

3. If you lived in the Village-Northton, how could you tell a mugger from a regular person?

An overwhelming number of young black males in the Village are committed to civility and law-abiding behavior. They often have a hard time convincing others of this, however, because of the stigma attached to their skin color, age, gender, appear-

ance, and general style of self-presentation. Moreover, most residents ascribe criminality, incivility, toughness, and street smartness to the anonymous black male, who
must work hard to make others trust his common decency.

This state of affairs is worth exploring [because]...the situation of young black
men as a group encapsulates the stigmatizing effect of "negative" status-determining
characteristics, in this case gender and race. Because public encounters between
strangers on the streets of urban America are by nature brief, the participants must
draw conclusions about each other quickly, and they generally rely on a small number of cues. This process is universal, and it unavoidably involves some prejudging—
prejudice—but its working out is especially prominent in the public spaces of the
Village-Northton....

The residents of the area, including black men themselves, are likely to defer to
unknown black males, who move convincingly through the area as though they
"run it," exuding a sense of ownership. They are easily perceived as symbolically in-
serting themselves into any available social space, pressing against those who might
challenge them. The young black males, the "big winners" of these little competi-
tions, seem to feel very comfortable as they swagger confidently along. Their looks,
their easy smiles, and their spontaneous laughter, singing, cursing, and talk about
the intimate details of their lives, which can be followed from across the street, all
convey the impression of little concern for other pedestrians. The other pedestrians,
however, are very concerned about them....

People, black or white, who are more familiar with the black street culture are
less troubled by sharing the streets with young black males. Older black men, for instance, frequently adopt a refined set of criteria. In negotiating the streets, they
watch out particularly for a certain *kind* of young black male: "jitterbugs" or those
who might belong to "wolf packs," small bands of black teenage boys believed to
travel about the urban areas accosting and robbing people.

Many members of the Village community, however, both black and white, lack
these more sophisticated insights. Incapable of making distinctions between law-
abiding black males and others, they rely for protection on broad stereotypes based
on color and gender, if not outright racism. They are likely to misread many of the
signs displayed by law-abiding black men, thus becoming apprehensive of almost
any black male they spot in public.... The "master status-determining characteristic" of race (Hughes 1945) is at work in the most casual street encounter. Becker's
application of Hughes's conception of the contradictions and dilemmas of status has
special relevance:

> Some statuses, in our society as in others, override all other statuses and have a certain
> priority. Race is one of these. Membership in the Negro race, as socially defined, will
> override most other status considerations in most situations; the fact that one is a phy-
> sician or middle class or female will not protect one from being treated as a Negro first
> and any of these other things second. The status of deviant (depending on the kind of

deviance) is this kind of master status. One receives the status as a result of breaking a rule, and the identification proves to be more important than most others. One will be identified as a deviant first, before other identifications are made. The question raised: "What kind of person would break such an important rule?" And the answer given: "One who is different from the rest of us, who cannot or will not act as a moral human being and therefore might break other important rules." The deviant identification becomes the controlling one.

Treating a person as though he were generally rather than specifically deviant produces a self-fulfilling prophecy. It sets in motion several mechanisms which conspire to shape the person in the image people have of him. (Becker 1963: 33, 34)

In the minds of many Village residents, black and white, the master status of the young black male is determined by his youth, his blackness, his maleness, and what these attributes have come to stand for in the shadow of the ghetto....

Because public interactions generally matter for only a few crucial seconds, people are conditioned to rapid scrutiny of the looks, speech, public behavior, gender, and color of those sharing the environment.... The central strategy in maintaining safety on the streets is to avoid strange black males. The public awareness is color-coded: white skin denotes civility, law abidingness, and trustworthiness, while black skin is strongly associated with poverty, crime, incivility, and distrust. Thus an unknown young black male is readily deferred to. If he asks for anything, he must be handled quickly and summarily. If he is persistent, help must be summoned.

This simplistic racial interpretation of crime creates a "we/they" dichotomy between whites and blacks. Yet here again the underlying issue is class.... Middle-income blacks in the Village, who also are among the "haves," often share a victim mentality with middle-income whites and appear just as distrustful of black strangers. Believing they are immune to the charge of racism, Village blacks make some of the same remarks as whites do, sometimes voicing even more incisive observations concerning "street blacks" and black criminality....

■ ■ ■ ■ STREET ETIQUETTE

A set of informal rules has emerged among residents and other users of the public spaces of the Village. These rules allow members of diverse groups orderly passage with the promise of security, or at least a minimum of trouble and conflict.... The process begins something like this. One person sees another walking down the street alone, with another person, or perhaps with a few others. Those seen might be getting out of an unusual car, riding a ten-speed bicycle, walking a dog, strolling on the grounds of a dwelling in the neighborhood, or simply crossing the street at the light or leaving a store carrying groceries. The sight of people engaging in such everyday activities helps to convey what may be interpreted as the usual picture of public life—what residents take for granted.

Skin color, gender, age, dress, and comportment are important markers that characterize and define the area. Depending on the observer's biases, such specific markers can become the most important characteristics determining the status of those being watched, superseding other meaningful attributes. However, the most important aspect of the situation is simply that the observer takes mental note of the other person: a significant social contact, though usually not a reciprocal one, is made. The person seen, and the category he or she is believed to represent, comes to be considered an ordinary part of the environment.

Although the initial observation is important, it is not the crucial element in "knowing about" others and feeling comfortable. Rather, it helps determine the social context for any other meaningful interactions, whether unilateral or bilateral. It gives users of the streets a sense of whom to expect where and when, and it allows them to adjust their plans accordingly.

The significance of the initial encounter is contingent upon subsequent meetings and interactions. If the person is never seen again, the encounter gradually loses significance. But if the observer sees the person again or meets others who are similar, the initial impression may become stronger and might develop into a theory about the category of people, a working conception of a social type. The strength of such impressions—nurtured and supported through repeated encounters, observations, and talk with other residents—gradually builds.

Background information and knowledge may provide a basis for social connection. A stranger may be seen in one context, then in another, then in a third. In time the observer might say to himself, "I know that person." Certainly he does know the person, if only by sight. He has noticed him many times in various neighborhood contexts, and with each successive encounter he has become increasingly familiar with him and the class he has come to represent. Probably the two are not yet speaking, though they may have exchanged looks that establish the minimal basis for trust. If asked directly, the observer might say, "Yeah, I've seen him around." In this way strangers may know each other and obtain a degree of territorial communion without ever speaking a word. It is quite possible that they will never reach speaking terms.

But there are circumstances where the social gap between visual and verbal interaction in public is pressed and the relationship between incomplete strangers is required to go further. People sometimes feel silly continually passing others they know well by sight without speaking to them. They may resolve their discomfort by greeting them or by contrived avoidance. If they choose to speak, they may commit themselves to a series of obligatory greetings.

Introductions may also occur when two people who have seen each other in the neighborhood for some time happen to meet in a different part of town; there, despite some awkwardness, they may feel constrained to greet each other like long-lost friends. Perhaps they had not yet reached the point of speaking but had only warily acknowledged one another with knowing looks, or even with the customary offensive/defensive scowl used on the street for keeping strangers at a distance. After this meeting, previously distant villagers may begin to speak regularly on the neighborhood streets. In this way trust can be established between strangers, who may then come to know each other in limited ways or very well.

Just the fact of their regular presence offers a sense of security, or at least continuity, to their neighbors. Thus, many people walk the streets with a confidence that belies their serious concerns. They use those they "know" as buffers against danger. Although they may still be strangers, they feel they can call on each other as allies when neighborhood crises emerge, when they would otherwise be seriously short of help, or when they must protect themselves or their loved ones. For example, during emergencies such as house fires, street crimes in which someone clearly needs help, or some other event where partial strangers have an opportunity to gather and compare notes with neighbors who seemed out of reach before, they may first provide help and only then reach out a hand and introduce themselves, saying, "Hello, my name is...."

Eye Work

Many blacks perceive whites as tense or hostile to them in public. They pay attention to the amount of eye contact given. In general, black males get far less time in this regard than do white males. Whites tend not to "hold" the eyes of a black person. It is more common for black and white strangers to meet each other's eyes for only a few seconds, and then to avert their gaze abruptly. Such behavior seems to say, "I am aware of your presence," and no more. Women especially feel that eye contact invites unwanted advances, but some white men feel the same and want to be clear about what they intend. This eye work is a way to maintain distance, mainly for safety and social purposes....

Many people, particularly those who see themselves as more economically privileged than others in the community, are careful not to let their eyes stray, in order to avoid an uncomfortable situation. As they walk down the street they pretend not to see other pedestrians, or they look right at them without speaking, a behavior many blacks find offensive.

Moreover, whites of the Village often scowl to keep young blacks at a social and physical distance. As they venture out on the streets of the Village and, to a lesser extent, of Northton, they may plant this look on their faces to ward off others who might mean them harm. Scowling by whites may be compared to gritting by blacks as a coping strategy. At times members of either group make such faces with little regard for circumstances, as if they were dressing for inclement weather. But on the Village streets it does not always storm, and such overcoats repel the sunshine as well as the rain, frustrating many attempts at spontaneous human communication.

Money

Naturally, given two adjacent neighborhoods representing "haves" and "have-nots," there is tremendous anxiety about money: how much to carry, how to hold it, how to use it safely in public. As in other aspects of Village life, shared anecdotes and group discussions help newcomers recognize the underlying rules of comportment.

Perhaps the most important point of etiquette with regard to money in public places is to be discreet. For example, at the checkout counter one looks into one's wallet or purse and takes out only enough to cover the charge, being careful that the remaining contents are not on display. Further, one attempts to use only small bills so as not to suggest that one has large ones.

When walling on the streets at night, it is wise to keep some money in a wallet or purse and hide the rest in other parts of ones clothing—some in a jacket pocket, some in the back pocket of one's jeans, maybe even some in a sock. In this way one would not lose everything in a mugging, yet the mugger would get something to appease him.

A final rule, perhaps the most critical, is that in a potentially violent situation it is better to lose one's money than one's life. Thus the person who plans to travel at dangerous times or in dangerous areas should have some money on hand in case of an assault:

> It was 9:00 P.M., and the Christmas party had ended. I was among the last to leave. John [a forty-five-year-old professional], the host, had to run an errand and asked if I wanted to go with him. I agreed. While I was waiting, Marsha, John's wife, said in a perfectly serious voice, "Now, John, before you go, do you have $10 just in case you get mugged "No, I don't have it, do you?"
>
> Marsha fetched $10 and gave it to John as what was in effect protection money, a kind of consolation prize designed to cool out a prospective mugger. As we walked the three blocks or so an the errand, John said, "We've come two blocks, and it's not so bad." His tone was that of a nervous joke, as though he really half expected to encounter muggers.

The reality of the Village is that residents can make their lives safer by "expecting" certain problems and making plans to cope with them. The mental preparation involved—imagining a bad situation and coming up with the best possible solution, acting it out in one's mind—may well be a valuable tool in learning to behave safely on the streets....

Other Safety Rules and Strategies

Dress is an important consideration when walling the Village streets, day or night. Women wear clothing that negates stereotypical "female frailty" and symbolizes aggressiveness. Unisex jackets, blue jeans, and sneakers are all part of the urban female costume. "Sexy" dresses are worn only when women are in a group, accompanied by a man, or traveling by car.

Village men also stick to practical, nonshowy clothing. Most times this means blue jeans or a sweat suit. More expensive clothing is relegated to day-time work hours or, as for females, travel by car.

The safety of cars and things in them is a major worry. Newcomers learn to park on the east-west streets to avoid nighttime vandalism and theft. They buy "crime locks" and hood locks for their cars. They learn, sometimes through painful error, to remove attractive items like tape decks and expensive briefcases, or anything that looks valuable, before they lock up and leave.

Their homes may be similarly barricaded. They sometimes have chains for their bicycles, bars for their first-floor windows, and dead bolts for their back doors. Some install elaborate and expensive burglar alarms or keep dogs for the same purpose.

They may build high fences to supplement the quaint waist-high wrought-iron fences from the early 1900s when the wealthy still claimed hegemony in the area.

Watching from the car as companions go into their houses is a standard precaution for city dwellers. The driver idles the motor out front and keeps an eye on the street until the resident has unlocked the door and is safely inside. This common practice has become ritualized in many instances, perhaps more important as a sign of a caring bond between people than as a deterrent of assault. It helps to make people feel secure, and residents understand it as a polite and intelligent action.

But some people are given to overreaction and to overelaboration of "mug-proofing" behaviors and are likely to see a potential mugger in almost anyone with certain attributes, most noticeably black skin, maleness, and youth. A middle-aged white woman told me this story:

> I had a white taxi driver drive me home once, and he was horrified at the neighborhood I lived in. It was night, and he told me what a horrible neighborhood I lived in, speaking of how dangerous it was here. He said, "This neighborhood is full of blacks. You'll get raped; you'll get murdered, or robbed." I replied, "I've lived here for a long time. I really like this neighborhood." He let me out on the opposite side of Thirty-fourth Street. He said, "OK, you go straight in your door, and I'll cover you." And he pulled out a gun. I said, "Please put it away." But he wouldn't. I was scared to death he was going to shoot me or something as I walked toward the house. It was so offensive to me that this man [did this], whom I trusted less than I trusted any of my neighbors, even those I knew only by sight. I felt sick for days.

The woman surmised that the taxi driver "must have been from a white ethnic and working-class background." It is commonly assumed among local blacks that such men feel especially threatened by blacks. But some middle- and upper-middle-class whites within the Village are susceptible to similar situational behavior.

■ ■ ■ ■ STREET WISDOM

...Street wisdom and street etiquette are comparable to a scalpel and a hatchet. One is capable of cutting extremely fine lines between vitally different organs; the other can only make broader, more brutal strokes....

The streetwise individual thus becomes interested in a host of signs, emblems, and symbols that others exhibit in everyday life. Besides learning the "safety signals" a person might display—conservative clothing, a tie, books, a newspaper—he also absorbs the vocabulary and expressions of the street. If he is white, he may learn for the first time to make distinctions among different kinds of black people. He may learn the meaning of certain styles of hats, sweaters, jackets, shoes, and other emblems of the subculture, thus rendering the local environment "safer" and more manageable....

A primary motivation for acquiring street wisdom is the desire to have the upper hand. It is generally believed that this will ensure safe passage, allowing one to outwit a potential assailant. In this regard a social game may be discerned. Yet it is a serious game, for failing could mean loss of property, injury, or even death. To prevail means simply to get safely to one's destination, and the ones who are most successful are those who are "streetwise." Street wisdom is really street etiquette wisely enacted....

Typically, those generally regarded as streetwise are veterans of the public spaces. They know how to get along with strangers, and they understand how to negotiate the streets. They know whom to trust, whom not to trust, what to say through body language or words. They have learned how to behave effectively in public. Probably the most important consideration is the experience they have gained through encounters with "every kind of stranger." Although one may know about situations through the reports of friends or relatives, this pales in comparison with actual experience. It is often sheer proximity to the dangerous streets that allows a person to gain street wisdom, and formulate some effective theory of the public spaces. As one navigates there is a certain edge to one's demeanor, for the streetwise person is both wary of others and sensitive to the subtleties that could salvage safety out of danger.

The longer people live in this locale, having to confront problems on the streets and public spaces every day, the greater chance they have to develop a sense of what to do without seriously compromising themselves. Further, the longer they are in the area, the more likely they are to develop contacts who might come to their aid, allowing them to move boldly.

This self-consciousness makes people likely to be alert and sensitive to the nuances of the environment. More important, they will project their ease and self-assurance to those they meet, giving them the chance to affect the interaction positively. For example, the person who is "streetdumb," relying for guidance on the most superficial signs, may pay too much attention to skin color and become needlessly tense just because the person approaching is black. A streetwise white who meets a black person will probably just go about his or her business. In both cases the black person will pick up the "vibe" being projected—in the first instance fear and hostility, in the second case comfort and a sense of commonality. There are obviously times when the "vibe" itself could tip the balance in creating the subsequent interaction.

Crisis and Adaptation

Sometimes the balance tips severely, and the whole neighborhood reacts with shock and alarm. A wave of fear surges through the community when violent crimes are reported by the media or are spread by word of mouth through the usually peaceful Village. One February a young woman, a new mother, was stabbed and left for dead in her home on one of the well-traveled north-south streets. Her month-old baby was unharmed, but it was weeks before the mother, recuperating in the hospital, remembered she had recently given birth. Word of how the stabbing occurred spread up and down the blocks of the Village. Neighbors said the woman often went out her back door to take out the garbage or call in the dog. But to uninitiated newcomers, the brick streets and large yards seem deceptively peaceful. Crises like these leave in their wake a deeper understanding of the "openness" that characterizes this quaint area of the city.

They also separate those who survive by brittle etiquette from those who—despite increased temporary precautions—can continue to see strangers as individuals. Less than half a block away from the scene of the attack, in a building facing an east-west street, a friend of the young mother was overcome with fear. Her husband was scheduled to go out of town the week after the vicious attack on her friend. She was so frightened that he had to arrange for a neighbor to "baby-sit" with his wife and children at night while he was away.

Security all over the Village was tightened for a time. People who used to go in and out, feeding the birds, shoveling walks, visiting their neighbors and friends, no longer came and went so carelessly. As the news traveled, fear rippled out from the young victim's immediate neighbors to affect behavior in other parts of the Village. One young black man reported that after the attack he was greeted with suspicious stares on his way to Mr. Chow's. "Everyone's looking over their shoulder suddenly," he said. "All black people are suspects."

"It makes you stop and wonder about living here," said one young mother shortly after the stabbing became the main item of conversation. "I've never lived in such a dangerous neighborhood. I run upstairs and leave my back door open sometimes. Like today, I got both kids and took them upstairs, and all of a sudden I said, "Oh, no! I left the door unlocked!" and I just stopped what I was doing and ran downstairs to lock it." This kind of fear-induced behavior occurs as neighbors work out their group perspective on what is possible, if not probable, in the aftermath of such a crime.

Violence causes residents to tense up and begin taking defensive action again. They may feel uncomfortable around strangers on the streets, particularly after dark. They become especially suspicious of black males. An interview with a young black man from the area sheds some light on how residents react to neighborhood blacks shortly after a violent incident:

> People come out of the door and they're scared. So when they see blacks on the streets they try to get away. Even ones who live right next door. All of a sudden they change attitudes toward each other. They're very suspicious. The guy that killed that lady and her husband down on Thirty-fourth in the Village, he from the Empire [gang]. He tried to rape the lady right in front of the husband—he stabbed the husband and killed him. He'll get the electric chair now; they gave him the death penalty. They caught him comin' out. Wouldn't been so bad, the cops got another call to next door where he did it at. She was screamin' and the cops heard and came around to the door.
>
> After that happened, you could feel the vibes from the whites. When things like that happen, things get very tense between blacks and whites. And you can feel it in the way they look at you, 'cause they think you might be the one who might do the crime. Every time they see a black they don't trust 'em. Should stay in their own neighborhood.
>
> That's the Village. They paranoid.

In time the fear recedes. Through successive documentations and neighborhood gossip, Villagers slowly return to some level of complacency, an acceptance of the risks of living in the city. Familiar people on the streets are "mapped" and associated with their old places, much as veteran Villagers have mapped them before. Streets, parks, and playgrounds are again made theirs. When these mental notations remain reliable and undisturbed for a time, a kind of "peace" returns. More and more can be taken for granted. Night excursions become more common. Children may be given a longer tether. Villagers gather and talk about the more pleasant aspects of neighborhood life. But they know, and are often reminded, that the peace is precarious....

REFERENCES

Becker, Howard S. 1963. *Outsiders: Studies in the sociology of deviance.* New York: Macmillan.

Hughes, Everett C. 1945. Dilemmas and contradictions of status. *American Journal of Sociology* 50:353–59.

The Great American Football Ritual

Douglas E. Foley

introduction ▪ ▪ ▪ ▪ ▪

Sports are important in human life. Over 2,000 years ago, the Greeks held the first Olympics. When Anglo explorers visited the New World, they found that Native Americans held athletic contests. Sports vary with cultures, and old forms have also changed through the years, making most of today's forms unrecognizable to the ancient Greeks or to tribal groups. They would recognize, however, the intense competition, the pride of victory, and the disappointment of defeat.

It would not take much of a trained sociological eye for a visitor to the United States to notice that some professional sports open with the singing of the national anthem, and to conclude from this that sports are linked to patriotism. Besides engendering national, regional, and local loyalties, sports have a deeper function. As Douglas Foley analyzes in this selection, high school football is a mechanism by which the adult generation reproduces its version of society—its status hierarchy, or customary divisions, of gender, race/ethnicity, and social class. Following the "first wisdom" of sociology—that things are not what they seem, that a deeper layer of reality underlies appearance—sociologists conclude that high school football is much more than a game, that it is one of the ways groups have of perpetuating inequalities across the generations.

Thinking Critically

As you read this selection, ask yourself:

1. Foley says that the high school football he observed is a mechanism by which the adult generation reproduces its version of society, its status divisions. What does he mean by this? What evidence does he offer for such a conclusion?

2. As you read this article, think about sports in your own high school. Can you see how the principles that Foley analyzes apply to your own high school sports?

3. The obvious "lessons" of high school football in the Texas town that Foley studied were teamwork and competitive success. What were the less obvious, or covert, lessons of the game?

The setting of this field study was "North Town," a small (8,000 population) South Texas farming/ranching community with limited industry, considerable local poverty, and a population that was 80% Mexican-American. "North Town High" had an enrollment of 600 students, and its sports teams played at the Triple-A level in a five level state ranking system.

During the football season described here, I attended a number of practices, rode on the players' bus, and hung out with the coaches at the fieldhouse and with players during extensive classroom and lunchtime observations. I also participated in basketball and tennis practices and interviewed students extensively about student status groups, friendship, dating, and race relations. The participant observation and interviewing in the sports scene involved hundreds of hours of fieldwork over a 12-month period....

■ ■ ■ THE WEEKLY PEP RALLY

Shortly after arriving in North Town I attended my first pep rally. Students, whether they liked football or not, looked forward to Friday afternoons. Regular 7th-period classes were let out early to hold a mass pep rally to support the team. Most students attended these events but a few used it to slip away from school early. During the day of this pep rally I overheard a number of students planning their trip to the game. Those in the school marching band (80) and in the pep club (50) were the most enthusiastic....

The Friday afternoon pep rally was age-graded. The older, most prominent students took the center seats, thus signaling their status and loyalty. Younger first- and second-year students sat next to the leaders of the school activities if they were protégés of those leaders. In sharp contrast, knots and clusters of the more socially marginal students, the "druggers" and the "punks and greasers," usually claimed the seats nearest the exits, thus signaling their indifference to all the rah-rah speeches they had to endure. The "nobodies" or "nerds," those dutiful, conforming students who were followers, tended to sit in the back of the center regions. Irrespective of the general territory, students usually sat with friends from their age group. Teachers strategically placed themselves at the margins and down in front to assist in crowd control.

The pep rally itself was dominated by the coaches and players, who were introduced to the audience to reflect upon the coming contest. In this particular pep rally the team captains led the team onto the stage. All the Anglo players entered first, followed by all the Mexicano players. Coach Trujillo started out with the classic pep talk that introduced the team captains, who in turn stepped forward and spoke in an awkward and self-effacing manner, thus enacting the ideal of a sportsman—a man of deeds, not words. They all stuttered through several "uhs" and "ers," then quickly said, "I hope y'all come support us. Thanks." Generally students expected their jocks to be inarticulate and, as the cliché goes, strong but silent types....

■ ■ ■ THE MARCHING BAND

The quality of the marching band was as carefully scrutinized as the football team by some community members. The band director, Dante Aguila, was keenly aware of maintaining an excellent winning band. Like sport teams, marching bands competed in local, district, and statewide contests and won rankings. The ultimate goal was winning a top rating at the state level. In addition, each band sent its best players of various instruments to district contests to compete for individual rankings. Individual band members could also achieve top rankings at the state level.

A certain segment of the student body began training for the high school marching band during their grade school years. Band members had a much more positive view of their participation in band than the players did. The band was filled with students who tended to have better grades and came from the more affluent families. The more marginal, deviant students perceived band members as "goodie goodies," "richies," and "brains." This characterization was not entirely true because the band boosters club did make an effort to raise money to help low-income students join the band. Not all band students were top students, but many were in the advanced or academic tracks. Band members were generally the students with school spirit who were proud to promote loyalty to the school and community. The marching band was also a major symbolic expression of the community's unity and its future generation of good citizens and leaders.

The view that band members were the cream of the crop was not widely shared by the football players. Many female band members were socially prominent and "cool," but some were also studious homebodies. On the other hand, "real men" supposedly did not sign up for the North Town band. According to the football players, the physically weaker, more effeminate males tended to be in the band. Males in the band were called "band fags." The only exceptions were "cool guys" who did drugs, or had their own rock and roll band, or came from musical families and planned to become professional musicians....

The main masculinity test for "band fags" was to punch their biceps as hard as possible. If the victim returned this aggression with a defiant smile or smirk, he was a real man; if he winced and whined, he was a wimp or a fag. The other variations on punching biceps were pinching the forearm and rapping the knuckles. North Town boys generally punched and pinched each other, but this kind of male play toward those considered fags was a daily ritual degradation. These were moments when physically dominant males picked on allegedly more effeminate males and reaffirmed their place in the male pecking order. Ironically, however, the players themselves rarely picked on those they called "band fags." Males who emulated jocks and hoped to hang out with them were usually the hit men. The jocks signalled their real power and prestige by showing restraint toward obviously weaker males.

■ ■ ■ CHEERLEADERS AND PEP SQUADS

As in most pep rallies, on the Friday I am describing, the cheerleaders were in front of the crowd on the gym floor doing dance and jumping routines in unison and shouting patriotic cheers to whip up enthusiasm for the team. The cheerleaders were acknowledged as some of the prettiest young women in the school and they aroused the envy of nobodies and nerds. Male students incessantly gossiped and fantasized about these young women and their reputations.... Students invariably had their favorites to adore and/or ridicule. Yet they told contradictory stories about the cheerleaders. When privately reflecting on their physical attributes and social status, males saw going with a cheerleader as guaranteeing their coolness and masculinity. Particularly the less attractive males plotted the seduction of these young women and reveled in the idea of having them as girlfriends. When expressing their views of these young women to other males, however, they often accused the cheerleaders of being stuck-up or sluts.

This sharp contradiction in males' discourse about cheerleaders makes perfect sense, however, when seen as males talking about females as objects to possess and dominate and through which to gain status. Conversations among males about cheerleaders were rhetorical performances that bonded males together and established their rank in the patriarchal order. In public conversations, males often expressed bravado about conquest of these "easy lays." In private conversations with intimate friends, they expressed their unabashed longing for, hence vulnerable emotional need for, these fantasized sexual objects. Hence, cheerleaders as highly prized females were dangerous, status-confirming creatures who were easier to relate to in rhetorical performances than in real life. Only those males with very high social status could actually risk relating to and being rejected by a cheerleader. The rest of the stories the young men told were simply male talk and fantasy.

Many young women were not athletic or attractive enough to be cheerleaders; nevertheless they wanted to be cheerleaders. Such young women often joined the pep squad as an alternative, and a strong esprit de corps developed among the pep squad members. They were a group of 50 young women in costume who came to the games and helped the cheerleaders arouse crowd enthusiasm. The pep squad also helped publicize and decorate the school and town with catchy team-spirit slogans such as "Smash the Seahawks" and "Spear the Javelinos." In addition, they helped organize after-the-game school dances. Their uniforms expressed loyalty to the team, and pep squad members were given a number of small status privileges in the school. They were sometimes released early for pep rallies and away games....

■ ■ ■ HOMECOMING: A RITE OF COMMUNITY SOLIDARITY AND STATUS

Ideally, North Town graduates would return to the homecoming bonfire and dance to reaffirm their support and commitment to the school and team. They would come back to be honored and to honor the new generation presently upholding the name and tradition of the community. In reality, however, few graduates actually attended the pregame bonfire rally or postgame school dance. Typically, the game itself drew a larger crowd and the local paper played up the homecoming game more. College-bound youth were noticeably present at the informal beer party after the game. Some townspeople were also at the pregame bonfire rally, something that rarely happened during an ordinary school pep rally....

Three groups of boys with pickup trucks...created a huge pile of scrap wood and burnable objects that had been donated. The cheerleaders, band, and pep squad members then conducted the bonfire ceremonies. Several hundred persons, approximately an equal number of Anglo and Mexicano students, showed up at the rally along with a fair sprinkling of older people and others who were not in high school. Nearly all of the leaders were Anglos and they were complaining that not enough students supported the school or them. The cheerleaders led cheers and sang the school fight song after brief inspirational speeches from the coaches and players....

The huge blazing fire in the school parking lot...added to the festive mood, which seemed partly adolescent high jinks and partly serious communion with the town's traditions. The collective energy of the youth had broken a property law or two to stage this event. Adults laughed about the "borrowed" packing crates and were pleased that others "donated" things from their stores and houses to feed the fire. The adults expressed no elaborate rationale for having a homecoming bonfire, which they considered nice, hot, and a good way to fire up the team. Gathering around the bonfire reunited all North Towners, past and present, for the special homecoming reunion and gridiron battle....

After the homecoming game, a school dance was held featuring a homecoming court complete with king and queen. The queen and her court and the king and his attendants, typically the most popular and attractive students, were elected by the student body. Ideally they represented the most attractive, popular, and successful youth. They were considered the best of a future generation of North Towners. Following tradition, the queen was crowned during halftime at midfield as the band played and the crowd cheered. According to tradition, the lovely queen and her court, dressed in formal gowns, were ceremoniously transported to the crowning in convertibles. The king and his attendants, who were often football players and dirty and sweaty at that, then came running from their halftime break to escort the young women from the convertibles and to their crowning. The king and his court lingered rather uneasily until the ceremony was over and then quickly returned to their team to rest and prepare for the second half....

■ ■ ■ THE POWDER-PUFF FOOTBALL GAME: ANOTHER RITE OF GENDER REPRODUCTION

A powder-puff football game was traditionally held in North Town on Friday afternoon before the seniors' final game. A number of the senior football players dressed up as girls and acted as cheerleaders for the game. A number of the senior girls dressed up as football players and formed a touch football team that played the junior girls. The male football players served as coaches and referees and comprised much of the audience as well. Perhaps a quarter of the student body, mainly the active, popular, successful students, drifted in and out to have a laugh over this event. More boys than girls, both Anglo and Mexicano, attended the game.

The striking thing about this ritual was the gender difference in expressive manner. Males took the opportunity to act in silly and outrageous ways. They pranced around in high heels, smeared their faces with lipstick, and flaunted their padded breasts and posteriors in a sexually provocative manner. Everything, including the cheers they led, was done in a very playful, exaggerated, and burlesque manner.

In sharp contrast, the females donned the football jerseys and helmets of the players, sometimes those of their boyfriends, and proceeded to huff and puff soberly up and down the field under the watchful eyes of the boys. They played their part in the game as seriously as possible, blocking and shoving with considerable gusto. This farce went on for several scores, until one team was the clear winner and until the females were physically exhausted and the males were satiated with acting in a ridiculous manner.

…Anthropologists…call such serious practices "rituals of inversion," specially marked moments when people radically reverse everyday cultural roles and practices. During these events people break, or humorously play with, their own cultural rules. Such reversals are possible without suffering any sanctions or loss of face. These moments are clearly marked so that no one familiar with the culture will misread such reversals as anything more than a momentary break in daily life.

Males of North Town High used this moment of symbolic inversion to parody females in a burlesque and ridiculous manner. They took great liberties with the female role through this humorous form of expression. The power of these young males to appropriate and play with female symbols of sexuality was a statement about males' social and physical dominance. Conversely, the females took few liberties with their expression of the male role. They tried to play a serious game of football. The females tried earnestly to prove they were equal. Their lack of playfulness was a poignant testimony to their subordinate status in this small town.…

PROMINENT CITIZENS AND THEIR BOOSTER CLUB: REPRODUCING CLASS PRIVILEGES

North Town was the type of community in which male teachers who had athletic or coaching backgrounds were more respected than other teachers. For their part, the other teachers often told "dumb coach" jokes and expressed resentment toward the school board's view of coaches. North Town school board members, many of them farmers and ranchers—rugged men of action—generally preferred that their school leaders be ex-coaches. Consequently a disproportionate number of ex-coaches became school principals and superintendents.… School board members invariably emphasized an ex-coach's ability to deal with the public and to discipline the youth.

Once gridiron warriors, coaches in small towns are ultimately forced to become organization men, budget administrators, and public relations experts.… Ultimately they must appease local factions, school boards, administrators, booster clubs, angry parents, and rebellious teenagers. The successful North Town coaches invariably become excellent public relations men who live a "down home" rural lifestyle; they like to hunt and fish and join local coffee klatches or Saturday morning quarterback groups. They must be real men who like fraternizing with the entrepreneurs, politicians, and good ole' boys who actually run the town. This role as a local male leader creates a web of alliances and obligations that puts most coaches in the debt of the prominent citizens and their booster club.

North Town's booster club, composed mainly of local merchants, farmers, and ranchers, had the all-important function of raising supplementary funds for improving the sports program and for holding a postseason awards banquet. The club was the most direct and formal link that coaches had with the principal North Town civic leaders. North Town had a long history of booster club and school board interference in coaching the team. One coach characterized North Town as follows: "One of the toughest towns around to keep a job. Folks here take their football seriously. They are used to winning, not everything, not the state, but conference and maybe bidistrict, and someday even regional. They put a lot of pressure on you to win here."...

The pattern of community pressures observed in North Town was not particularly exceptional. A good deal of the public criticism and grumbling about choices of players had racial overtones. The debate over which Anglo varsity quarterback to play also reflected community class differences among Anglos. North Town students and adults often expressed their fears and suspicion that racial and class prejudices were operating. It would be an exaggeration, however, to portray the North Town football team as rife with racial conflict and disunity. Nor was it filled with class prejudice. On a day-to-day basis there was considerable harmony and unity. Mexicanos and Anglos played side by side with few incidents. A number of working-class Mexicano youths and a few low-income Anglos were also members of the football program. At least in a general way, a surface harmony and equality seemed to prevail....

Local sports enthusiasts are fond of arguing that coaches select players objectively, without class or racial prejudices, because their personal interest, and that of the team, is served by winning. Unfortunately, this free-market view glosses over how sport actually functions in local communities. Small-town coaches are generally subjected to enormous pressures to play everyone's child, regardless of social class and race. Success in sport is an important symbolic representation of familial social position. Men can reaffirm their claim to leadership and prominence through the success of their offspring. A son's athletic exploits relive and display the past physical and present social dominance of the father. In displaying past and present familial prominence, the son lays claim to his future potential. Every North Town coach lived and died by his ability to win games *and* his social competence to handle the competing status claims of the parents and their children.

Socially prominent families, who want to maintain their social position, promote their interests through booster clubs. The fathers of future community leaders spend much time talking about and criticizing coaches in local coffee shops. These fathers are more likely to talk to the coaches privately. Coaches who have ambitions to be socially prominent are more likely to "network" with these sportsminded community leaders. A symbiotic relationship develops between coaches, especially native ones, and the traditional community leaders. Preferential treatment of the sons of prominent community leaders flows from the web of friendships, hunting privileges, Saturday morning joking, and other such exchanges.

The booster club that coach Trujillo had to deal with was run by a small clique of Anglos,... "good ole' boys and redneck types." They became outspoken early in the season against their "weak Mexican coach." They fanned the fires of criticism in the coffee-drinking sessions over which of the two freshman quarterbacks should start, the "strong-armed Mexican boy" of the "all-around, smart Anglo boy." The Anglo boy was the son of a prominent car dealer and...booster club activist. The Mexican boy was a son of a migrant worker and small grocery store manager. The freshman coach, Jim Ryan, chose the Anglo boy.... In a similar vein, conflict also surfaced over the selection of the varsity quarterback. Coach Trujillo chose the son of an Anglo businessman, an underclassman, over a senior, the son of a less prominent Anglo. The less educated Anglo faction lambasted the coach for this decision, claiming he showed his preference for the children of the more socially and politically prominent [families].

Moreover, considerable pressure to favor the sons of prominent citizens comes from within the school as well. The school and its classrooms are also a primary social stage upon which students enact their social privilege. These youths establish themselves as leaders in academic, political, and social affairs, and teachers grant them a variety of privileges. This reinforces the influence of their parents in the PTA, the sports and band booster clubs, and the school board. Both generations, in their own way, advance the interests of the family on many fronts.

■ ■ ■ THE SPECTATORS: MALE SOCIALIZATION THROUGH EX-PLAYERS

Another major aspect of the football ritual is how the spectators, the men in the community, socialize each new generation of players. In North Town, groups of middle-aged males with families and businesses were influential in socializing the new generation of males. These men congregated in various restaurants for the morning coffee and conversation about business, politics, the weather, and sports. Those leading citizens particularly interested in sports could be heard praising and criticizing "the boys" in almost a fatherly way. Some hired the players for part-time or summer jobs and were inclined to give them special privileges. Athletes were more like to get well-paying jobs as road-gang workers, machine operators, and crew leaders. Most players denied that they got any favors, but they clearly had more prestige than other high school students who worked. Nonplayers complained that jocks got the good jobs. On the job site the men regaled players with stories of male conquests in sports, romance, and business.

Many players reported these conversations, and I observed several during Saturday morning quarterback sessions in a local restaurant and gas station. One Saturday morning after the all-important Harris game, two starters and their good buddies came into the Cactus Bowl Café. One local rancher-businessman shouted,

"Hey, Chuck, Jimmie, get over here! I want to talk to you boys about the Harris game!" He then launched into a litany of mistakes each boy and the team had made. Others in the group chimed in and hurled jokes at the boys about "wearing skirts" and being "wimps." Meanwhile the players stood slope-shouldered and "uh-huhed" their tormentors. One thing they had learned was never to argue back too vociferously. The players ridiculed such confrontations with "old-timers" privately, but the proper response from a good kid was tongue-biting deference....,

Some ex-players led the romanticized life of tough, brawling, womanizing young bachelors. These young men seemed suspended in a state of adolescence while avoiding becoming responsible family men. They could openly do things that the players had to control or hide because of training rules. Many of these ex-players were also able to physically dominate the younger high school players. But ex-players no longer had a stage upon which to perform heroics for the town. Consequently they often reminded current players of their past exploits and the superiority of players and teams in their era. Current players had to "learn" from these tormentors and take their place in local sports history.

■ ■ ■ PLAYERS TALKING ABOUT THEIR SPORT: THE MEANING OF FOOTBALL

The preceding portrayal of the community sports scene has already suggested several major reasons why young males play football. Many of them are willing to endure considerable physical pain and sacrifice to achieve social prominence in their community. Only a very small percentage are skilled enough to play college football, and only one North Towner has ever made a living playing professional football. The social rewards from playing football are therefore mainly local and cultural.

However, there are other, more immediate psychological rewards for playing football. When asked why they play football and why they like it, young North Town males gave a variety of answers. A few openly admitted that football was a way for them to achieve some social status and prominence, to "become somebody in this town." Many said football was fun, or "makes a man out of you," or "helps you get a cute chick." Others parroted a chamber of commerce view that it built character and trained them to have discipline, thus helping them be successful in life. Finally, many evoked patriotic motives—to beat rival towns and to "show others that South Texas plays as good a football as East Texas."

These explicit statements do not reveal the deeper...lessons learned in sports combat, however. In casual conversations, players used phrases that were particularly revealing. What they talked most about was "hitting" or "sticking" or "popping" someone. These were all things that coaches exhorted the players to do in practice. After a hard game, the supreme compliment was having a particular "lick" or "hit" singled out. Folkloric immortality, endless stories about that one great hit in the big game, was what players secretly strove for. For most coaches and players, really "laying a lick on" or "knocking somebody's can off" or "taking a real lick" was that quintessential football moment. Somebody who could "take it" was someone who could bounce up off the ground as if he had hardly been hit. The supreme compliment, however, was to be called a hitter or head-hunter. A hitter made bone-crushing tackles that knocked out or hurt his opponent.

Players who consistently inflicted outstanding hits were called animals, studs, bulls, horses, or gorillas. A stud was a superior physical specimen who fearlessly dished out and took hits, who liked the physical contact, who could dominate other players physically. Other players idolized a "real stud," because he seemed fearless and indomitable on the field. Off the field a stud was also cool, or at least imagined to be cool, with girls. Most players expected and wanted strong coaches and some studs to lead them into battle. They talked endlessly about who was a real stud and whether the coach "really kicks butt."

The point of being a hitter and stud is proving that you have enough courage to inflict and take physical pain. Pain is a badge of honor. Playing with pain proves you are a man. In conventional society, pain is a warning to protect your body, but the opposite ethic rules in football. In North Town bandages and stitches and casts became medals worn proudly into battle. Players constantly told stories about overcoming injuries and "playing hurt." A truly brave man was one who could fight on; his pain and wounds were simply greater obstacles to overcome. Scars were permanent traces of past battles won, or at the very least fought well. They became stories told to girlfriends and relatives....

Many players, particularly the skilled ones, described what might be called their aesthetic moments as the most rewarding thing about football. Players sitting around reviewing a game always talked about themselves or others as "making a good cut" and "running a good route," or "trapping" and "blindsiding" someone. All these specific acts involved executing a particular type of body control and skill with perfection and excellence. Running backs made quick turns or cuts that left would-be tacklers grasping for thin air. Ends "ran routes" or a clever change of direction that freed them to leap into the air and catch a pass. Guards lay in wait for big opposing linemen or aggressive linebackers to enter their territory recklessly, only to be trapped or blindsided by them. Each position had a variety of assignments or moments when players used their strength and intelligence to defeat their opponents. The way this was done was beautiful to a player who had spent years perfecting the body control and timing to execute the play. Players talked about "feeling" the game and the ball and the pressure from an opponent.

Team sports, and especially American football, generally socialize males to be warriors. The young men of North Town were being socialized to measure themselves by their animal instincts and aggressiveness. Physicality, searching for pain, enduring pain, inflicting pain, and knowing one's pain threshold emphasize the biological, animal side of human beings. These are the instincts needed to work together and survive in military combat and, in capitalist ideology, in corporate, academic, and industrial combat. The language used—head-hunter, stick 'em, and various aggressive animal symbols—conjures up visions of Wall Street stockbrokers and real estate sharks chewing up their competition.

■ ■ ■ OTHER MALES: BRAINS, FARM KIDS, AND NOBODIES

What of those males who do not play high school football? Does this pervasive community ritual require the participation of all young males? Do all nonathletes end up in the category of effeminate "band fags"? To the contrary, several types of male students did not lose gender status for being unathletic. There were a small number of "brains" who were obviously not physically capable of being gridiron warriors. Some of them played other sports with less physical contact such as basketball, tennis, track, or baseball. In this way they still upheld the ideal of being involved in some form of sport. Others, who were slight of physique, wore thick glasses, lacked hand-eye coordination, or ran and threw poorly, sometimes ended up hanging around jocks or helping them with their schoolwork. Others were loners who were labeled nerds and weirdos.

In addition, there were many farm kids or poor kids who did not participate in sports. They were generally homebodies who did not participate in many extracurricular activities. Some of them had to work to help support their families. Others had no transportation to attend practices. In the student peer groups they were often part of the great silent majority called "the nobodies."

■ ■ ■ RESISTANCE TO THE FOOTBALL RITUAL: THE WORKING-CLASS CHICANO REBELS

There were also a number of Mexicano males who formed anti-school-oriented peer groups. They were into a "hip" drug-oriented lifestyle. These males, often called "vatos" (cool dudes), made it a point to be anti-sports, an activity they considered straight. Although some were quite physically capable of playing, they rarely tried out for any type of team sports. They made excuses for not playing such as needing a job to support their car or van or pickup. They considered sports "kids' stuff," and their hip lifestyle as more adult, cool, and fun.

Even for the vatos, however, sports events were important moments when they could publicly display their lifestyle and establish their reputation. A number of vatos always came to the games and even followed the team to other towns. They went to games to be tough guys and "enforcers" and to establish "reps" as fighters. The vatos also went to games to "hit on chicks from other towns." During one road game, after smoking several joints, they swaggered in with cocky smiles plastered on their faces. The idea was to attract attention from your women and hopefully provoke a fight while stealing another town's women. Unlike stealing watermelons or apples from a neighbor, stealing women was done openly and was a test of courage. A man faced this danger in front of his buddies and under the eyes of the enemy.

…[A]fter the game the vatos told many tales about their foray into enemy territory. With great bravado they recounted every unanswered slight and insult they hurled at those "geeks." They also gloried in their mythical conquests of local young women…. As the players battled on the field, the vatos battled on the sidelines.

They were another kind of warrior that established North Town's community identity and territoriality through the sport of fighting over and chasing young women.

■ ■ ■ THE CONTRADICTION OF BEING "IN TRAINING"

In other ways, even the straight young men who played football also resisted certain aspects of the game. Young athletes were thrust into a real dilemma when their coaches sought to rationalize training techniques and forbade various pleasures of the flesh. Being in training meant no drugs, alcohol, or tobacco. It also meant eating well-balanced meals, getting at least 8 hours of sleep, and not wasting one's emotional and physical energy chasing women. These dictates were extremely difficult to follow in a culture where drugs are used regularly and where sexual conquest and/or romantic love are popular cultural ideals. Add a combination of male adolescence and the overwhelming use of sex and women's bodies to sell commodities, and you have an environment not particularly conducive to making sacrifices for the coach and the team. North Town athletes envied the young bachelors who drank, smoked pot, and chased women late into the night. If they wanted to be males, American culture dictated that they break the rigid, unnatural training rules set for them.

…[M]any North Town football players…broke their training rules. They often drank and smoked pot at private teen parties. Unlike the rebellious vatos, who publicly flaunted their drinking and drugs, jocks avoided drinking in public. By acting like all-American boys, jocks won praise from adults for their conformity. Many of them publicly pretended to be sacrificing and denying themselves pleasure. They told the old-timers stories about their "rough practices" and "commitment to conditioning." Consequently, if jocks got caught breaking training, the men tended to overlook these infractions as slips or temptations. In short, cool jocks knew how to manage their public image as conformists and hide their private nonconformity.…

Fathers who had experienced this training contradiction themselves…gave their sons and other players stern lectures about keeping in shape, *but* they were the first to chuckle at the heroic stories of playing with a hangover. They told these same stories about teammates or about themselves over a cup of coffee or a beer. As a result, unless their youth were outrageously indiscreet—for example passing out drunk on the main street or in class, getting a "trashy girl" pregnant—a "little drinking and screwing around" was overlooked. They simply wanted the school board to stop being hypocritical and acknowledge that drinking was all part of growing up to be a prominent male.

In the small sports world of North Town, a real jock actually enhances his public image of being in shape by occasionally being a "boozer" or "doper." Indeed, one of the most common genres of stories that jocks told was the "I played while drunk/stoned," or the "I got drunk/stoned the night before the game" tale. Olmo, a big bruising guard who is now a hard-living, hard-drinking bachelor, told me a classic version of this tale before the homecoming game:

Last night we really went out and hung one on. Me and Jaime and Arturo drank a six-pack apiece in a couple of hours. We were cruising around Daly City checking out the action. It was really dead. We didn't see nobody we knew except Arturo's cousin. We stopped at his place and drank some more and listened to some music. We stayed there till his old lady [mom] told us to go home. We got home pretty late, but before the sun come up, 'cause we're in training, ha ha.

[CONCLUSION]

…[T]he football ritual remains a powerful metaphor of American capitalist culture. In North Town, football is still a popular cultural practice deeply implicated in the reproduction of the local ruling class of white males, hence class, patriarchal, and racial forms of dominance. Local sports, especially football, are still central to the socialization of each new generation of youth and to the maintenance of the adolescent society's status system. In addition, this ritual is also central to the preservation of the community's adult status hierarchy. The local politics of the booster club, adult male peer groups, and Saturday morning coffee klatches ensnare coaches and turn a son's participation in the football ritual into an important symbolic reenactment of the father's social class and gender prominence.…

Hanging Tongues:
A Sociological Encounter
with the Assembly Line

William E. Thompson

introduction

Few of us are born so wealthy that we do not have to work for a living. Some jobs seem to be of little importance, as with those we take during high school and college. We simply accept what is available and look at the job as a temporary activity to help us get by for the time being. When its time is up, we discard it as we would worn-out clothing. In contrast, the jobs we take after we have completed our education—those full-time, more or less permanent endeavors at which we labor so long and hard—in these we invest much of ourselves. In turn, as our schedules come to revolve around their demands, we become aware of how central these jobs are to our lives.

All jobs, however, whether full-time and permanent or temporary and discarded, are significant for our lives. Each contributes in its own way to our thinking and attitudes, becoming a part of the general stockpile of experiences that culminates in our basic orientation to life. Because of the significance of work for our lives, then, sociologists pay a great deal of attention to the work setting.

Of all jobs, one of the most demanding, demeaning, and demoralizing is that of the assembly line. Those of us who have worked on assembly lines have shared a work experience unlike any other, and for many of us education was the way by which we escaped from this wage slavery. As Thompson examines the assembly line in the meat-packing industry, he makes evident how this job affects all aspects of the workers' lives. His analysis provides a framework that you can use in reflecting on your own work experiences.

Thinking Critically

As you read this selection, ask yourself:

1. How does work at the meat-packing plant affect the lives of the workers? Since they face such rigorous, demanding work, why don't they simply quit?

2. How have jobs influenced your orientations to life? How about the job (position, work, or profession) that you are preparing for? (This takes you to the topic of reference groups, discussed in Chapter 5 of *Core Concepts*.)

3. Why would anyone engage in sabotage at work?

This qualitative sociological study analyzes the experience of working on a modern assembly line in a large beef plant. It explores and examines a special type of assembly line work which involves the slaughtering and processing of cattle into a variety of products intended for human consumption and other uses.

Working in the beef plant is "dirty work," not only in the literal sense of being drenched with perspiration and beef blood, but also in the figurative sense of performing a low-status, routine, and demeaning job. Although the work is honest and necessary in a society which consumes beef, slaughtering and butchering cattle is generally viewed as an undesirable and repugnant job. In that sense, workers at the beef plant share some of the same experiences as other workers in similarly regarded occupations (for example, ditch-diggers, garbage collectors, and other types of assembly line workers)....

■ ■ ■ THE SETTING

The setting for the field work was a major beef processing plant in the Midwest. At the time of the study, the plant was the third largest branch of a corporation which operated ten such plants in the United States....

The beef plant was organizationally separated into two divisions: Slaughter and Processing. This study focused on the Slaughter division in the area of the plant known as the *kill floor*. A dominant feature of the kill floor was the machinery of the assembly line itself. The line was composed of an overhead stainless steel rail which began at the slaughter chute and curved its way around every work station in the plant. Every work station contained specialized machinery for the job performed at that place on the line. Dangling from the rail were hundreds of stainless steel hooks pulled by a motorized chain. Virtually every part of the line and all of the implements (tubs, racks, knives, etc.) were made of stainless steel. The walls were covered with a ceramic tile and the floor was made of sealed cement. There were floor drains located at every work station, so that at the end of each work segment (at breaks, lunch, and shift's end) the entire kill floor could be hosed down and cleaned for the next work period.

Another dominant feature of the kill floor was the smell. Extremely difficult to describe, yet impossible to forget, this smell combined the smells of live cattle, ma-

From William E. Thompson, "Hanging Tongues: A Sociological Encounter with the Assembly Line," *Qualitative Sociology*, 6(3), pp. 215–237, 1983. Reprinted with kind permission of Springer Science and Business Media.

nure, fresh beef blood, and internal organs and their contents. This smell not only permeated the interior of the plant, but was combined on the outside with the smell of smoke from various waste products being burned and could be smelled throughout much of the community. This smell contributed greatly to the general negative feelings about work at the beef plant, as it served as the most distinguishable symbol of the beef plant to the rest of the community. The single most often asked question of me, during the research by those outside the beef plant was, "How do you stand the smell?" In typical line workers' fashion, I always responded, "What smell? All I smell at the beef plant is money."...

■ ■ ■ METHOD

The method of this study was nine weeks of full-time participant observation as outlined by Schatzman and Strauss (1973) and Spradley (1979; 1980). To enter the setting, the researcher went through the standard application process for a summer job. No mention of the research intent was made, though it was made clear that I was a university sociology professor. After initial screening, a thorough physical examination, and a helpful reference from a former student and part-time employee of the plant, the author was hired to work on the *Offal* crew in the Slaughter division of the plant....

■ ■ ■ THE WORK

...The line speed on the kill floor was 187. That means that 187 head of cattle were slaughtered per hour. At any particular work station, each worker was required to work at that speed. Thus, at my work station, in the period of one hour, 187 beef tongues were mechanically pulled from their hooks; dropped into a large tub filled with water; had to be taken from the tub and hung on a large stainless steel rack full of hooks; branded with a "hot brand" indicating they had been inspected by a USDA inspector, and then covered with a small plastic bag. The rack was taken to the cooler, replaced with an empty one, and the process began again.

It would be logical to assume that if a person worked at a steady, continuous pace of handling 187 tongues per hour, everything would go smoothly; not so. In addition to hanging, branding, and bagging tongues, the worker at that particular station also cleaned the racks and cleaned out a variety of empty stainless steel tubs used to hold hearts, kidneys, and other beef organs. Thus, in order to be free to clean the tubs when necessary, the "tongue-hanger" had to work at a slightly faster pace than the line moved. Then, upon returning from cleaning the tubs, the worker would be behind the line (*in a hole*) and had to work much faster to catch up with the line. Further, one fifteen-minute break and a thirty-minute lunch break were scheduled for an eight-hour shift. Before the "tongue-hanger" could leave his post for one of these, all tongues were required to be properly disposed of, all tubs washed and stored, and the work area cleaned.

My first two nights on the job, I discovered the consequences of working at the line speed (hanging, branding, and bagging each tongue as it fell in the tub). At the end of the work period when everybody else was leaving the work floor for break or lunch, I was furiously trying to wash all the tubs and clean the work area. Consequently, I missed the entire fifteen minute break and had only about ten minutes for lunch. By observing other workers, I soon caught on to the system. Rather than attempting to work at a steady pace consistent with the line speed, the norm was to work sporadically at a very frenzied pace, actually running ahead of the line and plucking tongues from the hooks before they got to the station. With practice, I learned to hang two or three tongues at a time, perform all the required tasks, and then take an unscheduled two or three minute break until the line caught up with me. Near break and lunch everybody worked at a frantic pace, got ahead of the line, cleaned the work areas, and even managed to add a couple of minutes to the scheduled break or lunch.

Working ahead of the line seems to have served as more than merely a way of gaining a few minutes of extra break time. It also seemed to take on a symbolic meaning. The company controlled the speed of the line. Seemingly, that took all element of control over the work process away from the workers.... However, when the workers refused to work at line speed and actually worked faster than the line, they not only added a few minutes of relaxation from the work while the line caught up, but they symbolically regained an element of control over the pace of their own work....

■ ■ ■ COPING

One of the difficulties of work at the beef plant was coping with three aspects of the work: monotony, danger, and dehumanization. While individual workers undoubtedly coped in a variety of ways, some distinguishable patterns emerged.

Monotony

The monotony of the line was almost unbearable. At my work station, a worker would hang, brand, and bag between 1,350 and 1,500 beef tongues in an eight-hour shift. With the exception of the scheduled fifteen-minute break and a thirty-minute lunch period (and sporadic brief gaps in the line), the work was mundane, routine, and continuous. As in most assembly line work, one inevitably drifted into daydreams (e.g., Garson, 1975; King, 1978; Linhart, 1981). It was not unusual to look up or down the line and see workers at various stations singing to themselves, tapping their feet to imaginary music, or carrying on conversations with themselves. I found that I could work with virtually no attention paid to the job, with my hands and arms automatically performing their tasks. In the meantime, my mind was free to wander over a variety of topics, including taking mental notes. In visiting with other workers, I found that daydreaming was the norm. Some would think about their families, while others fantasized about sexual escapades, fishing, or anything unrelated to the job. One individual who was rebuilding an antique car at home in his spare time would meticulously mentally rehearse the procedures he was going to perform on the car the next day.

Daydreaming was not inconsequential, however. During these periods, items were most likely to be dropped, jobs improperly performed, and accidents incurred. Inattention to detail around moving equipment, stainless steel hooks, and sharp knives invariably leads to dangerous consequences. Although I heard rumors of drug use to help fight the monotony, I never saw any workers take any drugs nor saw any drugs in any worker's possession. It is certainly conceivable that some workers might have taken something to help them escape the reality of the line, but the nature of the work demanded enough attention that such a practice could be ominous.

Danger

The danger of working in the beef plant was well known. Safety was top priority (at least in theory) and management took pride in the fact that only three employee on-the-job deaths had occurred in twelve years. Although deaths were uncommon, serious injuries were not. The beef plant employed over 1,800 people. Approximately three-fourths of those employed had jobs which demanded the use of a knife honed to razor-sharpness. Despite the use of wire-mesh aprons and gloves, serious cuts were almost a daily occurrence. Since workers constantly handled beef blood, danger of infection was ever present. As one walked along the assembly line, a wide assortment of bandages on fingers, hands, arms, necks, and faces could always be seen.

In addition to the problem of cuts, workers who cut meat continuously sometimes suffered muscle and ligament damage to their fingers and hands. In one severe case, I was told of a woman who worked in processing for several years who had to wear splints on her fingers while away from the job to hold them straight. Otherwise, the muscles in her hand would constrict her fingers into the grip position, as if holding a knife....

When I spoke with fellow workers about the dangers of working in the plant, I noticed interesting defense mechanisms.... After a serious accident, or when telling about an accident or death which occurred in years past, the workers would almost immediately dissociate themselves from the event and its victim. Workers tended to view those who suffered major accidents or death on the job in much the same way that nonvictims of crime often view crime victims as either partially responsible for the event, or at least as very different from themselves (Barlow, 1981). "Only a part-timer," "stupid," "careless" or something similar was used, seemingly to reassure the worker describing the accident that it could not happen to him. The reality of the situation was that virtually all the jobs on the kill floor were dangerous, and any worker could have experienced a serious injury at any time....

Dehumanization

Perhaps the most devastating aspect of working at the beef plant (worse than the monotony and the danger) was the dehumanizing and demeaning elements of the job. In a sense, the assembly line worker became a part of the assembly line. The assembly line is not a tool used by the worker, but a machine which controls him/her. A tool can only be productive in the hands of somebody skilled in its use, and hence becomes an extension of the person using it. A machine, on the other hand, performs specific tasks; thus its operator becomes an extension of it in the production process.... When workers are viewed as mere extensions of the machines with which they work, their human needs become secondary in importance to the smooth mechanical functioning of the production process. In a bureaucratic structure, when "human needs collide with systems needs, the individual suffers" (Hummel, 1977:65).

Workers on the assembly line are seen as interchangeable as the parts of the product on the line itself. An example of one worker's perception of this phenomenon at the beef plant was demonstrated the day after a fatal accident occurred. I asked the men in our crew what the company did in the case of an employee death (I wondered if there was a fund for flowers, or if the shift was given time off to go to the funeral, etc.). One worker's response was: "They drag off the body, take the hard hat and boots and check 'em out to some other poor sucker, and throw him in the guy's place." While employee death on the job was not viewed quite that coldly by the company, the statement fairly accurately summarized the overall result of a fatal accident, and importance of any individual worker to the overall operation of the production process. It accurately summarized the workers' perceptions about management's attitudes toward them....

■ ■ ■ SABOTAGE

It is fairly common knowledge that assembly line work situations often led to employee sabotage or destruction of the product or equipment used in the production process (Garson, 1975; Balzer, 1976; Shostak, 1980). This is the classic experience of alienation as described by Marx (1964a,b).... At the beef plant I quickly learned that there was an art to effective sabotage. Subtlety appeared to be the key. "The art lies in sabotaging in a way that is not immediately discovered," as a Ford worker put it (King, 1978:202). This seemed to hold true at the beef plant as well....

The greatest factor influencing the handling of beef plant products was its status as a food product intended for human consumption.... Though not an explicitly altruistic group, the workers realized that the product would be consumed by people (even family, relatives, and friends), so consequently, they rarely did anything to actually contaminate the product.

Despite formal norms against sabotage, some did occur. It was not uncommon for workers to deliberately cut chunks out of pieces of meat for no reason (or for throwing at other employees). While regulations required that anything that touched the floor had to be put in tubs marked "inedible," the informal procedural norms were otherwise. When something was dropped, one usually looked around to see if an inspector or foreman noticed. If not, the item was quickly picked up and put back on the line.

Several explanations might be offered for this type of occurrence. First, since the company utilized a profit-sharing plan, when workers damaged the product, or had to throw edible pieces into inedible tubs (which sold for pet food at much lower prices), profits were decreased. A decrease in profits to the company ultimately led to decreased dividend checks to employees. Consequently, workers were fairly careful not to actually ruin anything. Second, when something was dropped or mishandled and had to be rerouted to "inedible," it was more time-consuming than if the product had been handled properly and kept on the regular line. In other words, if no inspector noticed, it was easier to let it go through on the line. There was a third, and seemingly more meaningful, explanation for this behavior, however. It was against the rules to do it, it was a challenge to do it, and thus it was fun to do it.

The workers practically made a game out of doing forbidden things simply to see if they could get away with it.... New workers were routinely socialized into the subtle art of rulebreaking as approved by the line workers. At my particular work station, it was a fairly common practice for other workers who were covered with beef blood to come over to the tub of swirling water designed to clean the tongues, and as soon as the inspector looked away, wash their hands, arms, and knives in the tub. This procedure was strictly forbidden by the rules. If witnessed by a foreman or inspector, the tub had to be emptied, cleaned, and refilled, and all the tongues in the tub at the time had to be put in the "inedible" tub. All of that would be a time-consuming and costly procedure, yet the workers seemed to absolutely delight in successfully pulling off the act. As Balzer (1976:90) indicates:

> Since a worker often feels that much if not all of what he does is done in places designated by the company, under company control, finding ways to express personal freedom from this institutional regimentation is important.

Thus, artful sabotage served as a symbolic way in which the workers could express a sense of individuality, and hence, self-worth.

■ ■ ■ **THE FINANCIAL TRAP**

Given the preceding description and analysis of work at the beef plant, why did people work at such jobs? Obviously, there are a multitude of plausible answers to that question. Without doubt, however, the key is money. The current economic situation, the lack of steady employment opportunities (especially for the untrained and poorly educated), combined with the fact that the beef plant's starting wage exceeded the minimum wage by approximately $5.50 per hour emerge as the most important reasons people went to work there.

Despite the high hourly wage and fringe benefits, however, the monotony, danger, and hard physical work drove many workers away in less than a week. During my study, I observed much worker turnover. Those who stayed displayed an interesting pattern which helps explain why they did not leave. Every member of my work crew answered similarly my questions about why they stayed at the beef plant. Each of them took the job directly after high school, because it was the highest-paying job available. Each of them had intended to work through the summer and then look for a better job in the fall. During that first summer on the job they fell victim to what I label the "financial trap."

The "financial trap" was a spending pattern which demanded the constant weekly income provided by the beef plant job. This scenario was first told to me by an employee who had worked at the plant for over nine years. He began the week after his high school graduation, intending only to work that summer in order to earn enough money to attend college in the fall. After about four weeks' work he purchased a new car. He figured he could pay off the car that summer and still save enough money for tuition. Shortly after the car purchase, he added a new stereo sound system to his debt; next came a motorcycle; then the decision to postpone school for one year in order to continue working at the beef plant and pay off his debts. A few months later he married; within a year purchased a house; had a child; and bought another new car. Nine years later, he was still working at the beef plant, hated every minute of it, but in his own words "could not afford to quit." His case was not unique. Over and over again, I heard stories about the same process of falling into the "financial trap." The youngest and newest of our crew had just graduated from high school and took the job for the summer in order to earn enough money to attend welding school the following fall. During my brief tenure at the beef plant, he purchased a new motorcycle, a new stereo, and a house trailer. When I left, he told me he had decided to postpone welding school for one year in order "to get everything paid for." I saw the financial trap closing in on him fast; he did, too....

■ ■ ■ SUMMARY AND CONCLUSIONS

There are at least three interwoven phenomena in this study which deserve further comment and research.

First is the subtle sense of unity which existed among the line workers.... The line both symbolically and literally linked every job, and consequently every worker, to each other.... A system of "uncooperative teamwork" seemed to combine simultaneously a feeling of "one for all, all for one, and every man for himself." Once a line worker made it past the first three or four days on the job which "weeded out" many new workers, his status as a *beefer* was assured and the sense of unity was felt as much by the worker of nine weeks as it was by the veteran of nine years. Because the workers maintained largely secondary relationships, this feeling of unification is not the same as the unity typically found on athletic teams, in fraternities, or among various primary groups. Yet it was a significant social force which bound the workers together and provided a sense of meaning and worth. Although their occupation might not be highly respected by outsiders, they derived mutual self-respect from their sense of belonging.

A second important phenomenon was the various coping methods...the beef plant line workers developed and practiced...for retaining their humanness. Daydreaming, horseplay, and occasional sabotage protected their sense of self. Further, the prevailing attitude among workers that it was "us" against "them" served as a reminder that, while the nature of the job might demand subjugation to bosses, machines, and even beef parts, they were still human beings....

A third significant finding was that consumer spending patterns among the beefers seemed to "seal their fate" and make leaving the beef plant almost impossible. A reasonable interpretation of the spending patterns of the beefers is that having a high-income/low-status job encourages a person to consume conspicuously. The prevailing attitude seemed to be "I may not have a nice job, but I have a nice home, a nice car, etc." This conspicuous consumption enabled workers to take indirect pride in their occupations. One of the ways of overcoming drudgery and humiliation on the job was to surround oneself with as many desirable material things as possible off the job. These items (cars, boats, motorcycles, etc.) became tangible rewards for the sacrifices endured at work.

The problem, of course, is that the possession of these expensive items required the continual income of a substantial paycheck which most of these men could only obtain by staying at the beef plant. These spending patterns were further complicated by the fact that they were seemingly "contagious." Workers talked to each other on breaks about recent purchases, thus reinforcing the norm of immediate gratification. A common activity of a group of workers on break or lunch was to run to the parking lot to see a fellow worker's new truck, van, car, or motorcycle. Even the seemingly more financially conservative were usually caught up in this activity and often could not wait to display their own latest acquisitions. Ironically, as the workers cursed their jobs, these expensive possessions virtually destroyed any chance of leaving them.

Working at the beef plant was indeed "dirty work." It was monotonous, difficult, dangerous, and demeaning. Despite this, the workers at the beef plant worked hard to fulfill employer expectations in order to obtain financial rewards. Through a variety of symbolic techniques, they managed to overcome the many negative aspects of their work and maintain a sense of self-respect about how they earned their living.

REFERENCES

Balzer, Richard (1976). *Clockwork: Life In and Outside an American Factory*. Garden City, NY: Doubleday.

Barlow, Hugh (1981). *Introduction to Criminology*. 2d ed. Boston: Little, Brown.

Garson, Barbara (1975). *All the Livelong Day: The Meaning and Demeaning of Routine Work*. Garden City, NY: Doubleday.

Hummel, Ralph P. (1977). *The Bureaucratic Experience*. New York: St. Martin's Press.

King, Rick (1978). "In the sanding booth at Ford," Pp. 199–205 in John and Erna Perry (eds.), *Social Problems in Today's World*. Boston: Little, Brown.

Linhart, Robert (translated by Margaret Crosland) (1981). *The Assembly Line*. Amherst: University of Massachusetts Press.

Marx, Karl (1964a). *Economic and Philosophical Manuscripts of 1844*. New York International Publishing (1844).

———— (1964b). *The Communist Manifesto*. New York: Washington Square Press (1848).

Schatzman, Leonard, and Anselm L. Strauss (1973). *Field Research*. Englewood Cliffs, NJ: Prentice-Hall.

Shostak, Arthur (1980). *Blue Collar Stress*. Reading, MA: Addison-Wesley.

Spradley, James P. (1979). *The Ethnographic Interview*. New York: Holt, Rinehart & Winston.

———— (1980). *Participant Observation*. New York: Holt, Rinehart & Winston.

Just Another
Routine Emergency

Daniel F. Chambliss

introduction ▪ ▪ ▪ ▪

In social life, appearances may not be everything, but they certainly are essential for getting along. Just as buildings have façades—attractive front exteriors that are designed to give a good impression of what might be inside—so social groups and organizations have façades. Some organizations even hire public relations firms to put out favorable messages to the public. To cultivate images of caring, others contribute to charitable causes. Oil companies that exploit the environment publish expensive, glossy ads and brochures to convince the public that they care more about the environment than does *Greenpeace* or *The Sea Shepherds*.

As mentioned in the introduction to an earlier reading, some say that the first rule of sociology is that nothing is as it appears. If so, the first task of sociology is to look behind the scenes. Behind the social façade put out for public consumption lies a different reality. As in the case of some oil companies, the reality may conflict greatly with their cultivated public image. But in the typical case, the hidden reality has more to do with dissension among the group's members, or with less dedication to the group's goals or to the public welfare, than the organization wants to reveal. At times, the façade may be giving an appearance of competence and order, while the hidden reality is a looming incompetence and disorder. This selection by Daniel Chambliss takes a look behind the social façade of the hospital, revealing a reality unfamiliar to most of us.

Thinking Critically

As you read this selection, ask yourself:

1. How do hospital workers keep outsiders from seeing past their social façade?

2. Why are the public and private realities of hospitals so different?

3. From information in this reading, prove or disprove this statement: From their callous and inappropriate humor, we can see that doctors and nurses don't really care about their patients.

*E*very unit in the hospital…has its own normality, its own typical patients, number of deaths, and crises to be faced. But just as predictably, every unit has its emergencies that threaten the routine and challenge the staff's ability to maintain workaday attitudes and practices. Emergencies threaten the staff's ability to carry on as usual, to maintain their own distance from the patient's suffering, and to hold at bay their awe at the enormity of events. Occasionally breakdowns occur in unit discipline or the ability to do the required work.

Staff follow several strategies when trying to manage the threat of breakdowns: they will keep outsiders outside, follow routinization rituals, or use humor to distance themselves. Finally, even when all efforts fail, they will keep going, no matter what. Consider in turn each of these implicit maxims:

■ ■ ■ 1. KEEP OUTSIDERS OUTSIDE

Every hospital has policies about visiting hours, designed not only to "let patients rest" but also to protect staff from outsiders' interference in their work. Visitors are limited to certain hours, perhaps two to a patient room for fifteen-minute visits; they may have to be announced before entering the unit or may be kept waiting in a room down the hall. No doubt many such policies are good for the patient. No doubt, too, they keep visitors out of the nurse's way, prevent too many obtrusive questions or requests for small services, and prevent curious laypersons from seeing the messier, less presentable sides of nursing care.

When visitors cannot be physically excluded, they can still be cognitively controlled, that is, prevented from knowing that something untoward is happening. Typically, the staff behave in such episodes as if everything were OK, even when it is not. This is similar to what Erving Goffman observed in conversations: when the shared flow of interaction is threatened by an accidental insult or a body failure such as a sneeze or flatulence, people simply try to ignore the break in reality and carry on as if nothing has happened. Such "reality maintenance" is often well-orchestrated, requiring cooperation on the part of several parties. For Goffman, normal people in normal interactions accept at face value each other's presentation of who they are:

> A state where everyone temporarily accepts everyone else's line is established. This kind of mutual acceptance seems to be a basic structural feature of interaction, especially the interaction of face-to-face talk. It is typically a "working" acceptance, not a "real" one.[1]

And when this routine breaks down, the immediate strategy is simple denial:

> When a person fails to prevent an incident, he can still attempt to maintain the fiction that no threat to face has occurred. The most blatant example of this is found where the person acts as if an event that contains a threatening expression has not occurred at all.[2]

From *Beyond Caring: Hospitals, Nurses, and the Social Organization of Ethics,* by Daniel F. Chambliss. Copyright © 1986 by Daniel F. Chambliss. Reprinted by permission of the University of Chicago Press.

In the hospital, the unexpected entrance of outsiders into a delicate situation can disrupt the staff's routine activities and create unmanageable chaos. To avoid this, the staff may pretend to outsiders that nothing special is happening; this pretense itself can be part of the routine. During a code (resuscitation) effort I witnessed, there were three such potential disruptions by outsiders: another patient calling for help, a new incoming patient being wheeled in, and the new patient's family members entering the unit. All three challenges were handled by the staff diverting the outsiders from the code with a show, as if nothing were happening:

> Code in CCU [Cardiac Care Unit]…woman patient, asystole [abnormal ventricle contractions]. Doc (res[ident]) pumping chest—*deep* pumps, I'm struck by how far down they push. Serious stuff. Matter of factness of process is striking. This was a surprise code, not expected. Patient was in Vtak [ventricular fibrillation], pulse started slowing, then asystole. N[urse]s pumping for a while, RT [Respiratory Therapist] ambu-bagging [pumping air into lungs]. Maybe 7–8 people in patient's room working. Calm, but busy. Occasionally a laugh.
>
> Pt in next room (no more than 10 feet away) called for nurse—a doc went in, real loose and casual, strolled in, pt said something; doc said, "There's something going on next door that's taking people's time; we'll get to you"—real easy, like nothing at all happening. Then strolls back to code room. Very calm…
>
> Two N[urse]s came into unit wheeling a new patient. One said, "Uh, oh, bad time," very quietly as she realized, going in the door, that a code was on. Somebody said, "Close the door"—the outside door to the unit, which the Ns with the new pt were holding open…
>
> When the new pt was brought in and rolled into his room, the family with him was stopped at unit door, told to stay in waiting room and "we'll call you" with a casual wave of hand, as if this is routine. [No one said a code was on. Patient lying on gurney was wheeled in, went right by the code room and never knew a thing.] [Field Notes]

This is a simple example of protecting the routine from the chaos of a panicking patient or a horrified family; the outsiders never knew that a resuscitation was occurring fifteen feet away. The staff's work was, in their own eyes, routine; their challenge was protecting that routine from outside disruption.

■ ■ ■ 2. FOLLOW ROUTINIZATION RITUALS

The staff's sense of routine is maintained by the protective rituals of hospital life. Under stress, one may use them more and more compulsively, falling back on the old forms to reconvince oneself that order is still present. Frantic prayers in the foxhole are the prototype cases.

Most prominent of such rituals in hospitals are "rounds," the standard ritual for the routine handling of patient disasters in the hospital. "Rounds" is the generic term for almost any organized staff group discussion of patients' conditions. "Walking rounds" refers to a physician walking through the hospital, usually trailed by various residents and interns, going from patient to patient and reviewing their condition. "Grand rounds" are large meetings of the medical staff featuring the presentation of an interesting case, with elaborate discussion and questions, for the purpose of education and review of standard practices. Nursing rounds usually consist of a meeting between the staff for one (outgoing) shift reporting to the staff of the next (incoming) shift on the condition of all patients on the floor. Here the staff collectively explains what has happened and why, bringing every case into the staff's framework of thinking, and systematically enforcing the system's capability for handling medical problems without falling to pieces. In rounds, the staff confirm to each other that things are under control. Once a week, for instance, the Burn Unit at one hospital holds rounds in their conference room with a group of residents, one or two attending, several nurses, the social workers, dieticians, and physical therapists. The patients here are in terrible shape; one can sometimes hear moans in the hallway outside as patients are taken for walks by the nurses. But rounds continue:

> Macho style of the docs very evident.... Resident will present a case, then the attendings take rapid-fire shots at what he [the resident] had done: wrong dressing, wrong feeding schedule, failure to note some abnormality in the lab results. Much of the talk was a flurry of physiological jargon, many numbers and abbreviations. The intensity of the presentation, the mercilessness of the grilling, is surprising.... Focus is on no errors made in situation of extreme pressure—i.e., both in patient treatment and then here in rounds presenting the case. Goal here is to be predictable, *controlled,* nothing left out. [Field Notes]

■ ■ ■ 3. USE HUMOR TO DISTANCE YOURSELF

Keeping outsiders away and following the standard rituals for maintaining normality can help, but sometimes the pathos of hospital life becomes psychologically threatening to staff members. One response is to break down, cry, and run out, but this is what they are trying to avoid; the more common reaction is the sort of black humor that notoriously characterizes hospitals and armies everywhere. Humor provides an outlet; when physical space is not available, humor is a way to separate oneself psychologically from what is happening. It says both that I am not involved and that this really isn't so important. (In brain surgery, when parts of that organ are, essentially, vacuumed away, one may hear comments like "There goes 2d grade, there go the piano lessons," etc.) With laughter, things seem less consequential, less of a burden. What has been ghastly can perhaps be made funny:

> Today they got a 600-gram baby in the Newborn Unit. When Ns heard [the baby] was in Delivery, they were praying, "Please God let it be under 500 grams"—because that's the definite cutoff under which they won't try to save it—but the doc said admit it anyway. Ns unhappy.
> I came in the unit tonight; N came up to me and said brightly, with a big smile, "Have you seen our fetus?" Ns on the Newborn Unit have nicknames for some. There's "Fetus," the 600-gram one; "Munchkin"; and "Thrasher," in the corner, the one with constant seizures. Grim humor, but common. ["Fetus" was born at 24 weeks, "Munchkin" at 28.] [Field Notes]

The functions of such humor for medical workers have been described in a number of classic works of medical sociology. Renée Fox, writing in her book *Experiment Perilous* about physicians on a metabolic research unit, says, "The members of the group were especially inclined to make jokes about events that disturbed them a good deal," and she summarizes that

> by freeing them from some of the tension to which they were subject, enabling them to achieve greater detachment and equipoise, and strengthening their resolve to do something about the problems with which they were faced, the grim medical humor of the Metabolic Group helped them to come to terms with their situation in a useful and professionally acceptable way.[3]

Fox and other students of hospital culture (notably Rose Coser)[4] have emphasized that humor fills a functional purpose of "tension release," allowing medical workers to get on with the job in the face of trauma; their analyses usually focus on jokes explicitly told in medical settings. This analysis is correct as far as it goes, but in a sense I think it almost "explains away" hospital humor—as if to say that "these people are under a lot of strain, so it's understandable that they tell these gruesome jokes." It suggests, in a functionalist fallacy, that jokes are made because of the strain and that things somehow aren't "really" funny.

But they are. An appreciation of hospital life must recognize that funny things—genuinely funny, even if sometimes simultaneously horrible—do happen. Hospitals are scenes of irony, where good and bad are inseparably blended, where funny things happen, where to analytically excuse laughter as a defense mechanism is simultaneously to deny the human reality, the experience, that even to a non-stressed outsider *this is funny*.[5] The humor isn't found only in contrived jokes but in the scenes one witnesses; laughter can be spontaneous, and it's not always nervous. True, one must usually have a fairly normalized sense of the hospital to laugh here, but laugh one does.

Certainly, the staff make jokes:

> In the OR [operating room]:
> "This is his [pt's] 6th time [for a hernia repair]."
> "After two, I hear you're officially disabled."
> "Oh good, does that mean he gets a special parking place?"
> [Field Notes]
> In the ICU [Intensive Care Unit], two Ns—one male, one female—working on pt.
> Nurse 1 (male): "This guy has bowel sounds in his scrotum."
> Nurse 2 (female): "In his scrotum?"
> Nurse 1: "Yeah, didn't you pick that up?"
> Nurse 2: "I didn't put my stethoscope there!" (Big laughs.) [Field Notes]

Sometimes jokes are more elaborate and are obviously derived from the tragedy of the situation:

> In another ICU, staff member taped a stick to the door of the unit, symbolizing (for them) "The Stake," a sign of some form of euthanasia [perhaps the expression sometimes used, "to stake" a patient, derives from the myth that vampires can only be killed

by driving a stake through the heart]. Periodically word went around that a resident had just won the "Green Stake Award," meaning that he or she had, for the first time, allowed or helped a patient to die. [Field Notes]

Some colorful balloons with "Get Well Soon" were delivered to a patient's room. The patient died the following night. Someone on the staff moved the balloons to the door of another patient's room; that patient died! Now the staff has put the balloons at the door of the patient they believe is "most likely to die next." [Field Notes]

But jokes have to be contrived; they are deliberate efforts at humor and so make a good example of efforts to distance oneself, or to make the tragic funny. But the inherent irony of the hospital is better seen in situations that spontaneously provoke laughter. These things are funny in themselves; even an outsider can laugh at them:

Nurse preparing to wheel a patient into the OR tells him, "Take out your false teeth, take off your glasses…," and continuing, trying to make a joke, "Take off your leg, take out your eyes." The patient said, "Oh, I almost forgot—" and pulled out his [false] eye! [Interview]

Or:

Lady patient [Geriatric floor] is upset because she called home, there's no answer; she's afraid her husband has died. Sylvia [a nurse] told her he probably just went somewhere for lunch, but patient said he would have called. She's afraid.

[Later] Sylvia went back in lady's room—she's crying. Husband called! Sylvia happy, smiling, "You should be happy!" "But," says the old lady, "he called to say he was out burying the dog!"

Sylvia had to leave the room because she was starting to laugh; she and Janie laughing at this at the N's station, saying it's really sad but funny at the same time. [Field Notes]

Or:

In looking at X-rays of a patient's colon, the resident explains to the team a shadow on the film: "Radiology says it could be a tumor, or it might just be stool." Jokes all around about how "helpful" Rays [Radiology] is. [Field Notes]

One needn't be under pressure to find such things funny. People do laugh to ease pressure or to distance oneself. But sometimes the distance comes first: laughter is made possible by the routinization that has gone before.

■ ■ ■ 4. WHEN THINGS FALL APART, KEEP GOING

Sometimes routinization fails: outsiders come into the room and, seeing their dead mother, break down, screaming and wailing; or a longtime, cared-for patient begins irretrievably to "decompensate" and lose blood pressure, sliding quickly to death; or emergency surgery goes bad, the trauma shakes the staff, and there are other patients coming in from the ambulances. Any of these can destroy the staff's sense of "work as usual." In such cases, the typical practice seems to be, remarkably: just keep going. Trauma teams specialize in the psychological strength (or cold-bloodedness, perhaps) to continue working when the world seems to be falling apart. Finally, nurses and physicians are notable for continuing to work even, in the final case, after the patient is for almost all purposes dead, or will be soon.

> A resident said to the attending [physician] on one floor, discussing a terminal patient: "If we transfuse him, he might get hepatitis."
> Another resident: "By the time he gets hepatitis he'll be dead."
> Attending: "OK, so let's transfuse." [Field Notes]

Perseverance is a habit; it's also a moral imperative, a way of managing disaster as if it were routine.

In every unit there are nurses known for being good under pressure. These are people who, whatever their other skills (and, typically, their other skills are quite good), are able to maintain their presence of mind in any crisis. Whereas "being organized" is a key quality for nurses in routine situations, staying calm is crucial in emergency situations. Compare two nurses known for remaining calm (Mavis and Anna) to two others who are prone to alarm (Linda and Julie):

> Mavis [in Neonatal ICU] is cited as a good nurse (great starting IVs, e.g.) who doesn't get shook, even in a code, even if her pt is dying, she still keeps doing what you're supposed to do. Linda, by contrast, is real smart, very good technically, but can freak out, start yelling, etc., if things are going badly. [Field Notes]
> Julie [in Medical ICU], hurrying around, looks just one step ahead of disaster, can't keep up, etc. Doc says something about the patient in room 1. Julie says, walking past, "He's not mine," keeps going. But Anna, calm, walks in pt's room—pt with oxygen mask, wants something. Anna goes out, calmly, comes back in a minute w/cup of crushed ice, gives pt a spoonful to ease thirst. She *always* seems to be doing that little thing that others "don't have time for"—never flustered and yet seems to get more done than anyone else. [Field Notes, Interview]

But to "keep going" depends not so much on the individual fortitude of nurses such [as] Mavis and Anna, but on the professional and institutional habits of the nursing staff and the hospital. The continuance of care even in the face of obvious failure of efforts is itself a norm. Whatever one's personal disposition, one keeps working; the staff keep working, often when the patient is all but dead, or "dead" but not officially recognized as such:

> Dr. K., walking rounds with four residents, discussing a 30-year-old male patient, HIV-positive, gone totally septic [has bloodstream infection, a deadly problem], no hope at all of recovery—Dr. K. says this is a "100 percent mortality" case; so they decide how to proceed with minimal treatment, at the end of which Dr. K. says brightly, "And if he codes—code him!" [Field Notes]

Coding such a patient is an exercise in technique; there is no hope entailed, no optimism, no idea that he might be saved. There is only the institutional habit which substitutes for hope, which in many cases obviates the staff's pessimism or lack of interest. When standard procedure is followed, courage is unnecessary. It is one thing to be routinely busy, caring for vegetative patients; it happens every day. It is quite another to handle emergency surgery with no time and a life at stake. Sometimes such a case will challenge all the staff's resources—their personal fortitude, their habitualization of procedures, the self-protection offered by an indefatigable sense of humor. To maintain one's composure while under tremendous pressures of time and fatefulness requires all the courage a staff can muster.

One such case was that of emergency surgery on a thirty-five-year-old woman who came to Southwestern Regional hospital in severe abdominal pain; she was diagnosed with a ruptured ectopic [tubal] pregnancy estimated at sixteen weeks. The case provides us with a dramatic example of the pressure placed on the staff to retain their composure in the face of disaster.

The long description which follows is graphic. The scene was more than bloody; it was grotesque. More than one staff member—including one member of the surgical team itself—left the room during the operation, sickened. Other nurses, even very experienced ones, told me they have never witnessed such a scene and hope never to witness one. I include it here, in some detail, to exemplify both what health professionals face in their work and how, incredibly, some of them can carry on. The description is reconstructed from Field Notes (some written at the time on the inside of a surgical mask, some on sheets of paper carried in a pocket), and from interviews afterward with participants:

> Saturday night OR suite; hasn't been busy. Only one case so far, a guy who got beat up with a tire iron (drug deal), finished about 8:30 P.M. It's about 10:00. 2 Ns—the Saturday night staff—sitting around in the conference room, just chatting and waiting for anything that happens.
>
> Call comes over intercom: ruptured tubal (pregnancy) just came in OR, bringing to the crash room. 35-year-old black woman, very heavy—250 pounds maybe—apparently pregnant for 16 weeks, which means she's been in pain for 10 weeks or more without coming in. Friends brought her to ER screaming in pain. Blood pressure is at "60 over palpable," i.e., the diastolic doesn't even register on the manometer. She's obviously bleeding bad internally, will die fast if not opened up. Ns run to OR and set up fast. I've never seen people work so quickly here, no wasted motion at all. This is full speed *emergency.*
>
> When patient is rolled in, fully conscious, there are more than a dozen staff people in the room, including three gynecological surgery residents, who will operate; all three are women. The surgeons are scrubbed and gowned and stand in a line, back from the table, watching without moving, the one in charge periodically giving orders to the nurses who are setting up. At one point there are twelve separate people working on the patient—IVs going into both arms, anesthesiologist putting mask on pt to gas, nurse inserting a Foley [bladder] catheter, others tying pt's arms to the straightout arms of the table, others scrubbing the huge belly, an incredible scene. The patient is shaking terribly, in pain and fear. Her eyes are bugging out, looking around terribly fast. She's whimpering, groaning as needles go in, crying out softly. No one has time even to speak to her; one nurse briefly leans over and speaks into her ear something like "try not to worry, we're going to take care of you," but there is no time for this. I've never seen anyone so afraid, sweating and crying and the violent shaking.
>
> As soon as they have prepped her—the belly cleansed and covered with Opsite, in a matter of minutes, very, very fast, the anesthesiologist says, "All set?" And someone says "yes," and they gas her. I'm standing right by her head, looking to the head side of the drape which separates her head from her body; the instant that her eyes close, I look

to the other side—and the surgeon has already slit her belly open. No hesitation at all, maybe before the patient was out.

What happened next, more extraordinary than the very fast prep, was the opening. Usually in surgery the scalpel makes the skin cut, then slowly scissors are used, snipping piece by piece at muscle, the Bovie cauterizing each blood vessel on the way, very methodical and painstaking. This was nothing like that. It was an entirely different style. They cut fast and deep, sliced her open deep, just chopped through everything, in a—not a panic, but something like a "blitzkrieg," maybe—to get down into the Fallopian tube that had burst and was shooting blood into the abdomen.

When they first got into the abdominal cavity, usually there would be some oozing blood; here as they opened blood splattered out all over the draping on the belly. It was a godawful mess, blood everywhere. They had one surgeon mopping up with gauze sponges, another using a suction pump, a little plastic hose, trying to clean the way. Unbelievable. They got down to the tubes, reaching down and digging around with their hands. And then they found it—suddenly out of this bloody mess down in the abdomen, with the surgeons groping around trying to feel where things were, out of this popped up, right out of the patient and, literally, onto the sheet covering her, the 16-week fetus itself. Immediately one surgeon said mock-cheerfully, "It's a boy!" "God, don't do that," said the scrub tech, turning her head away.

The scrub tech then began to lose it, tears running down her cheeks. Two other people on the team—there were maybe six around the table—said about the same time, nearly together, "Damien!" and "Alien!" recalling recent horror movies, "children of the devil" themes. The fetus lay on the sheet just below the open abdomen for a few moments. The head surgery resident, working, just kept working. The scrub tech should have put the fetus into a specimen tray, but she was falling to pieces fast, crying, and starting to have trouble handing the proper tools to the surgeon, who said something like, "What are you doing?" At this point the circulating nurse, a man, said, "If nobody else will do it," picked up the fetus and put it in a specimen tray, which he then covered with a towel and put aside. He then told another nurse to help him into a gown—he wasn't scrubbed. This violates sterile technique badly, for him to start handling tools, but the scrub tech was becoming a problem. The circulating nurse then quickly gowned and gloved, gently pulled the scrub tech aside and said, "I'll do it." The scrub tech ran out of the room in tears. And the circulating nurse began passing tools to the surgeons himself. It is the circulating nurse's responsibility to handle problems this way, and he did. Another nurse had gone out to scrub properly, and when she came back, maybe ten minutes later, she gowned and gloved and relieved him; so he (the circulating nurse) went back to his regular job of charting the procedure, answering the phone, etc.

By this time, things were under control; the bleeding was stopped, the tube tied off. The other tube was OK and left alone so the pt can get pregnant again. The blood in the abdomen was cleaned up—over 1500 cc's were lost, that's just under a half-gallon of blood. The pt would have died fast if they hadn't gotten in there.

Within two hours after the patient had first rolled in, the room was quiet, only three staff members left, two surgeons and the scrub nurse closing up and talking quietly. Most of the mess—the bloody sponges, the used tools, and all—was gone, cleared away, and all the other staff people, including the chief surgeon, had left. Very calm. The patient, who two hours ago was on the end of a fast terrible death, will be out of the hospital in two days with no permanent damage beyond the loss of one Fallopian tube. [Field Notes, Interviews]

In this situation, we can see two somewhat distinct problems in maintaining the routine order of things: first, the challenge simply in getting the work done; and second, the challenge of upholding the moral order of the hospital.[6] The first issue was resolved by replacing the scrub tech so the operation could continue. The second issue is trickier. The scrub tech's response appeared to be set off not by the horror of what she saw—the bloody fetus—but by the reaction of the assisting surgeon—"It's a boy!" I can only guess that the joke was too much for her. In continuing to work without her, and continuing without noticeable change of demeanor, the surgical team was asserting not only the imperative to protect the operational routine but also, I think, to protect the moral order of emergency surgery as well. That order includes:

1. The job comes first, before personal reactions of fear or disgust.
2. Cynicism is an acceptable form of expression if it helps to maintain composure and distance.
3. The medical team is rightfully in charge and above what may be happening in the OR [operating room].
4. Preserving life is the central value; others (such as niceties of language or etiquette) fall far behind.

There is clearly a morality here. Just as clearly, it is not the morality of everyday life.

NOTES

1. Erving Goffman, "On Face-Work," in *Interaction Ritual: Essays on Face-to-Face Behavior* (New York: Pantheon Books, 1967), p. 11.
2. Ibid., pp. 17–18
3. Renée C. Fox, *Experiment Perilous* (New York: Free Press, 1959; reprint ed., Philadelphia: University of Pennsylvania Press, 1974), pp. 80–82.
4. Rose Laub Coser, "Some Social Functions of Laughter," in Lewis Coser, *The Pleasures of Sociology,* edited and with an introduction and notes by Lewis Coser (New York: New American Library, 1980), pp. 81–97.
5. The genius of Shem's *House of God* is that it accepts this fact and presents it honestly.
6. I am indebted to Robert Zussman, who suggested these in his review of the manuscript.

Becoming a Prostitute

Nanette J. Davis

introduction ■ ▪ ▪ ▪

Society is set up to produce conforming individuals. As we learn the ways of our culture, we learn how we *ought* to act, think, and evaluate people, events, and ourselves. We learn what is expected of us if we are to be considered members of society in good standing. We learn this lesson as we are socialized within our family and later within other social institutions. The overall message we receive is to conform—in behavior and thought. And conformity is necessary, because if society is to survive, there must be rules, or norms, that allow its members to interact cooperatively with one another. This requires that people know what to expect of one another.

Most of us do conform most of the time, but not always. All of us break at least some of the rules, and some of us seem to break most of the rules. Most of us manage to skirt the rules when we want to, yet conform sufficiently to remain members of society in good standing. Some, however, flout the norms to such a degree that they are labeled outsiders. They know the label they receive, and this, in turn, affects how they think of themselves. Note how the women that Davis analyzes gradually move from one set of norms to another.

Thinking Critically

As you read this selection, ask yourself:

1. Why did these young women become prostitutes?

2. How does identifying with hustler norms facilitate entry into prostitution?

3. If you were appointed by the mayor of Minneapolis to develop a program to decrease the prostitution of young women, based on this article what program would you propose?

The source of data for this study is provided by a jail sample of thirty prostitutes from three correctional institutions (reformatory, workhouse, and training school) in Minnesota. Included are seventeen white women, twelve black women, and one Indian woman. The age range was fifteen to thirty-four, with an average age of twenty-one.

From "Becoming a Prostitute," by Nanette J. Davis. In James M. Henslin (Ed.), *Studies in the Sociology of Sex*. Copyright © 1971 by James M. Henslin. Reprinted by permission of James M. Henslin.

All of the thirty women were legally classified as "common prostitute," although only twenty-four of the thirty informants reported that they were professional prostitutes. The women operated at the "street-walker" level of prostitution, that is lounging in bars or on streetcorners and openly soliciting clients. Data were elicited through structured interviews with emphasis, however, on the informants' verbalized statements. The interviews averaged one and one-half to two hours in length. Official records also were used. Further, informal data were gained through participant observation....

THE PROCESS OF DRIFT FROM PROMISCUITY
■ ■ ■ TO THE FIRST ACT OF PROSTITUTION

Age at First Sexual Experience

The women in this sample were initiated into sexual experiences at an early age. The mean age at which they first had sexual intercourse was 13.6, with a range of seven to eighteen. Rape experiences, reported by two women, account for the lower age level (seven and nine years, respectively). Three other informants noted traumatic sexual experiences with brothers, step-father, or father, at age twelve or under. Nineteen of the thirty women report they had sexual intercourse by age thirteen, although almost one-half of the white girls had experienced intercourse by age twelve. The most characteristic pattern was coitus with a boyfriend, who was typically five or six years older than the girl was. Four informants were sexually initiated by another girl with heterosexual relations occurring within a year after such lesbian contacts.... First sexual contacts typically involved sexual intercourse, with only one girl reporting an initial petting experience.

Preconditions for those characterized by "early sexuality" are: (1) high levels of familial permissiveness led to association with older males at parties, neighboring houses, or street pickups, (2) familial social control was often lacking or inconsistent, (3) peer group norms encouraged early sexuality, and (4) sexuality was associated with freedom (a movement away from a disliked family) or, conversely, security (the certainty of male companionship). Three girls, on the other hand, did not experience their first sexual intercourse until age seventeen or eighteen. Those having this "late sexuality" experienced these typical conditions: (1) sexual matters were taboo areas in the family, (2) the mother was highly protective, exerting strong religious and familial controls with consequent little freedom of opportunity in early adolescence, and (3) a rebellion pattern eventually developed in opposition to the rigidity of the controls.

Almost all of the women (twenty-eight of thirty) report that their first sex experience was either meaningless or distasteful; for example, "It was nothing," "I did it just to please him," "I really didn't like it," "I disliked it," "It was awful," "I was scared," "It made me sick." A need for conformity seems to be the most salient motive for this first sexuality, as:

> I did it just to belong. Everybody was doing it.

> I was the only virgin in the crowd (age fifteen). Five of my girlfriends had kids at sixteen....

The promiscuous pattern which developed for most girls (three women had early pregnancies which were followed by marriage, with promiscuity and prostitution occurring *after* these events) seems to reflect associates' expectations, the desire to attract males ("The boys were always hot after me"), and an opportunity structure which facilitated the behavior.

Perception of Childhood and Adolescent Years

The promiscuous pattern may provide one condition which can lead to informal labeling ("bad" girl, "easy mark") and subsequent stigmatization by parents, teachers, and conventional associates. But other circumstances may arise, prior to or following this sexual behavior.... These women perceived their childhood and adolescent years as marked by negative or degrading interactions with society, as the following data indicate:

1. Familial instability was typical for almost all of the white girls (sixteen of seventeen) and two-thirds of the blacks (eight of twelve). Such instability included a drunken, violent or absentee parent (usually the father), extreme poverty, or families larger than the parents could cope with. Conditions within the family were eventually brought to the attention of neighbors, welfare board, or court. Such attention was defined as humiliating or demoralizing.

2. More than half of the informants (eighteen of thirty) have spent one year or more of their childhood (under twelve) in foster homes, living with relatives, or in other separations from the nuclear family.

3. Almost all of the informants (twenty-eight) report that parents, neighbors, and/or teachers considered them "trouble-makers," "slow learners," or generally inadequate in relation to expectations.

4. The black women (nine of twelve), especially, reported "unfair" treatment by white teachers or students, inability to gain and/or hold a job, and frustration in cases where self-improvement was attempted.

5. Twenty-three of the thirty informants reported that they had been sentenced to a juvenile home or training school as adolescents for truancy, incorrigibility, or sex delinquency....

In the interactional processes with significant others (parents, teachers, neighbors, and friends), the girl [is seen as] "different." She is a person who is expected to behave in unconventional ways. Absenteeism from school, chronic disobedience at home, and later, promiscuity, categorize the girl as difficult, if not impossible to control. Low family cohesion with consequent weak affectional ties between parents and daughter leads the girl to seek street associates....

[T]he rationale for promiscuity, and initially for prostitution, is a hedonistic concern for fun, new experiences, excitement, and a response to peer group expectations. Sex as a status tool is exploited to gain male attention. The adolescent urge for liberation from the confines of the family and controls of school and job leads to involvement in drinking parties or hustler groups, where differential identification with sophisticated delinquents occurs.

The Drift from Promiscuity to First Act of Prostitution

Regardless of the age at which the girl first experienced intercourse, there then followed a *"drift" or "slide" process from promiscuity to prostitution,* with the girl first prostituting herself in late adolescence (mean = 17.3 years). There was a range, however, of fourteen to twenty-five years. The early age of prostitution was facilitated by a definition of the deviant situation as similar to sexual promiscuity—excitement and desire for male attention:...

> It was either jump in bed, and go with every Tom, Dick, and Harry, and just give it away, so I decided to turn tricks instead.... The money was so easy to get....

My data strongly suggest that the movement from casual delinquency to the first phase of [prostitution] is facilitated by the policy of confining deviants to correctional institutions. The adolescent girl who is labeled a sex offender for promiscuity or "mixing" (white girls associating with black males) may initially experience a conflict about her identity. Intimate association with sophisticated deviants, however, may provide an incentive to learn the hustler role ("The girls told me about it—I was such an avid listener."), and thus resolve the status anxiety by gaining prestige through association with deviants, and later, experimentation in the deviant role. Frequent and predictable escapes from the open institution are common. Lines of communication between urban vice neighborhoods and training school inmates assures the escapee of finding accommodations during a "run."

As an outlaw, the girl cannot seek the security of parents or the home neighborhood. Thus, isolated from conventional associates or activities, and dependent on deviant contacts for financial and social support, the girl may come to define the situation as one that inevitably leads her into enacting the deviant role, as:

> I ran away from the institution. I went and visited my girlfriends. I was out of the institution about a month, just loafing around. I talked to some friends of mine who were hustlers. Someone suggested I try it. I had been sponging off everybody. I got sick of sponging. I'd sleep here one night, and there another....

> I had run away (from the training school). I had no money or anything. I went walking the street. The older girls (institutionalized associates) told me about it.

Roads to Recruitment

Adolescent institutionalization, then, often prior to the actual commitment of a deviant act, may act as a structural condition which facilitates the learning of a deviant role. Induction into the career, on the other hand, proceeds through alternative routes, chief of which are: (1) response to peer group expectations, (2) involvement in a pimp-manager relationship, and (3) adolescent rebellion.

Response to *peer group expectations* undoubtedly provides the major avenue to recruitment ("It's the environment. Everyone is doing it.") Associating with hustlers, "party girls," or pimps, while viewed as prestigious, can only be maintained by "trying out" the behavior. Clearly, for twenty-eight of the thirty informants, differential identification with deviant associates accounts, in part, for the movement into prostitution.

> I was on run…I didn't get up until 3 P.M. I was staying with my boyfriend. He was unemployed. He was planning to set me up [for prostitution]. We had been talking about it. I took long precautions…. A friend helped me out. Everything happened so fast. It was kind of like prearranged for me. Crazy! We were staying in a hotel with lots of pimps and prostitutes living there. The first time was at the World's Series. I was dressed like a normal teenager….

Involvement in a *pimp-manager relationship* provides a typical method of entrance for some under-age girls (eight informants.) In other instances, the pimp may not have initially arranged the first contact, but he typically appears relatively early on the scene to direct the girl's activities. The uninitiated girl views the pimp relationship as a means of security in an otherwise rejecting world.

> I always had a need to belong…. A pimp moves in, and he sees you're attractive, and he sees you want to belong. Pimps are the most understanding. They're the least educated persons, though. I thought my pimp was my knight in shining armor….

The pimp's ability to "set the girl up" by arranging clients is a measure of the girl's arrival on the deviant scene. One informant, whose first experience was such an arrangement, recalled how the system operated.

> I was living with a girlfriend…. She wasn't a hustler—and started going with this one boy. He introduced me to this pimp. He asked me if I would [hustle]. I was against it, but they all said how easy it was. I went to this pimp's house. I was a call girl. There were three of us [hustlers]. The pimps would come in. They got all the contacts, and they'd say to the tricks, "Lookee here, I got these girls, see," and he'd line up the tricks. Then he'd say to the girls that there was a trick in this hotel, and you'd go to a room number.

Another girl commented that the pimp used alternate techniques of violence ("He hit me on the head when I said no") and persuasion: "He told me, 'I can put you in big business. You won't have to hustle hard.' I saw the girls and how they did it. It was like a dream."

Adolescent rebellion operates for girls who have experienced oppressive familial controls (six women), forming another typical pattern.

> Well, I started hustling, I suppose, because the party group I ran around with were always talking about it. My mother had always picked my friends. She wouldn't allow any bad influences—the square friends only, the goody-goody club activities at church. My parents were very old-fashioned. They didn't drink or smoke, and were very church-going. But when I got in with this group, it was really different, man!…

Dominant Motives during the First Stage

Underlying these main roads to recruitment into prostitution are curiosity and a desire for new experience, defined idleness, identification with hustler norms, and a strong present-time orientation.

Curiosity and access to new experiences (or "kicks") act as a dominant motive to the naive girl who seeks esteem from the hustler group. "I was unemployed at the time, just hanging around with a group. I wanted some excitement—kicks, you know."

Remarks such as, "It was the glamor and game of it," "I did it just for the fun of it," "There's a lot of excitement to that—the cops on you and everything," indicate a perception of deviance as part of the excitement and risk of street life....

Idleness is typical for most of the women (twenty-three of thirty). Separations from family, school, job, or other conventional activities characterize this first deviant phase. For the runaway training school girl, prostitution may relieve the dullness of an otherwise undirected existence.

> I was sixteen and on the run, just loafing around my girlfriend's house. One of my girlfriends gave me the pointers, so I decided to try it.

> I had run away—like I was lost or something. I had been walking the streets all day, and at 6 P.M. I met this guy. I was really looking for love and attention, but not necessarily the men.

Identification with hustler norms undoubtedly accounts for the frequently expressed (twenty-seven of thirty) money rationale. However, economic deprivation is not the dominant element for most girls. Only two women, for instance, expressed intense financial need because of child support. Independence, isolation from conventional supports, and the lure of "easy" money, were major considerations.

> I was on run—no job or anything. I was by myself. It was about 8. I went out, went downtown. My boyfriend worked in the _____ Hotel. He called me up to say that he had a man who had fifty dollars to get a girl, and so there it was. I got forty-five dollars the first night—for four men. Everyone was doing it, anyway. Then I walked back downtown, and had three more, and then went back to my apartment.

A strong present-time orientation characterizes the younger girl particularly, who conceives of the act as satisfying immediate needs only, without considering long-range implications.

> The first time I did it was to buy a present for my boyfriend. The next time just to have some spending money. I've been asked to hustle lots of times. I know all the gimmicks, and how to do it...all that stuff.

> I was going to school and I wanted to go to this dance the night after. I needed new clothes. I went out at ten o'clock and home at twelve. I had three tricks the first time, and fifteen dollars for every trick.

Whatever the mode of recruitment, or the dominant motives involved, this study shows certain common elements present at this state of deviant involvement.

These generally include: informal labeling which early categorizes the girl as unconventional or "troublemaker"; isolation from conventional family, friends, or associates; response to deviant associates' expectations; and expressed need for economic self-sufficiency while "on run" or probation. Such motives indicate that: (1) episodic involvement, or *a drift into deviance,* is characteristic of prostitutes and is related to hedonistic and short-term concerns; and (2) stigmatized persons may respond to a morally degraded status by seeking associates who may reward the deviant behavior.

Transitional Deviance and Professionalization

Twenty-one of the thirty women interviewed experienced an "occasional" or "transitional" stage of deviance. Of the nine other labeled prostitutes, four repudiated the role after three or more deviant episodes, while five women moved directly into full-time deviance. The transitional stage lasted an average of six months (with a range from two weeks to four years). It could be viewed as an on-the-job learning period....

Motivational ambivalence during the transitional phase creates a zig-zag pattern of deviance for most prostitutes. They vacillate between conventionality and deviance. The conventional life, for instance, is not yet denied. Some girls make verbal commitments to stop, or even attempt to return to home, school, job or to set themselves up in an apartment with conventional associates. Conventional motives involve expressed reluctance to move into the act because of fear of discovery, interracial contacts, or belief that such conduct is immoral. ("It's not the right thing to do. I would get a bad reputation.")...

During this phase, they indicate indecision and confusion regarding their role. By hustling only occasionally, not more than two or three times a week, or engaging in prostitution "only when I wanted to," or "sometimes when I'm lonesome," or for "just something to do," the individual perceives that she is in control of the situation....

[T]he drift into deviance...occurs through *normalization of the act*.... [This] may occur through rationalizations appropriate for promiscuity—the desire for male attention....

> I'm a person who likes to walk. There's nothing wrong with picking somebody up while you're walking. I always like walking around at night, and girls will be tempted. Girls like the offer. They like to see what the guy is going to say.

The "gaming" element, which revolves around the excitement of the "pickup" and independence on the street, is also linked to a promiscuous, rather than deviant, orientation. The promiscuous girl with conventional in-group supports may not define herself as a prostitute at this point.

In certain cases, role ambivalence may even lead to repudiation of the "trial" role after a few experiences (four informants). Negative experiences with a client, pimp, or policeman, for instance, may lead her to reject the role. Inadequate motivation is a typical condition leading to role failure in many areas of life. It was expressed by one seventeen-year old informant who had hustled on-and-off for about a month before her career had been interrupted by jail:

> Hustling—I don't get no kicks from it. I wouldn't go out and do it for a living. There are better ways to make money. I couldn't go through everything a prostitute goes through. I really don't have the guts for it. A prostitute picks up anyone off the street and gets money for it. The tricks I had it with I did it just for sex, but not for me—not the whole self. I knew I couldn't make a career out of it. When you don't care about the guy, sex isn't for that.

Sex with affection, uncontaminated by money, still operates as a norm for the deviant dropout.

Their continuation in this sexually deviant behavior, on the other hand, is contingent on strong economic motivation (twenty-one women), loneliness (three), and/ or expressed entrapment because of pimp control (six). For two girls, drug addiction acted as an inducement for continuation of the deviant role. Continuation in the deviant role is further contingent on an adequate learning period uninterrupted by police harassment or jail sentencing....

Delayed definitions of the act as immoral, degrading or repulsive (fifteen women report intense dissatisfaction or disgust with the situation) can no longer be postponed if situations occur that force unequivocal perception of a deviant self. Self-discovery, for instance, may be inevitable for some prostitutes when the pimp's behavior shifts from lover to exploiter, and, for example, nightly money quotas become the primary condition for the relationship ("I was just another one of his hustlers").... Another typical experience is contact with the police, court, or jail, where the label "common prostitute" is assigned. After the legal confrontation, public exposure proceeds in rapid order. Listing the girl's name in the paper, or passing the information to parents from "inside" sources, implies that, as a consequence, the girl soon renounces the pretense of conventional commitments. At this point, she may cut herself off from family and conventional others' support. Informants report such responses to the labeling procedure:

> They sent me up for something I didn't do, so I might as well do it. I wasn't afraid of anything.

> Society is really uninformed. They don't put themselves to the trouble to understand. There are lots worse things besides prostitution that happen. Society isn't helping at all. There's not a chance to be decent. Society has put the brand on us.

Personal integrity at earlier phases of the career had been maintained by secrecy regarding the deviant behavior. Role segmentation breaks down, however, if the woman has internalized the streetwalker's myth—"once a girl is on the streets, everyone knows what she is." For example,

> At first I was scared. The news gets out so fast. Everyone knows when a girl's on the streets a couple of nights. I thought about stopping, you know, but I just went on....

In-service training for this streetwalker group during the transitional period includes: (1) willingness to satisfy a broad range of client requests, requiring certain social and sexual skills; (2) elimination of fears regarding clients who are defined as "odd" (sadomasochists); (3) adaptation to police surveillance and entrapment procedures; (4) avoidance of drunken clients, or those unable or unwilling to pay; and (5) substitution of a "business" ethic for the earlier one of "gaming" or excitement....

[After a woman has gone through this process of learning and of making the required adjustment in her identity, she has *become* a prostitute. Sex has become her vocation.]

NOTE

This study is based on an unpublished Master's thesis, "Prostitution and Social Control: An Empirical Inquiry into the Socialization Process of Deviant Behavior" (1967) University of Minnesota, under the direction of Professor David A. Ward.

The writer wishes to express appreciation to James M. Henslin, Peter K. Manning, Bernard N. Meltzer, John Petras, and Ira Reiss for their helpful comments.

The selection is a condensed version of the author's more detailed analysis appearing in *Studies in the Sociology of Sex,* James M. Henslin, ed. New York: Appleton-Century-Crofts, 1971: 297–322, and the revised edition, *The Sociology of Sex: An Introductory Reader,* James M. Henslin and Edward Sagarin, eds. New York: Schocken Books, 1978: 195–222.

Outlaw Motorcyclists

J. Mark Watson

introduction

Who are those strange people? You occasionally see them riding on the highways, or perhaps lounging outside some seedy bar, or grouped somewhere in a public park. Almost without exception, when you see them they are part of a group, and the appearance of each person is remarkably similar. Their demeanor, as well as their uniform of denim and insignia, make a lot of people nervous, and most people steer a wide path around them.

What do they represent, these dirty, unkempt men? Why do they look so different from most people? What is it about big, noisy motorcycles that so attracts them? How do they feel about the rest of us? What women would ever be attracted to them? And for those who are, what is it like to live as a woman among these men? Mark Watson answers these questions. As he does so, he provides us a glimpse inside one of the most intriguing—and feared—groups in U.S. society.

Thinking Critically

As you read this selection, ask yourself:

1. If you are a man, would you like to be an outlaw biker? Why or why not? If you are a woman, would you like to be a biker's woman? Why or why not?

2. What are the essential characteristics of this group? That is, what are their values and goals, and how do their behaviors match those values and goals? How do their values differ from mainstream society?

3. How do outlaw bikers see the world? How do they see themselves?

Walter Miller's (1958) typology of focal concerns of lower-class culture as a generating milieu for gang delinquency is by most standards a classic in explaining gang behavior among juvenile males. Its general heuristic value is here demonstrated by the striking parallel between this value system and that of adult outlaw motorcyclists.

The reader may remember Miller's general schema, which concerned the strain between the value system of youthful lower class males and the dominant, middle-class value system of those in a position to define delinquent behavior.... Because the typology itself is contained in the discussion of biker values, it will not be discussed separately here.

■ ■ ■ **METHODOLOGY**

The findings of the paper are based on my three years of participant observation in the subculture of outlaw motorcyclists. Although I am not a member of any outlaw clubs, I am or have been acquainted with members and officers of various clubs, as well as more loosely organized groups of motorcyclists for ten years. I am myself a motorcycle enthusiast, which facilitated a natural entry into the biker scene. I both build and ride bikes and gained direct access to local biker groups by frequenting places where bikers congregate to work on their bikes. Building a bike gave me legitimation and access to local biker groups and eventually led to contact with other bikers, including outlaws. Groups observed varied from what could be classified as clubs to loose-knit groups of associated motorcyclists. Four groups were studied in depth. Two small local groups in middle Tennessee were subjects of direct participation. Here they are given the fictional names of the Brothers and the Good Old Boys. In addition, one regional group from North Carolina, given the fictional name of Bar Hoppers, was studied through interviews with club officers and members. One national level group, one of the largest groups of outlaw motorcyclists, was extensively observed and interviewed, primarily at regional and national events. This group is given the fictional name of the Convicts....

Interviews were informally administered in the sense that no formal interview schedule was used. Instead, bikers were queried in the context of what would pass for normal conversation.... Notes and impressions were taken at night and/or after the events. Groups and individuals were generally not aware that they were being studied, although I made no attempt to hide my intentions. Some bikers who came to know me were curious about a university professor participating in such activities and accordingly were told that a study was being conducted. This honesty was prompted by fear of being suspected of being a narcotics agent. Such self-revelation was rarely necessary as the author affected the clothing and jargon of bikers and was accepted as such. Frequent invitations to engage in outrageous and illegal behavior (e.g., drug use and purchase of stolen parts) that would not be extended to outsiders were taken as a form of symbolic acceptance. My demeanor and extensive association with lower-class gangs in adolescence combined with the type of mechanical skills necessary to build bikes mentioned earlier may have contributed to an ability to blend in. Reactions to self-revelation, when necessary, generally ranged from amazement to amusement. I suspect that, as is true with the general population, most bikers had no idea what a sociologist was, but the presence of a professor in their midst was taken as a sort of legitimation for the group....

It must be kept in mind that research conducted with this kind of deviant subculture can be dangerous. Because many outlaws do not welcome scrutiny and carefully avoid those who they feel may not be trusted, which includes most nonbikers, I remained as unobtrusive as possible.... Generally, I felt my presence was accepted.... This acceptance can be symbolized by my receiving a nickname (Doc) and eventually being defined as an expert in a certain type of obsolete motorcycle (the Harley-Davidson 45-cubic-inch side-valve model). I assumed the role of an inside outsider.

■ ■ ■ THE BIKER SUBCULTURE

We may locate outlaw bikers in the general spectrum of bikers as the most "outrageous" (their own term, a favorite modifier indicating something distinctively appealing to their own jaded sense of values) on the continuum of bikers, which extends from housewives on mopeds to clubs that actually engage in illegal behavior with a fair degree of frequency, thus the term "outlaws" (Thompson, 1967:9). Outlaws generally adopt certain symbols and lead a life-style that is clearly defined and highly visible to other bikers. Symbols include extensive tattooing, beard, dirty jeans, earrings, so-called stroker caps and quasi-military pins attached, engineer's boots, and cut-off jackets with club emblems, called "colors," sewn on the back. Weapons, particularly buck knives and guns of any sort, and chains (motorcycle or other types) are favorite symbols as well (*Easyriders,* February 1977:28, 29, 55). By far the most important symbol, however, is the Harley-Davidson V-twin motorcycle. It should be kept in mind that many other motorcyclists affect these symbols, although they are by no means outlaws....

■ ■ ■ OUTLAW LIFE-STYLE

...This life-style is in many respects a lower-class variation of bohemian, "dropout" subcultures. Such similarities include frequent unemployment and disdain for cleanliness, orderliness, and other concerns of conventional culture. For example, I have observed bikes being built and stored in living rooms or kitchens, two nonessential rooms in the subculture. This is apparently a common practice. Parts may be stored in an oil bath in the bathtub, also a nonessential device....

Although individual freedom and choice are also emphasized, the clubs actually suppress individual freedom, while using the value to defend their life-style from outsiders. For example, when the Convicts take a club trip called a "run," all members must participate. Those whose bikes are "down" for repairs are fined and must find a ride in a truck with the women. Many club rules require members to follow orders as prescribed by club decisions upon threat of violence and expulsion. Club rules generally include a constitution and bylaws that are surprisingly elaborate and sophisticated for groups of this nature. Many club members express pride in their written regulations. It seems likely that the basic format is borrowed from that developed by the Hell's Angels (Thompson, 1967:72). Most club decisions are made in a democratic way, but minority rights are not respected. Once such a decision is made, it is imperative to all members, with risk of physical retribution for failure to conform. Typical rules include care of colors, which are to never touch the ground or be washed. They are treated essentially as a flag....

Masculinity as a dominant value is expressed in many ways, including toughness and a general concern with looking mean, dirty, and "outrageous."... Some other biker-associated values include racism, concern with Nazism, and in-group superiority. "Righteousness" is achieved through adherence to these values. One celebrity member of the Brothers had been convicted of killing a young black man in a street confrontation. He is reported to have jumped bail and lived with a Nazi couple in South America, where he worked as a ranch hand: This particular member spoke some German and frequently spouted racist and Nazi doctrine. A typical righteous outlaw belongs to a club, rides an American-made motorcycle, is a white male, displays the subculture's symbols, hates most if not all nonwhites and Japanese motorcycles, works irregularly at best, dresses at all times in dirty jeans, cut-off denim jacket, and engineer's boots, drinks beer, takes whichever drugs are available, and treats women as objects of contempt.

■ ■ ■ ■ OUTLAW BIKER WORLD VIEW AND SELF-CONCEPT

The outlaw biker generally views the world as hostile, weak, and effeminate. Perhaps this view is a realistic reaction to a working-class socialization experience. However, the reaction contains certain elements of a self-fulfilling prophecy. Looking dirty, mean, and generally undesirable may be a way of frightening others into leaving one alone, although, in many senses such an appearance arouses anger, hostility, and related emotions in the observer and results in the persecution that such qualities are intended to protect one from.

Bikers tend to see the world in terms of here and now. They are not especially hostile toward most social institutions such as family, government, and education. Most of the local group members had finished high school and had been employed from time to time, and some had been college students. Some were veterans, and nearly all had been married more than once. Few had been successful in these endeavors, however. They are generally not capable of establishing the temporal commitments necessary for relating to such institutions. For example, marriages and similar relationships rarely last more than a few years, and education requires concentrated effort over a time span that they are generally not willing or in many cases not capable of exerting. Most of them drift from one job to another or have no job at all. Simply keeping up with where the informants were living proved to be a challenge. I frequently had a call from a local biker relating that he was "on his way over" only to find that he did not arrive at all or arrived hours or days later. I have been on runs that were to depart in the early morning and that did not in fact depart until hours later. The biker's sense, of time and commitment to it is not only lower class, but more typical of preliterate societies. The result is frequent clashes with bureaucratically organized institutions, such as government and economy, which are oriented toward impulse control, commitment, and punctuality, and failure in organizations that require long-term commitments or interpersonal relations, such as family and education....

Outlaw bikers generally view themselves as outsiders. I have on occasion invited local bikers to settings that would place them in contact with members of the middle class. Their frequent response is that they would "not fit in" or would "feel out of place." Basically, they seem to feel that they cannot compete with what sociologists define as the middle class although I have never heard the term used by bikers. Outlaws see themselves as losers, as symbolized by tattoos, patches, and even their humor, which portrays them as ignorant. "One percenter" is a favorite patch, referring to its wearers as the most deviant fraction of the biker fraternity. In effect, the world that they create for themselves is an attempt to suspend the rules of competition that they cannot win by and create a world where one does not compete but simply exists (Montgomery, 1976, 1977). Pretense and self-importance are ways to lose acceptance quickly in such a situation. One does not compete with or "put down" a fellow biker, for he is a "brother."

It is not that bikers are uniformly hostile toward the outside world; they are indifferent toward, somewhat threatened by, and contemptuous of it.

■ ■ ■ MILLER'S FOCAL CONCERNS AS EXPRESSED IN OUTLAW BIKER CULTURE

Trouble

Trouble is a major theme of the outlaw biker culture as illustrated by the very use of the term "outlaw." The term refers to one who demonstrates his distinctiveness (righteousness) by engaging in outrageous and even illegal behavior. Trouble seems to serve several purposes in this subculture. First, flirting with trouble is a way of demonstrating masculinity—trouble is a traditionally male prerogative. Trouble also enforces group solidarity through emphasizing the outsider status of the outlaw, a status that can be sustained only by the formation of counterculture. Given the outlaw biker's world view and impulsiveness, trouble comes without conscious effort. Trouble may come over drug use, stolen bikes or parts, possession of fire-arms, or something as simple as public drunkenness. Some of the local bikers whom I knew well had prison records for manslaughter (defined as self-defense by the subjects), receiving stolen property, drug possession, statutory rape, and assault on an officer. All saw these sentences as unjust and claimed that the behavior was justifiable or that they were victims of a case of overzealous regulation of everyday activities or deliberate police harassment....

Toughness

In addition to trouble, toughness is at the heart of the biker emphasis on masculinity and outrageousness. To be tough is to experience trouble without showing signs of weakness. Therefore, the objective of trouble is to demonstrate the masculine form of toughness. Bikers have contempt for such comforts as automobiles or even devices that increase biking comfort or safety such as eye protection, helmets, wind-shields, farings, or even frames with spring rear suspension (a so-called hardtail is the preferred frame). Bikers wear denim or leather, but the sleeves are generally removed to show contempt for the danger of "road rash," abrasions caused by contact with the road surface at speed, which protective material can prevent.

Part of toughness is the prohibition against expressing love for women and children in any but a possessive way. Women are viewed with contempt and are regarded as a necessary nuisance (generally referred to as "cunts," "whores," or "sluts"), as are children ("rug rats"). Curiously, bikers seem to attract an adequate supply of women despite the poor treatment they receive from them.... When asked about the female's motivation for participation in the subculture, one (male) informant stated simply "they're looking for excitement." The women attracted to such a scene are predictably tough and hard-bitten themselves. Not all are unattractive, but most display signs of premature aging typical of lower-class and deviant life-styles. All work to keep up their mate and his motorcycle. I must admit that my interviews with biker women were limited lest my intentions be misinterpreted. I could have hired some of them under sexual pretenses, as many may be bought, but ethical and financial considerations precluded this alternative. My general impression is that these women generally come from lower-class families in which the status of the female is not remarkably different from that they currently enjoy. Being a biker's "old lady" offers excitement and opportunities to engage in exhibitionist and outlandish behavior that in their view contrasts favorably with the lives of their mothers. Many are mothers of illegitimate children before they resort to bikers and may view themselves as fallen women who have little to lose in terms of respectability. Most seem to have fairly low self-concepts, which are compatible with their status as bikers' old ladies.

Of course, the large, heavy motorcycles bikers ride are symbolic of their toughness as well. Not everyone can ride such a machine because of its sheer weight. Many models are "kick start," and require some strength and skill just to start. A certain amount of recklessness is also used to express toughness.... [T]he ability to ride it, wreck it, and survive demonstrates toughness in a very dramatic way. An example of my experience in this regard may be illuminating. Although I had ridden motorcycles for years, I became aware of the local biker group while building my first Harley-Davidson. Full acceptance by this group was not extended until my first and potentially fatal accident, however. Indeed, local bikers who had only vaguely known me offered the gift of parts and assistance in reconstructing my bike and began to refer to me by a new nickname, "Doc." I sensed and was extended a new degree of acceptance after demonstrating my "toughness" by surviving the accident. Toughness, in this sense, is a combination of stupidity and misfortune, and hardly relates to any personal virtue.

Smartness

On this characteristic, biker values seem to diverge from general lower-class values as described by Miller. The term "dumb biker" is frequently used as a self-description. Given the choice of avoiding, outsmarting, or confronting an opponent, the biker seems to prefer avoidance or confrontation. Confrontation gives him the opportunity to demonstrate toughness by generating trouble. Avoidance is not highly valued, but no one can survive all the trouble he could generate, and the stakes are frequently the highest—life itself or at least loss of freedom. The appearance of toughness and outlandishness mentioned above make confrontation a relatively infrequent occurrence, as few outsiders will challenge a group of outlaw bikers unless the issue is of great significance. Smartness, then, does not seem to be an emphasized biker value or characteristic. Gambling on outsmarting an opponent is for low stakes such as those faced by the adolescents Miller studied.

Excitement

One of the striking things about the outlaw life-style is its extremes. Bikers hang out at chopper (motorcycle) shops, clubhouses, or bars during the day, except when they are in prison or jail, which is not uncommon. Places frequented by bikers are generally located in lower-class neighborhoods. A clubhouse, for example, is generally a rented house which serves as a headquarters, party location, and place for members to "crash" when they lack more personal accommodations. They are not unlike a lower-class version of a fraternity house. Outlaws tend to designate bars as their own. This involves taking over bars to the exclusion of their usual lower- or working-class clientele. Such designations are frequently short-lived, as the bars may be closed as a public nuisance or the proprietor may go out of business for economic or personal reasons as a result of the takeover. I know of at least one such bar that was burned by local people to rid the neighborhood of the nuisance. Its owner relocated the business some 40 miles away.

Local bikers who worked generally had unskilled and semi-skilled jobs, which are dull in themselves. Examples include laborers, factory workers, construction workers, and hospital orderlies. Many do not work regularly, being supported by their women.[1] In any case most of their daylight hours are spent in deadly dull environment where the most excitement may be a mechanical problem with a bike. Escape from this dull life-style is dramatic in its excesses. Drugs, alcohol, and orgiastic parties are one form of escape. Other escapes include the run or simply riding the bikes for which the subculture is named. Frequently both forms of escape are combined, and such events as the Daytona and Sturgis runs are remarkable, comparing favorably to Mardis Gras as orgiastic events. Living on the edge of trouble, appearing outlandish, fierce, and tough, itself yields a form of self-destructive excitement, especially when it can be used to outrage others.

Unlike the situation that Miller studied, excitement and trouble rarely seem to center around women, as their status among bikers is even lower than in the lower class in general. I have never seen a conflict over a woman among bikers and am struck by the casual manner in which they move from one biker to another. The exchange of women seems to be the male's prerogative, and women appear to be traded or given away as casually as pocket knives are exchanged among old men. I have on occasion been offered the use of a female for the duration of a run. This offer was always made by the male and was made in the same manner that one might offer the use of a tool to a neighbor. (I have never been offered the loan of a bike, however.) The low regard for women combined with the traditional biker's emphasis on brotherhood seems to minimize conflicts over women. Those conflicts that do occur over women seem to occur between clubs and are a matter of club honor rather than jealousy or grief over the loss of a relationship.

Fate

Because bikers do not emphasize smartness to the extent that Miller perceived it among the lower class, the role of fate in explaining failure to succeed is somewhat different for them. In Miller's analysis fate was a rationalization used when one was outsmarted. The biker's attitude toward fate goes much deeper and could be described as figuratively and literally fatalistic. The theme of death is central to their literature and art.[2] A biker who becomes economically successful or who is too legitimate is suspect. He is no longer one of them. He has succeeded in the outside and in a sense has sold out. His success alone shows his failure to subscribe to the basic values that they hold. He is similar to a rich Indian—no longer an Indian but a white man with red skin. Members of local groups, the Brothers and the Good Old Boys, came and went. Membership fluctuated. Few members resigned because of personal difficulty. However, many former members were still around. The single characteristic that they all shared was economic success. Although these former members tended to be older than the typical member, many current members were as old or older. Success in small businesses were typical. Some former members had been promoted to lower management positions in local factories and related businesses, apparently were no longer comfortable in their former club roles, and so resigned. Some kept their bikes, others exchanged them for more respectable touring bikes, and others sold their bikes. In any case, although some maintained limited social contact and others participated in occasional weekend runs, their success appeared to make them no longer full participants in group activities and resulted ultimately in their formal resignation from the clubs. Bikers basically see themselves as losers and affect clothing, housing, and other symbols of the embittered and dangerous loser. They apparently no longer dream the unrealistic adolescent dreams of the "big break." Prison and death are seen as natural concomitants of the biker life-style. Fate is the grim reaper that so often appears in biker art.

Autonomy

Autonomy in the form of freedom is central to the outlaw biker's expressed philosophy and in this respect closely parallels the lower-class themes outlined by Miller. A studied insistence that they be left alone by harassing law enforcement agencies and overregulating bureaucrats is a common theme in biker literature and personal expressions. The motorcycle itself is an individual thing, begrudgingly including an extra seat for an "old lady" or "down" brother. Ironically, the outlaw biker life-style is so antisocial vis-à-vis the wider society that it cannot be pursued individually. A lone outlaw knows he is a target, an extremely visible and vulnerable one. Therefore, for purposes of self-protection, the true outlaw belongs to a club and rarely makes a long trip without the company of several brothers.

Outlaw clubs are themselves both authoritarian and democratic. Members may vote on issues or at least select officers, but club policy and rules are absolute and may be enforced with violence (*Choppers*, March 1978:36–39). Antisocial behavior associated with the outlaw life-style itself frequently results in loss of autonomy. Most prisons of any size not only contain a substantial biker population but may contain local (prison) chapters of some of the larger clubs (*Life*, August 1979:80–81). *Easyriders*, a biker magazine, regularly contains sections for pen pals and other requests from brothers in prison (*Easyriders*, October 1977b:16–19, 70). So, although autonomy in the form of the right to be different is pursued with a vengeance, the ferocity with which it is pursued ensures its frequent loss.

Miller noted an ambivalent attitude among lower-class adolescents toward authority: They both resented it and sought situations in which it was forced on them. The structure of outlaw clubs and the frequent incarceration that is a result of their life-style would seem to be products of a similar ambivalence. Another loss of autonomy that Miller noted among lower-class gangs was a dependence on females that caused dissonance and was responsible for lower-class denigration of female status. Outlaws take the whole process a step further, however. Many of their women engage in prostitution, topless waitressing, or menial, traditionally female labor. Some outlaws live off the income of several women and in this sense are dependent on them but only in the sense that a pimp is dependent on his string of girls. From their point of view, the females see themselves as protected by and dependent on the male rather than the other way around.

Conclusion

Miller's typology of lower-class focal concerns appears to be a valid model for analyzing outlaw biker cultures; just as it was for analyzing some forces behind juvenile gang delinquency. Although there are some differences in values and their expression, the differences are basically those occurring by the transferring of the values from street-wise adolescents to adult males. [My] experiences with bikers indicate a working-class family background with downward mobility. A surprising proportion of the bikers interviewed indicated respectable working-class or lower-middle-class occupations for their fathers. Examples included postal worker, forestry and lumber contractor, route sales business owner, and real estate agency owner. They are definitely not products of multigenerational poverty. I would classify them as nonrespectable working-class marginals.

The study is presented primarily as an ethnographic description of a difficult and sometimes dangerous subculture to study, which when viewed from the outside appears as a disorganized group of deviants but when studied carefully with some insider's insights is seen to have a coherent and reasonably consistent value system and a life-style based on that value system.

NOTES

1. Outlaw bikers sometimes support themselves by dealing in drugs, bootleg liquor, and prostitution of their women.

2. Of the fiction in the entire 1977 issue of *Easyriders,* 40 percent of the articles concerned themselves with death.

REFERENCES

Choppers (1978). "Club profile: Northern Indiana Invaders M/C." (March):36.

Easyriders (1977a). "Gun nut report." (February):28, 29, 55.

Easyriders (1977b). "Man is the ruler of woman." (October):15.

———. (1977c). "Jammin in the joint." (October):16–19 (Also "Mail call").

———. (1977c). "Gun nut report."

Life (1979). "Prison without stripes." (August):80–81.

Miller, Walter B. (1958). "Lower class culture as a generating milieu for gang delinquency." *Journal of Social Issues* 14:5–19.

Montgomery, Randall (1976). "The outlaw motorcycle subculture." *Canadian Journal of Criminology and Corrections* 18.

———. (1979). "The outlaw motorcycle subculture II." *Canadian Journal of Criminology and Corrections* 19.

Thompson, Hunter (1967). *Hell's Angels: A Strange and Terrible Saga.* New York: Random House.

The Uses of Poverty: The Poor Pay All

Herbert J. Gans

introduction ▪ ▪ ▪ ▪

Of the several social classes in the United States, sociologists have concentrated their studies on the poor. The super-rich and, for the most part, the ordinarily wealthy are beyond the reach of researchers. Sociologists are not members of the wealthy classes or of the power elite, and members of these groups have the means to insulate themselves from the prying eyes (and questionnaires and tape recorders) of sociologists. When it comes to the middle classes, sociologists are likely to take their members for granted. The middle classes are part of their everyday life, and, like others, sociologists often overlook the things closest to them. The characteristics and situations of the poor, however, are different enough to strike the interests of sociologists. And the poor are accessible. People in poverty are generally willing to be interviewed. They are even a bit flattered that sociologists, for the most part members of the upper middle class, will take the time to talk to them. Hardly anyone else takes them seriously.

A couple of thousand years ago, Jesus said, "The poor you'll always have with you." In this selection, as Herbert Gans places the sociological lens yet again on people in poverty, he uses a functionalist perspective to explain why we always will have people in poverty. Simply put, from a functionalist perspective, we *need* the poor.

Thinking Critically

As you read this selection, ask yourself:

1. What functions (or uses) of poverty does Gans identify?

2. Of the functions of poverty that Gans identifies, which two do you think are the most important? Which two the least important? Why?

3. Do you think that Gans has gone overboard with his analysis? That he has stretched the functionalist perspective beyond reason? Or do you agree with him? Why or why not?

Some years ago Robert K. Merton applied the notion of functional analysis to explain the continuing though maligned existence of the urban political machine: If it continued to exist, perhaps it fulfilled latent—unintended or unrecognized—positive functions. Clearly it did. Merton pointed out how the political machine provided central authority to get things done when a decentralized local government could not act, humanized the services of the impersonal bureaucracy for fearful citizens, offered concrete help (rather than abstract law or justice) to the poor, and otherwise performed services needed or demanded by many people but considered unconventional or even illegal by formal public agencies.

Today, poverty is more maligned than the political machine ever was; yet it, too, is a persistent social phenomenon. Consequently, there may be some merit in applying functional analysis to poverty, in asking whether it also has positive functions that explain its persistence.

Merton defined functions as "those observed consequences [of a phenomenon] which make for the adaptation or adjustment of a given [social] system." I shall use a slightly different definition; instead of identifying functions for an entire social system, I shall identify them for the interest groups, socioeconomic classes, and other population aggregates with shared values that "inhabit" a social system. I suspect that in a modern heterogeneous society, few phenomena are functional or dysfunctional for the society as a whole, and that most result in benefits to some groups and costs to others. Nor are any phenomena indispensable; in most instances, one can suggest what Merton calls "functional alternatives" or equivalents for them, i.e., other social patterns or policies that achieve the same positive functions but avoid the dysfunction. (In the following discussion, positive functions will be abbreviated as functions and negative functions as dysfunctions. Functions and dysfunctions, in the planner's terminology, will be described as benefits and costs.)

Associating poverty with positive functions seems at first glance to be unimaginable. Of course, the slumlord and the loan shark are commonly known to profit from the existence of poverty, but they are viewed as evil men, so their activities are classified among the dysfunctions of poverty. However, what is less often recognized, at least by the conventional wisdom, is that poverty also makes possible the existence or expansion of respectable professions and occupations, for example, penology, criminology, social work, and public health. More recently, the poor have provided jobs for professional and para-professional "poverty warriors," and for journalists and social scientists, this author included, who have supplied the information demanded by the revival of public interest in poverty.

Clearly, then, poverty and the poor may well satisfy a number of positive functions for many nonpoor groups in American society. I shall describe 13 such functions—economic, social and political—that seem to me most significant.

■ ■ ■ **THE FUNCTIONS OF POVERTY**

First, the existence of poverty ensures that society's "dirty work" will be done. Every society has such work: physically dirty or dangerous, temporary, dead-end and underpaid, undignified, and menial jobs. Society can fill these jobs by paying higher wages than for "clean" work, or it can force people who have no other choice to do the dirty work—and at low wages. In America, poverty functions to provide a low-wage labor pool that is willing—or rather, unable to be *un*willing—to perform dirty work at low cost. Indeed, this function of the poor is so important that in some Southern states, welfare payments have been cut off during the summer months when the poor are needed to work in the fields. Moreover, much of the debate about the Negative Income Tax and the Family Assistance Plan [welfare programs] has concerned their impact on the work incentive, by which is actually meant the incentive of the poor to do the needed dirty work if the wages therefrom are no larger than the income grant. Many economic activities that involve dirty work depend on the poor for their existence: restaurants, hospitals, parts of the garment industry, and "truck farming," among others, could not persist in their present form without the poor.

Second, because the poor are required to work at low wages, they subsidize a variety of economic activities that benefit the affluent. For example, domestics subsidize the upper-middle and upper classes, making life easier for their employers and freeing affluent women for a variety of professional, cultural, civic, and partying activities. Similarly, because the poor pay a higher proportion of their income in property and sales taxes, among others, they subsidize many state and local governmental services that benefit more affluent groups. In addition, the poor support innovation in medical practice as patients in teaching and research hospitals and as guinea pigs in medical experiments.

Third, poverty creates jobs for a number of occupations and professions that serve or "service" the poor, or protect the rest of society from them. As already noted, penology would be minuscule without the poor, as would the police. Other activities and groups that flourish because of the existence of poverty are the numbers game, the sale of heroin and cheap wines and liquors, Pentecostal ministers, faith healers, prostitutes, pawn shops, and the peacetime army, which recruits its enlisted men mainly from among the poor.

Fourth, the poor buy goods others do not want and thus prolong the economic usefulness of such goods—day-old bread, fruit and vegetables that otherwise would have to be thrown out, secondhand clothes, and deteriorating automobiles and buildings. They also provide incomes for doctors, lawyers, teachers, and others who are too old, poorly trained or incompetent to attract more affluent clients.

In addition to economic functions, the poor perform a number of social functions.

Fifth, the poor can be identified and punished as alleged or real deviants in order to uphold the legitimacy of conventional norms. To justify the desirability of hard work, thrift, honesty, and monogamy, for example, the defenders of these norms must be able to find people who can be accused of being lazy, spendthrift, dishonest, and promiscuous. Although there is some evidence that the poor are about as moral and law-abiding as anyone else, they are more likely than middle-class transgressors to be caught and punished when they participate in deviant acts. Moreover, they lack the political and cultural power to correct the stereotypes that other people hold of them and thus continue to be thought of as lazy, spendthrift, etc., by those who need living proof that moral deviance does not pay.

Sixth, and conversely, the poor offer vicarious participation to the rest of the population in the uninhibited sexual, alcoholic, and narcotic behavior in which they are alleged to participate and which, being freed from the constraints of affluence, they are often thought to enjoy more than the middle classes. Thus many people, some social scientists included, believe that the poor not only are more given to uninhibited behavior (which may be true, although it is often motivated by despair more than by lack of inhibition) but derive more pleasure from it than affluent people (which research by Lee Rainwater, Walter Miller and others shows to be patently untrue). However, whether the poor actually have more sex and enjoy it more is irrelevant; so long as middle-class people believe this to be true, they can participate in it vicariously when instances are reported in factual or fictional form.

Seventh, the poor also serve a direct cultural function when culture created by or for them is adopted by the more affluent. The rich often collect artifacts from extinct folk cultures of poor people; and almost all Americans listen to the blues, Negro spirituals, and country music, which originated among the Southern poor. Recently they have enjoyed the rock styles that were born, like the Beatles, in the slums, and in the last year, poetry written by ghetto children has become popular in literary circles. The poor also serve as culture heroes, particularly, of course, to the left; but the hobo, the cowboy, the hipster, and the mythical prostitute with a heart of gold have performed this function for a variety of groups.

Eighth, poverty helps to guarantee the status of those who are not poor. In every hierarchical society, someone has to be at the bottom; but in American society, in which social mobility is an important goal for many and people need to know where they stand, the poor function as a reliable and relatively permanent measuring rod for status comparisons. This is particularly true for the working class, whose politics is influenced by the need to maintain status distinctions between themselves and the poor, much as the aristocracy must find ways of distinguishing itself from the *nouveaux riches.*

Ninth, the poor also aid the upward mobility of groups just above them in the class hierarchy. Thus a goodly number of Americans have entered the middle class through the profits earned from the provision of goods and services in the slums, including illegal or nonrespectable ones that upper-class and upper-middle-class businessmen shun because of their low prestige. As a result, members of almost every immigrant group have financed their upward mobility by providing slum housing, entertainment, gambling, narcotics, etc., to later arrivals—most recently to blacks and Puerto Ricans.

Tenth, the poor help to keep the aristocracy busy, thus justifying its continued existence. "Society" uses the poor as clients of settlement houses and beneficiaries of charity affairs; indeed, the aristocracy must have the poor to demonstrate its superiority over other elites who devote themselves to earning money.

Eleventh, the poor, being powerless, can be made to absorb the costs of change and growth in American society. During the nineteenth century, they did the backbreaking work that built the cities; today, they are pushed out of their neighborhoods to make room for "progress." Urban renewal projects to hold middle-class taxpayers in the city and expressways to enable suburbanites to commute downtown have typically been located in poor neighborhoods, since no other group will allow itself to be displaced. For the same reason, universities, hospitals, and civic centers also expand into land occupied by the poor. The major costs of the industrialization of agriculture have been borne by the poor, who are pushed off the land without recompense; and they have paid a large share of the human cost of the growth of American power overseas, for they have provided many of the foot soldiers for Vietnam and other wars.

Twelfth, the poor facilitate and stabilize the American political process. Because they vote and participate in politics less than other groups, the political system is often free to ignore them. Moreover, since they can rarely support Republicans, they often provide the Democrats with a captive constituency that has no other place to go. As a result, the Democrats can count on their votes, and be more responsive to voters—for example, the white working class—who might otherwise switch to the Republicans.

Thirteenth, the role of the poor in upholding conventional norms (see the *fifth* point, above) also has a significant political function. An economy based on the ideology of laissez-faire requires a deprived population that is allegedly unwilling to work or that can be considered inferior because it must accept charity or welfare in order to survive. Not only does the alleged moral deviancy of the poor reduce the moral pressure on the present political economy to eliminate poverty but socialist alternatives can be made to look quite unattractive if those who will benefit most from them can be described as lazy, spendthrift, dishonest and promiscuous.

■ ■ ■ ■ THE ALTERNATIVES

I have described 13 of the more important functions poverty and the poor satisfy in American society, enough to support the functionalist thesis that poverty, like any other social phenomenon, survives in part because it is useful to society or some of its parts. This analysis is not intended to suggest that because it is often functional, poverty *should* exist, or that it *must* exist. For one thing, poverty has many more dysfunctions than functions; for another, it is possible to suggest functional alternatives.

For example, society's dirty work could be done without poverty, either by automation or by paying "dirty workers" decent wages. Nor is it necessary for the poor to subsidize the many activities they support through their low-wage jobs. This would, however, drive up the costs of these activities, which would result in higher prices to their customers and clients. Similarly, many of the professionals who flourish because of the poor could be given other roles. Social workers could provide counseling to the affluent, as they prefer to do anyway; and the police could devote themselves to traffic and organized crime. Other roles would have to be found for badly trained or incompetent professionals now relegated to serving the poor, and someone else would have to pay their salaries. Fewer penologists would be employable, however. And Pentecostal religion could probably not survive without the poor—nor would parts of the second- and third-hand-goods market. And in many cities, "used" housing that no one else wants would then have to be torn down at public expense.

Alternatives for the cultural functions of the poor could be found more easily and cheaply. Indeed, entertainers and adolescents are already serving as the deviants needed to uphold traditional morality and as devotees of orgies to "staff" the fantasies of vicarious participation.

The status functions of the poor are another matter. In a hierarchical society, some people must be defined as inferior to everyone else with respect to a variety of attributes, but they need not be poor in the absolute sense. One could conceive of a society in which the "lower class," though last in the pecking order, received 75 percent of the median income, rather than 15–40 percent, as is now the case. Needless to say, this would require considerable income redistribution.

The contribution the poor make to the upward mobility of the groups that provide them with goods and services could also be maintained without the poor's having such low incomes. However, it is true that if the poor were more affluent, they would have access to enough capital to take over the provider role, thus competing with, and perhaps rejecting, the "outsiders."... Similarly, if the poor were more affluent, they would make less willing clients for upper-class philanthropy, although some would still use settlement houses to achieve upward mobility, as they do now. Thus "Society" could continue to run its philanthropic activities.

The political functions of the poor would be more difficult to replace. With increased affluence the poor would probably obtain more political power and be more active politically. With higher incomes and more political power, the poor would be likely to resist paying the costs of growth and change. Of course, it is possible to imagine urban renewal and highway projects that properly reimbursed the displaced people, but such projects would then become considerably more expensive, and many might never be built. This, in turn, would reduce the comfort and convenience of those who now benefit from urban renewal and expressways.

In sum, then, many of the functions served by the poor could be replaced if poverty were eliminated, but almost always at higher costs to others, particularly more affluent others. Consequently, a functional analysis must conclude that poverty persists not only because it fulfills a number of positive functions but also because many of the functional alternatives to poverty would be quite dysfunctional for the affluent members of society. A functional analysis thus ultimately arrives at much the same conclusion as radical sociology, except that radical thinkers treat as manifest what I describe as latent: that social phenomena that are functional for affluent or powerful groups and dysfunctional for poor or powerless ones persist; that when the elimination of such phenomena through functional alternatives would generate dysfunctions for the affluent or powerful, they will continue to persist; and that phenomena like poverty can be eliminated only when they become dysfunctional for the affluent or powerful, or when the powerless can obtain enough power to change society.

■ ■ ■ **POSTSCRIPT***

Over the years, this article has been interpreted as either a direct attack on functionalism or a tongue-in-cheek satirical comment on it. Neither interpretation is true. I

---

*A note from the author to the editor.

wrote the article for two reasons. First and foremost, I wanted to point out that there are, unfortunately, positive functions of poverty which have to be dealt with by antipoverty policy. Second, I was trying to show that functionalism is not the inherently conservative approach for which it has often been criticized, but that it can be employed in liberal and radical analyses.

The U.S. Upper Class

Stephen Higley

introduction

As stressed in *Core Concepts,* social inequality is a fact of life in all societies. Some people receive more of their society's goods and services, others far less. This is the way it has been in every known society of the past, is now, and—despite people's hopes to the contrary—likely always will be. As much as many of us wish it were different, our own society is no exception to this universal principle.

Although equality is held as an ideal, the social divisions of the United States are deep and extensive. They also persist decade after decade. The disparity is especially great between those who live in wealth and are powerful and those who live in poverty and are powerless. The wealthy are much less accessible to sociologists than are the poor. The more wealth, the greater the privacy. The wealthy live behind gated enclaves and send their children to exclusive schools where they don't have to mix with ordinary folk. As a result, sociologists who do research on social inequality usually focus on the poor. Consequently, we have many more studies and much greater understanding of people in poverty than of people in wealth. Yet, it is the rich who are the powerful in society, they who make the decisions that affect the lives of the rest of us. In contrast to the usual studies, in this selection Higley examines the life situation of the very rich, focusing on how they glide through life with little contact with people in classes below them—and how their insulation gives them cohesion.

Thinking Critically

As you read this selection, ask yourself:

1. In what ways would your life be different if you had been born into one of the families on which this article focuses?

2. The significance of wealth and poverty goes far beyond the differences in what people own. In many ways, such differences are superficial. What are some of the more significant ways that wealth and power affect people's lives?

3. The U.S. upper class does not meet together as a group. Nor does it send representatives to meetings to work out differences and flex its muscle. By what mechanisms, then, does it maintain cohesiveness?

From a class perspective, the American upper class exhibits a class solidarity derived from the group awareness that they share a common fate. They consider one another equals, and their voting behavior in support of the Republican Party and their charitable efforts are the most obvious manifestations of their ability for joint action in the pursuit of common interests.

Those who are listed in the *Social Register* are chosen primarily for the style of life (and, implicitly, the system of values) they exhibit. The main purpose of the *Social Register* is to restrict social intercourse for the members by acting as a ready reference as to who is "in" and who is "out" of proper society. Although it is hard to confirm (because of the *Social Register's* policy of not responding to inquiries), the *Social Register* strives to "confine normal marriage to within the status circle" by requiring members who marry outside the *Register* to resubmit themselves and their bride or groom for membership. And the *Social Register* is but one element of the upper class's complete system of socialization. The American upper class has attempted to separate itself socially from the *hoi polloi* literally from birth to death—from favored maternity hospitals and attending physicians to specific retirement homes such as Dunwoody Village in Newtown Square, Pennsylvania, and Cathedral Village in Washington, D.C.... Between birth and retirement is a full array of socializing institutions: prep schools, Ivy League schools, debutante balls, and metropolitan clubs, to name a few.

The upper-class families listed in the *Social Register* are direct descendants of the men who made great fortunes during the Gilded Age (1870–1910).... The short-term and long-term economic success of the upper class is fundamentally important to maintaining the style of life that differentiates the upper class from the other classes in society. Once a family no longer has the economic resources to give its members the advantages that money can buy in the United States, the fall from social grace is swift and sure. The family that is reduced to "shabby gentility" is an often-used literary device that, underlines the importance of liquid assets to continued good standing in American society.

The men and women who defined late-nineteenth- and early-twentieth-century American upper-class society were overwhelmingly white, Anglo-Saxon, and Protestant. As the personal, ethnic, and religious characteristics were unofficially codified, social and generational seasoning became equally important for acceptance into upper-class society. No amount of improperly socialized new money could buy its way into "proper" upper-class society....

If one subscribes to the Weberian theory that status is ultimately dependent on economic control and wealth, there are clear implications that the influence of white, Anglo-Saxon Protestants will inevitably decline in the twenty-first century. Although "WASP" and "upper class" have been synonymous in the past, it is apparent that the ethnic definition of upper class will be transformed and redefined in the future.

From *Privilege, Power and Place* by Stephen Higley, pp. 14–22. Reprinted with permission of Rowman & Littlefield Publishers.

The transformation, or de-WASPing, of the upper class that is now taking place in the United States is not easily evident to the casual observer. The status order will eventually reflect the economic order, although there are a multitude of cultural bulwarks that make the change slower and more subtle than [some] anticipate. There is a powerful WASP cultural inertia in the United States, and it will take decades to effect changes in the way Americans define themselves culturally. WASP culture is essentially derivative of the English nobility, and to this day, Anglophilia continues to pervade the American upper class. Because the upper class provides a value and consumptive role model for the American upper-middle class, upper-class values are in turn transmitted to the rest of American society—the upper-middle class being relatively large and visible to the rest of society....

■ ■ ■ ■ THE ELEMENTS OF UPPER-CLASS COHESION

The American upper class has a large number of institutions and associational arrangement that have made it possible for members to pass through life with very little significant contact with other social classes. This section reviews the most important of these institutions: private boarding schools (prep schools), colleges, metropolitan and country clubs, and the Episcopal and Presbyterian churches. The role of debutante balls, service organizations, and charitable organizations as contributing factors in maintaining upper-class cohesion will also be explored. Finally, an in-depth look at the *Social Register* will examine the role of neighborhood and community in upper-class cohesiveness.

Private Preparatory Schools

Of all of the institutions that inculcate upper-class values, private preparatory schools may have the greatest role (Cookson and Persell 1985, 13–30). The role of private education begins with upper-class day schools. Baltzell, in his examination of the role of education, termed the local institutions *provincial family surrogates* in that their outlooks were local in nature (Baltzell 1958, 292–300). Baltzell chronicles the changing role and fortunes of the Protestant Episcopal Academy, the first educator of large numbers of Philadelphia's young male upper class. The Episcopal Academy was founded in 1785 and began catering consciously to the upper class in 1846. The institution's move in 1921 to the suburban Main Line in pursuit of its clientele maintained its primacy in Philadelphia. The Episcopal Academy was not without competitors, however; other day schools were Haverford, Penn Charter, and Chestnut Hill. There were also day schools (such as Springside, Shipley, and Agnes Irwin) for upper-class girls in Philadelphia that served the same socializing functions as the boys' schools (Baltzell 1958, 300–301).

The day schools' popularity began to wane in the second half of the nineteenth century as boarding schools became the preferred method of educating young upper-class men and women. Boarding schools made it possible to completely control the social and educational environment of the students (Cookson and Persell

1985, 31–48). Parents could be assured that their child would be raised away from the distractions of the large cities and their hordes of newly arrived aliens. The prep schools were staffed with teachers who could be relied on to transmit the values of the upper class. The WASP ethic of civility, honesty, principle, and service was imparted within a totally structured environment. The schools, particularly the Episcopalian schools, were modeled after the public schools of England, complete with "forms" for grades and "headmasters" for principals.

The day schools increasingly turned to the nouveau riche to fill the slots left by the defections of some of their constituency. In his 1980 article, "The Rise of American Boarding Schools and the Development of a National Upper Class," Levine writes that the original purpose of the schools was to protect the "old guard" of the upper class from the arrivistes, [the "newly arrived"—people who only recently became rich] with their newly minted family fortunes created during the last quarter of the nineteenth century. He theorizes that New England led the way in the creation of boarding schools as the Boston Brahmins reacted to their imminent social eclipse by the much larger fortunes the Gilded Age was producing. The elites of cities such as New York and Philadelphia were able to participate in the industrialization of America, whereas the Boston Brahmins, whose fortunes were grounded largely in the trade from the Far East, were not as effective in gaining a share of the new wealth. The boarding schools were but one of a series of institutions founded during this era to create social distance between old money and new money. Country clubs and metropolitan clubs were other examples. It was also during this time that books such as the *Social Register* and various blue books were published to provide a scorecard as to who was in and who was out of proper society.

More important than the social distancing function prep schools provide is the common socializing force they exert on young men and women of the upper class. C. Wright Mills felt that prep schools were an essential element in the calculus of preserving privilege. He wrote:

> As a selection and training place of the upper classes, both old and new, the private school is a unifying influence, a force for the nationalization of the upper classes. The less important the pedigreed family becomes in the careful transmission of moral and cultural traits, the more important the private school—rather than the upper-class family—as the most important agency for transmitting the traditions of the upper social classes and regulating the new admission of wealth and talent. It is the characterizing point in the upper-class experience. (Mills 1956, 64–65)

Although upper-class schools were originally conceived to buffer the old guard from the nouveau riche, the need to infuse the upper class with new talent and money and the need to socialize the parvenus into the minutiae of upper-class culture led to the acceptance of some newly moneyed families. As sociologist Randall Collins notes, "Schools primarily teach vocabulary and inflection, styles of dress, aesthetic tastes, values and manners" (Collins 1971, 101). Levine's 1980 study found that, in general, it took one generation to socialize upper-class fortunes. The sons of fathers who acquired large fortunes in the early twentieth century often placed their children in the most prestigious boarding schools. The fathers were not above building a new library or classroom building to ensure their son's entrance. In most cases, the sons went on to Ivy League schools and became members of the upper-class secret societies and eating clubs. They were also likely to be listed in the *Social Register.* Gaining membership in upper-class secret societies and eating clubs would not present a problem because sponsorship would come easily from former schoolmates who were already members of the clubs.

Although there were literally hundreds of schools founded in the Gilded Age, a hierarchy of preferred schools quickly developed. At the top of the list in terms of prestige are the five Episcopalian boarding schools known collectively as St. Grottlesex (St. Paul's, St. Mark's, St. George's, Groton, and Middlesex). St. Paul's is often held up as the quintessential upper-class school (Domhoff 1983). Located in Concord, New Hampshire, it has a campus of eighty buildings (for six hundred students) and is situated on two thousand acres of woods and open land. In 1981, the student-faculty ratio was 6.3 to 1 and the average class size was twelve.

The second group of prestigious prep schools is represented by Choate, Hotchkiss, and Kent—nondenominational schools that were founded specifically to cater to the burgeoning market for private, exclusive education at the turn of the century.

The two oldest schools are usually put in a class by themselves. The Phillips Academy (commonly called Andover) and the Phillips Exeter Academy were founded originally to provide secondary education for a large array of students before the advent of the public school system. With the growth of the public school systems, Andover and Exeter became oriented strictly to preparing students for college. Both schools are larger and less aristocratic and have higher academic standards than the other boarding schools mentioned (Cookson and Persell 1985, 38).

In summary, boarding schools offered a place where the upper class could rest assured that class-supportive values would be instilled in their young. Their children would be exposed to only those nouveau riche children who were "acceptable" and to none of the perceived evils of the city. They would make valuable social and business friendships that would be nourished in college and in the world of private clubs during their adult lives.

An Upper-Class College Education

Just as there are preferred upper-class boarding schools to attend, there are preferred universities for young men and women of the upper class. The three universities that are considered most desirable by upper class parents are Harvard, Yale, and Princeton. These three are followed by any other schools in the Ivy League (Brown University has become increasingly popular among students) or any number of small prestigious schools located primarily in New England (for example, Williams, Amherst, or Trinity). If an upper-class family lives in a state with an academically prestigious public university, such as Wisconsin, Michigan, or California, it is increasingly considered appropriate to attend those universities. In addition, there are selected private regional universities that are considered acceptable as one's first choice. Examples of these schools are Duke, Stanford, and Northwestern.

Fraternities and Eating Clubs

Once a young man has been accepted at Harvard, Princeton, or Yale, he is confronted with a large university that is dominated in numbers, if not tone, by members of other social classes. The solution to the problem of having to mix with the upper-middle class (or worse) is a system of private clubs similar to the fraternities and sororities found on many American campuses. The system of private clubs is best described in the words of Baltzell:

> An intricate system of exclusive clubs, like the fraternities on less rarefied American campuses, serve to insulate the members of the upper class, from the rest of the students at Harvard, Princeton, and Yale. There are virtually "two nations" at Harvard. The private-school boys, with their accents, final clubs, and Boston debutante parties— about one-fifth of the student body—stand aloof and apart from the ambitious, talented, and less polished boys who come to Cambridge each year from public schools over the nation. (Baltzell 1958, 329–330)

The private eating clubs of Princeton were formed in the years following Woodrow Wilson's 1906 ban on fraternities. Juniors and Seniors joined eating clubs that had a "pecking order" based on social status. Upper-class young men usually joined the Ivy Club or the Cottage Club. The exclusivity of the eating clubs ended in the 1960s when the university compelled the clubs to accept all who had applied but had not been accepted.

At Harvard, Porcellian is the club of the most prestigious boarding schools such as St. Paul's and Groton. Other social clubs that are notable but of slightly less status are A. D., Fly, Spee, Delphic, and Owl. Porcellian's counterpart at Yale is the Fence Club. As at Harvard, there are a host of slightly prestigious clubs to join. Perhaps the senior societies are even more important than the social clubs at Yale. The two most important are the elite and meritorious Skull and Bones Club (of which former President George Bush is a member) and the more socially exclusive Scroll and Key Club. The purpose of these clubs is to build class solidarity and personal alliances that will be translated into lifetime friendships and business relationships at graduation (Baltzell 1958, 330–334).

At each critical juncture of a young person's life, the upper class has developed a series of supporting institutions to link individuals with a shared outlook and value system. By carefully molding young upper-class people into the established value system, the upper class assures its own continuity.

The Upper-Class World of Private Clubs

On graduation, young men and women begin their careers with yet another array of private clubs that will act as an extended class-oriented family. One can differentiate between two types of private clubs, the metropolitan dining clubs and the more familiar suburban country clubs. Baltzell maintains that the metropolitan clubs are much more important than country clubs in terms of the social ascription of status.

Unlike the American middle classes, and resembling the lower classes, in fact, the Philadelphia upper class is largely male dominated and patriarchal. The social standing of the male family head, the best index of which is his metropolitan club affiliation, usually determines the social position of the family as a whole (Baltzell 1958, 336).

The first American metropolitan club, following the British experience with such clubs, grew out of an informal gathering of the leading citizens to discuss daily affairs over coffee. In the days before reliable newspapers, it was a way to pass on news and keep informed of current events. The first club formed in the United States was the Philadelphia Club in 1835. It was closely followed by the Union Club of New York City, which was founded in 1836 (Baltzell 1958, 335–363). The metropolitan club subculture, with its distinctive mores and value rituals, was perceptively outlined by Wecter:

> The social club in America has done a great deal to keep alive the gentleman in the courtly sense. Here is a peculiar asylum from the Pandemonium of commerce, the bumptiousness of democracy, and the feminism of his own household. Here he is technically invisible from the critical female eye—a state of bliss reflected in the convention that a gentleman never bows to a lady from a club window and does not, according to best form, discuss ladies there. The club is the Great Good Place with its comfortable and slightly shabby leather chairs, the pleasant malt-like effluvium of its bar, the newspaper room with a club servant to repair quickly the symptoms of disarray, the catholicity of magazines from highbrows to *La Vie Parisienne* which in less stately company would seem a trifle sophomoric, the abundant newspaper, the good cigars and hearty carnivorous menus....
>
> With what Henry James called "a certain light of fine old gentlemenly prejudice to guide it," the preeminently social club welcomes the serious frivolity of horses, hounds, foxes, and boats, but not the effeminate frivolity of aestheticism. Pedantry is also frowned upon; except for the *Social Register*, the *World Almanac*, and *Lloyd's Register of American Yachts*, not a volume in the club library has been taken down since the cross-word puzzle craze. It is comforting to think that one's sons and grandsons will sit in these same chairs, and firelight will flicker on the same steel engravings and oil portraits of past presidents—and though the stars may wheel in their courses and crowned heads totter to the guillotine, this little world will remain, so long as first mortgages and government bonds endure. (Wecter 1937, 253–255)

This evocative description of metropolitan clubs was written in 1937 and is dated in some details but still accurate in its main thrust.

There have been several recent legal challenges to the all-male membership policies of metropolitan clubs. The Supreme Court has ruled against the males-only policies of the clubs. The main argument made by female complainants was that women are excluded from important business transactions that are discussed in the clubs. Aldrich maintains that the women's victory will be mainly Pyrrhic because it is considered extremely bad form to discuss business in metropolitan clubs (Aldrich 1988, 122–123). However, Aldrich does not address the valuable alliances made in leisure that lead to business deals later, outside the confines of the club.

The suburban country club is less important than the metropolitan club, but it is significant in that the entire family are members and there are facilities and activities for all. The first American country club was established in 1882 in Brookline, Massachusetts; it is simply called The Country Club. These clubs are most frequently associated with golf, but they may include facilities for swimming, tennis, and, in some cases, polo. Americans are familiar with suburban country clubs, which have been enthusiastically established by the upper-middle class throughout the country.

As in the case of the metropolitan clubs, there is a status hierarchy among the country clubs. Because of the relatively small number of upper-class families, upper-class country clubs make up only a small portion of the private equity country clubs in the United States.

Yacht clubs are also an integral part of upper-class social life. Again, only a select few of the yacht clubs in America are favored by the American upper class. Similarly, there are a large number of historically oriented clubs, such as the well-known Daughters of the American Revolution and more obscure clubs such as the American Association of the Sovereign Military Order of Malta.

Religion and the Upper Class

Observers of the American scene have long commented on the status differentiation of Protestant denominations. The upper class has had a long association with the Protestant Episcopal Church and to a lesser degree with the Presbyterian Church. The Episcopalian connection is a logical extension of the Anglophilia of the American upper class because the church has a number of characteristics that make it attractive to upper-class men and women. The richness of the church's ritual, the classic traditionalism of most Episcopalian architecture, and the sophisticated, urbane, and intellectual nature of its leaders have great appeal to the upper class (Cookson and Persell 1985, 44–48). The Episcopalian Church was very close to an established church for some parts of colonial America and was, in fact, the established church of the state of Virginia until 1786. Although the church suffered during and immediately following the Revolutionary War because of its close association with England and her Loyalists, it quickly recovered its status as a church of the educated elite in the postwar period.

Baltzell confirmed the alliance statistically by analyzing the church membership of those people in the upper class who were in both the 1940 edition of *Who's Who in America* and the 1940 Philadelphia *Social Register*. *Who's Who's* listing of church membership enabled Baltzell to determine religious affiliation for 226 upper-class heads of households. Although 35 percent did not acknowledge a church membership, 42 percent were affiliated with the Episcopalian Church (compared with 1.0 percent of the total U.S. population). An additional 13 percent of those in *Who's Who* listed the Presbyterian Church as their place of worship (compared to 1.2 percent of the general population). Because of the general privacy of religious information, it is difficult to verify Baltzell's findings. However, it is fair to say that the subjective information on the relationship is indeed overwhelming. Of course, not all Episcopalians are upper class. The actual number of upper-class families within the church is small compared to the total membership of Episcopalian churches;

however, the church carries the distinctive imprint of upper-class support, philanthropy, and values.

Debutante Balls

The debutante season consists of a series of parties, teas, and dances held by upper-class families to formally announce the arrival and availability of their daughters for suitable matrimonial partners. Each major city holds a grand ball that is the highlight of the season. Debutante "coming-out" parties are yet another means of reinforcing class solidarity because the young women and men who participate are carefully screened to ensure upper-class exclusivity. Because upper-class endogamy is highly valued, the debutante season is a formal process, the sole purpose of which is to encourage and create upper-class familial unions. Although there is often a philanthropic cause behind the tens of thousands of dollars spent for each coming out, none of the participants are under any illusion as to the real purpose behind the festivities. The debutante season strengthens the bonds of intermetropolitan upper-class social relationships just as, shared summer resort holidays strengthen intermetropolitan alliances.

The *Social Register*

Before the Civil War, "society" in most large American cities, including New York City, was small enough that members of the upper class knew each other informally. Invitations to balls and other "serious" social events were handled either by personal secretaries or by the hostess herself. There were also self-appointed social arbiters whose dictates could help the unsure hostess in determining who was "in" and who was "out" of society.

The role of individual society kingmakers would soon be eclipsed with the appearance of the first *Social Register* in 1886. Hundreds of new fortunes were being made (and lost) during the last two decades of the nineteenth century, and a book was needed to take the place of personal knowledge as to a family's acceptability in polite society.

The first edition of the *Social Register* was a listing of society in Newport, Rhode Island. The next year, 1887, saw the first appearance of the New York City edition. It has been published continuously ever since that date. The *Social Register* was not the first of its kind; there were many books that purported to list society in the 1880s. The secret of success for the founder, Louis Keller, was the quality of his list and his refusal to clutter the book with advertisements for wine merchants; dressmakers, and the like.

Another component of Keller's success was a strict code of secrecy that has been conscientiously maintained to the present. The all-enveloping veil of secrecy has given the book a mystique that has made it all the more alluring to those who aspire to join. The aura of exclusivity is enhanced by the *Social Register's* policy of rarely speaking to the press or publicly commenting on itself in any way.

Keller incorporated his idea as the Social Register Association; new editions quickly followed the New York City volume in Philadelphia and Boston (1890), Baltimore (1892), Chicago (1893), Washington, D.C. (1903), St. Louis and Buffalo (1903), Pittsburgh (1904), San Francisco (1906), and Cleveland and Cincinnati-Dayton (1910). At its height in the 1920s, there were 24 volumes. Many of these editions failed during the Great Depression because of the lack of a large and sophisticated industrial elite and/or insufficient interest on the part of the local population. This would explain the absence of a large number of *Social Register* families from Detroit, a city that made its fortune in the 1920s, and the three post–World War II growth centers of Dallas, Houston, and Los Angeles. The families that dominate the *Social Register* were created during the Gilded Age, and the sunbelt families would have to wait for their generational acculturation into upper-class mores.

The *Social Register* has remained the only social listing for the thirteen cities listed above since 1939. In 1977, the twelve editions were combined into one large book—a reflection of the national solidarity of the upper class and also of cost considerations (Birmingham 1978). The *Social Register* has subsequently become an address and telephone book for the American upper class. Along with this basic information, the *Register* also lists which boarding school and which university members attended, the year in which he or she graduated, and their club memberships. Members may also list their children and the schools they are attending or their current addresses. It has several useful appendices: "Married Maidens," a listing of the maiden names of the wives (very helpful in a divorce-prone culture), and "Dilatory Domiciles," for those who are late in returning their annual questionnaires. There is also a separate volume published each summer called the *Summer Social Register*. The summer edition lists summer homes and also has a yacht registry that lists the home port, tonnage, and year built for each yacht. As the upper class has added winter homes in the post–World War II period, they have tended to list those addresses in the main *Social Register*.

Getting into the *Social Register* and being dropped from the book have been subjects of endless speculation among the upper class and among gossip columnists. The best term to describe the process is *idiosyncratic*. There are three methods for obtaining membership. The most likely way to get in is to be born into it. The second is to marry into a listed family. However, a new bride or groom who is not in the *Register* must submit a new application to be accepted or rejected (without comment) by the "advisory committee." (The makeup of the committee has been the subject of much speculation, and some have questioned if there really is one.) The third way to gain a listing in the *Social Register* is to apply for membership. The prospective member fills out an application and if it passes initial review, he or she must then supply the committee with four or five recommendations from current listees. The application then goes to the advisory committee and the applicant is either accepted or rejected without comment. It is believed that the number that gain membership through this process is extremely limited (Winfrey 1980).

Even the ownership of the *Social Register* is veiled in mystery. When Keller died in 1924, he left the Association to several heirs. It was purchased by Malcolm

Forbes in 1977 and remained in his family after his death in 1989, but who actually owns it is not known.

The reasons why members are dropped from the *Social Register* has also been the subject of much musing. Perhaps the surest way to guarantee elimination is to publicly disparage the *Social Register* or to be publicly disgraced. As long as one's personal foibles do not become public knowledge, one seems to be immune from being dropped. Another way to be banished is to marry an entertainer—one of the many groups of people who are *personae non gratae* in the *Social Register*.

The largest groups that are systematically excluded from the *Social Register* are Jews, African Americans, and Asian Americans. Although there are one known Black and several Jewish members, the *Social Register* remains a compendium that is overwhelming white, Anglo-Saxon, and Protestant American (*Newsday*, December 12, 1984, 10–11). A small percentage of the listees have French and Dutch surnames, but it is a challenge to find German, Scandinavian, or southern European surnames anywhere in the *Social Register*.

There are members of the upper class who have asked to have their names removed from the *Social Register* because of the *Register*'s discriminatory practices. Alfred Gwynne Vanderbilt and "Jock" Whitney were among the notable society people who asked to be deleted. It is politically astute for politicians to request that their names be deleted. George Bush had his name deleted before he received his complimentary listings as vice president and president. Former presidents and the chief justice of the Supreme Court are also given complimentary listings. There are many retired senators who are listed once it is "safe" to be associated with an organization that is so blatant in its discrimination.

[SUMMARY]

The upper class has a distinct set of institutions that provide social and physical separation from the rest of society, and these institutions inculcate an intricate set of values and beliefs in both young and old. They affirm cultural and group solidarity within the upper class and clearly delineate class boundaries.

REFERENCES

Aldrich, N. W., Jr. 1988. *Old Money: the Mythology of America's Upper Class*. New York: Knopf.

Baltzell, E. D. 1958. *Philadelphia Gentlemen: The Making of a National Upper Class*. New York: Free Press.

Birmingham, N. 1978. "Ask Me No Secrets." *Town and Country* vol. 132, October, 181.

Collins, R. 1971. "Functional and Conflict Theories of Educational Stratification." *American Sociological Review* 36: no. 6, December 1,002–1,019.

Cookson, P. W., 3rd, and C. H. Persell, 1985. *Preparing for Power*. New York: Basic.

Domhoff, G. W. 1983. *Who Rules America Now?* New York: Touchstone.

Levine, S. B. 1980. "The Rise of American Boarding Schools and the Development of a National Upper Class." *Social Problems* 28, no. 1: 63–94.

Mills, C. W. 1956. *The Power Elite*. London: Oxford University Press.

Social Register Association. 1986. *Social Register 1887, Facsimile Edition*. New York: Social Register Association.

Social Register Association. 1987. *Social Register 1988*, Vol. CII. New York: Social Register Association.

Social Register Association. 1987. *Social Register, Summer 1988*, Vol. CII. New York: Social Register Association.

Wecter, D. 1937. *The Saga of American Society*. New York: Charles Scribner's Sons.

Winfrey, C. 1980. "Society's 'In' Book: Does It Still Matter?," *New York Times*, 2 February.

READING 15

Learning Silence: Girls and Boys in School

Peggy Orenstein

introduction

Many experiences from grade school remain firmly embedded in our memories—friendships, embarrassments, and perhaps times of pride and triumph. We all remember some of our teachers, the good and the bad. We all saw bullies push others around. We all had crushes—on teachers, perhaps, and on classmates. We all found ourselves at moments of clumsiness, awkwardness, shyness. All of us were socialized by our grade schools into the dominant expectations of our society, with teachers doing their best to weed out our tendencies toward deviance.

One of the main lessons we learned in grade school had nothing to do with the school's curriculum. It was part of the *hallway curriculum*, what we learned about life from one another. Especially significant was *gender*, what others expected of us because we were a boy or a girl—and what we expected of our classmates for the same reason. We learned—rather quickly—to what extent we were living up to those expectations. Lessons in gender were ongoing, a part of our everyday lives, and they weren't always subtle. Pity the poor kids who didn't learn their gender lessons well, those who violated the fiercely delimited social boundaries that marked female from male.

From Orenstein's analysis, you can observe some of the gender lessons that children teach one another. As boys and girls socialize one another into gender, they are helping to write the "scripts" they will follow as adults.

Thinking Critically

As you read this selection, ask yourself:

1. How do your experiences in grade school compare with those reported in this selection? Were your question and answer sessions similar to those reported here? Did your teachers respond in similar ways?

2. What did you learn about gender from grade school? How have those lessons become a part of your current life?

3. Why do attempts by adults to make children unisexual (making both boys and girls similar) fail?

*W*eston, California, sits at the far reaches of the San Francisco Bay Area. The drive from the city takes one through a series of bedroom communities, carefully planned idylls in which, as the miles roll by, the tax brackets leap upward, the politics swing right, and the people fade to white. But Weston is different: once an oddly matched blend of country folk and chemical plant workers, this is an old town, the kind of place where people still gather curbside under the bunting-swathed lampposts of Maple Street to watch the Fourth of July parade. Many of the businesses in Weston's center—doughnut shops, ladies' clothing stores, a few hard drinkers' bars, and picked-over antiquaries—haven't changed hands in over thirty years. There are a few fern bars and one café serving expresso here, but if people want high tone, they go to the city. . . .

The only place where Weston's two populations converge regularly is at Weston Middle School, a crumbling Spanish-style edifice just up the street from the post office, city hall, and, more important to the student body, a McDonalds. This is the town's sole middle school, and as such, it serves nearly nine hundred students a year from this disparate population. The bumper stickers on the cars dropping off the children reflect the mix: Toyota vans advertising the local NPR affiliate pull up behind rusty pickups that proclaim: "My wife said if I buy another gun she'll divorce me; God, I'll miss her!" There is also a staunch Christian population here—Mormons, Seventh-Day Adventists, and other, less austere sects whose cars remind other residents that "Jesus Loves You!"

In recent years, Weston Middle School has fulfilled its mandate well: the school entrance is draped with a "California Distinguished School" banner, earned last year by the students' estimable standardized test scores as well as the staff's exemplary performance. The teachers are an impressive, enthusiastic group who routinely seek methods of instruction that will inspire a little more engagement, a little more effort on the part of their pupils: an eighth-grade history teacher uses a karaoke microphone to juice up his lessons; an English teacher videotapes students performing original poems to bring literature to life; a science teacher offers extra credit to students who join him in cleaning up the banks of a local river. There is also some concern about gender issues in education: Weston's history teachers have embraced the new, more inclusive textbooks adopted by the state of California; in English, students write essays on their views about abortion and read, among other books, *Streams to the River, River to the Sea,* a historical novel which recasts Sacagawea as an intrepid female hero.

Yet the overt curriculum, as fine as it may be, is never the only force operating in a classroom. There is something else as well. The "hidden curriculum" comprises the unstated lessons that students learn in school: it is the running subtext through which teachers communicate behavioral norms and individual status in the school culture, the process of socialization that cues children into their place in the hierarchy of larger society. Once used to describe the ways in which the education system works to reproduce class systems in our culture, the "hidden curriculum" has recently been applied to the ways in which schools help reinforce gender roles, whether they intend to or not.

■ ■ ■ THE DAILY GRIND: LESSONS IN THE HIDDEN CURRICULUM

Amy Wilkinson has looked forward to being an eighth grader forever—at least for the last two years, which, when you're thirteen, seems like the same thing. By the second week of September she's settled comfortably into her role as one of the school's reigning elite. Each morning before class, she lounges with a group of about twenty other eighth-grade girls and boys in the most visible spot on campus: at the base of the schoolyard, between one of the portable classrooms that was constructed in the late 1970s and the old oak tree in the overflow parking lot. The group trades gossip, flirts, or simply stands around, basking in its own importance and killing time before the morning bell.

At 8:15 on Tuesday the crowd has already convened, and Amy is standing among a knot of girls, laughing. She is fuller-figured than she'd like to be, wide-hipped and heavy-limbed with curly, blond hair, cornflower-blue eyes, and a sharply upturned nose. With the help of her mother, who is a drama coach, she has become the school's star actress: last year she played Eliza in Weston's production *of My Fair Lady*. Although she earns solid grades in all of her subjects—she'll make the honor roll this fall—drama is her passion, she says, because "I love entertaining people, and I love putting on characters."

Also, no doubt, because she loves the spotlight: this morning, when she mentions a boy I haven't met, Amy turns, puts her hands on her hips, anchors her feet shoulder width apart, and bellows across the backyard, "Greg! Get over here! You have to meet Peggy."

She smiles wryly as Greg, looking startled, begins to make his way across the schoolyard for an introduction. "I'm not exactly shy," she says, her hands on her hips. "I'm *bold*."...

Mrs. Richter, a ruddy, athletic woman with a powerful voice, has arranged the chairs in a three-sided square, two rows deep. Amy walks to the far side of the room and, as she takes her seat, falls into a typically feminine pose: she crosses her legs, folds her arms across her chest, and hunches forward toward her desk, seeming to shrink into herself. The sauciness of the playground disappears, and, in fact, she says hardly a word during class. Meanwhile, the boys, especially those who are more physically mature, sprawl in their chairs, stretching their legs long, expanding into the available space.

Nate, a gawky, sanguine boy who has shaved his head except for a small thatch that's hidden under an Oakland As cap, leans his chair back on two legs and, although the bell has already rung, begins a noisy conversation with his friend Kyle. Mrs. Richter turns to him, "What's all the discussion about, Nate?" she asks.

"*He's* talking to *me*," Nate answers, pointing to Kyle. Mrs. Richter writes Nate's name on the chalkboard as a warning toward detention and he yells out in protest. They begin to quibble over the justice of her decision, their first—but certainly not their last—power struggle of the day. As they argue, Allison, a tall, angular girl who once told me, "My goal is to be the best wife and mother I can be," raises her hand to ask a question. Mrs. Richter, finishing up with Nate, doesn't notice.

"Get your homework out, everyone!" the teacher booms, and walks among the students, checking to make sure no one has shirked on her or his assignment. Allison, who sits in the front row nearest both the blackboard and the teacher, waits patiently for another moment, then, realizing she's not getting results, puts her hand down. When Mrs. Richter walks toward her, Allison tries another tack, calling out her question. Still, she gets no response, so she gives up.

As a homework assignment, the students have divided their papers into one hundred squares, color-coding each square prime or composite—prime being those numbers which are divisible only by one and themselves, and composite being everything else. Mrs. Richter asks them to call out the prime numbers they've found, starting with the tens.

Nate is the first to shout, "Eleven!" The rest of the class chimes in a second later. As they move through the twenties and thirties, Nate, Kyle, and Kevin, who sit near one another at the back of the class, call out louder and louder, casually competing for both quickest response and the highest decibel level. Mrs. Richter lets the boys' behavior slide, although they are intimidating other students.

"Okay," Mrs. Richter says when they've reached one hundred. "Now, what do you think of one hundred and three? Prime or composite?"

Kyle, who is skinny and a little pop-eyed, yells out, "Prime!" but Mrs. Richter turns away from him to give someone else a turn. Unlike Allison, who gave up when she was ignored, Kyle isn't willing to cede his teacher's attention. He begins to bounce in his chair and chant, *Prime! Prime! Prime!"* Then, when he turns out to be right, he rebukes the teacher, saying, *"See,* I told you."

When the girls in Mrs. Richter's class do speak, they follow the rules. When Allison has another question, she raises her hand again and waits her turn; this time, the teacher responds. When Amy volunteers her sole answer of the period, she raises her hand, too. She gives the wrong answer to an easy multiplication problem, turns crimson, and flips her head forward so her hair falls over her face.

Occasionally, the girls shout out answers, but generally they are to the easiest, lowest-risk questions, such as the factors of four or six. And their stabs at public recognition depend on the boys' largess: when the girls venture responses to more complex questions the boys quickly become territorial, shouting them down with their own answers. Nate and Kyle are particularly adept at overpowering Renee, who, I've been told by the teacher, is the brightest girl in the class. (On a subsequent visit, I will see her lay her head on her desk when Nate overwhelms her and mutter, "I hate this class.")

Mrs. Richter doesn't say anything to condone the boys' aggressiveness, but she doesn't have to: they insist on—and receive—her attention even when she consciously tries to shift it elsewhere in order to make the class more equitable. . . .

■ ■ ■ **VOICE AND SILENCE**

I had chosen Amy, along with two of her friends, Evie DiLeo and Becca Holbrook, as three of the subjects for this book partly because, within minutes of our first meeting—and months before I ever saw them in a classroom—they announced to me that they were not like other girls at Weston: they were, they proudly announced, feminists. Amy explained that to them "feminism" meant that as adults they plan to be economically independent of men. Until that time, though, it means "knowing that the boys aren't all they're cracked up to be.". . .

Yet although they spoke of themselves in terms of grit and independence, those qualities were rarely on display in the classroom. Whereas their male classmates yelled out or snapped the fingers of their raised hands when they wanted to speak, these girls seemed, for the most part, to recede from class proceedings, a charge they didn't deny.

"I don't raise my hand in my classes because I'm afraid I have the wrong answer and I'll be embarrassed," Becca, who is gangly and soft-spoken, explains one day during lunch. "My self-confidence will be taken away, so I don't want to raise my hand even if I really do know.". . .

Girls' hesitance to speak out relative to boys is not mere stylistic difference; speaking out in class—and being acknowledged for it—is a constant reinforcement of a student's right to be heard, to take academic risks. Students who talk in class have more opportunity to enhance self-esteem through exposure to praise; they have the luxury of learning from mistakes and they develop the perspective to see failure as an educational tool. Boys such as Kyle and Nate feel internal permission to speak out whether they are bright or not, whether they are right or wrong, whether their comments are insightful, corrosive, combative, or utterly ridiculous. The important thing is to be recognized, to assert the "I am."

"I think my opinions are important, so I yell them out," Nate tells me one day after Mrs. Richter's math class. "The teacher'll tell you not to do it, but they answer your question before the people who raise their hands. Girls will sit there until the bell rings with their hands up and never get their question answered." He waves his hand in the air as if brushing the girls aside and says contemptuously, "Forget that.". . .

Several days after joining Amy in her math class, I visit Ms. Kelly's English class. Ms. Kelly is a second-year teacher: freckle-faced and snub-nosed, dressed in a T-shirt and khaki skirt, she barely looks older than her students. The class has been studying Greek mythology; today Ms. Kelly, who has placed the desks in clusters of six, instructs the students to write out the discussion they imagine took place between Zeus and Hera when she discovered he had fathered an illegitimate child.

"Any questions?" she asks, after explaining the assignment.

Two girls, Kathy and Amanda, raise their hands and she calls on Amanda. Amanda glances at Kathy, who sits in the group of desks next to hers. "Well, can you help me when you've answered her question?" she says politely. The teacher tends to Kathy, and then to a boy in another group who is misbehaving; she never returns to Amanda, who becomes frustrated. . . .

Certainly some girls at Weston act out, demand attention, clown in class, but when they try those tactics, using disruption as a tool to gain individual attention and instruction, they are not met with the same reward as boys.

In mid-November, Mrs. Richter is giving out grades to Amy's class. The teacher sits at her desk in the back corner of the room, and the students come up one by one, in reverse alphabetical order; their faces are tense on the way up, then pleased or disappointed on the way back.

When Dawn's turn comes, Mrs. Richter speaks sharply to her.

"You're getting a B," the teacher says, "but for citizenship, you're getting 'disruptive.' You've been talking a lot and there have been some outbursts."

Dawn scrunches her mouth over to one side of her face, lowers her eyes, and returns to her seat.

"Disruptive?" yells Nate from across the room where the teachers voice has carried. "*She's* not disruptive, *I'm* disruptive."

Mrs. Richter laughs. "You've got that right," she says.

When his turn comes, Nate gets a B plus. "It would've been an A minus if you turned in your last homework assignment," Mrs. Richter says. As predicted, his citizenship comment is also 'disruptive,' but the bad news isn't delivered with the same sting as it was to Dawn—it's conferred with an indulgent smile. There is a tacit acceptance of a disruptive boy, because boys *are* disruptive. Girls are too, sometimes, as Dawn illustrates, but with different consequences.

So along with fractions and exponents, Dawn has learned that she has to tamp down assertive behavior, that she has to diminish herself both to please the teacher and to appease the boys, with whom she cannot compete. Meanwhile, Nate has learned that monopolizing the class period and defying the teacher gets him in trouble, but he also garners individual attention, praise, and answers to his questions.

Over the course of the semester, Dawn slowly stops disrupting; she stops participating, too. At the semester break, when I check with Mrs. Richter on the classes' progress, she tells me, "Dawn hardly talks at all now because she's overpowered by the boys. She can't get the attention in class, so she's calmed down."

Nate, however, hasn't changed a bit, but whereas Dawn's behavior is viewed as containable, the teacher sees Nate's as inevitable, "I'll go through two weeks of torture before I'll give him detention." Mrs. Richter says. "But you have to tolerate that behavior to a certain extent or he won't want to be there at all; he'll get himself kicked out.

"I know his behavior works for him, though," she continues. "He talks more, he gets more answers out there, and he does well because of it. I try to tell him that we need to let others talk so they can understand, too. But when I do, I begin and end with positive things about his behavior and sandwich the bad stuff in the middle. I'm never sure which part he really hears."...

■ ■ ■ **YOU CAN SAY "I THINK" IN THERE**

Teachers at Weston varied tremendously in their reactions to boys' dominance in their classroom. Some, like Mr. Sinclair, simply didn't see it. Others fought the boys for control: one eighth-grade history teacher—who proudly told me that his wife had founded the local NOW chapter—would break into class discussions to say, "We haven't heard from any of the girls in the room. What do you think?" The girls seemed to be uncomfortable with such attention at first, but, as the year progressed, they became increasingly vocal. During a lesson on England's debtor's prisons one girl even yelled out, "What about the women? What happened to them?"

Another teacher, Liz Muney, who runs the district's gifted program and teaches sixth grade at Weston, told me that...from now on, she was going to call equally on girls and boys, and, just to make sure that she did, she held her attendance roster during class.

"After two days the boys blew up," she told me one afternoon during a break between classes. "They started complaining and saying that I was calling on the girls more than them. I showed them it wasn't true and they had to back down. I kept on doing it, but for the boys, equality was hard to get used to; they perceived it as a big loss."

Like the teachers, the girls I interviewed were not always aware that they were being ignored in class (in some classes, such as math, they even preferred it), but their favorite teachers just happened to be the ones who actively wrestled with the hidden curriculum. For Amy, Evie, and Becca that teacher is Ms. Nellas, with whom they study American history.

"She teaches good," Becca assures me one day during lunch.

"Yeah," Evie says. "She makes you want to strive to be better. She'll do 'the power clap' and say how good you're doing..."

"Even if your work sucks," interrupts Amy, whose work rarely "sucks." "So you try really hard. And you can say what you want in there and no one ever says you're wrong; it's like, you're not afraid to say 'I think.'"

Becca returns to her original assessment: "She teaches good," she says, nodding her head.

Amy's demeanor in Ms. Nellas' class is utterly different than it is in math, science, or even English: she uncrosses her legs and plants both feet on the floor. She sits up straight, leans forward, and thrusts her hand in the air. Once, she even gives an impatient (and uncharacteristic) little wave for attention.

This is election year, and when I first visit Ms. Nellas' class in late October, she is discussing the electoral college. She stands at the front of the room, a craggy faced woman with an easy smile, and offer a blunt explanation of that esoteric organization: "The reason there's an electoral college is that people who wrote the constitution—who were all men—*didn't* really want everyone to participate in electing officials," she says. "They only trusted people like themselves, so they said, 'We don't want the common people to vote. They can't read or write and we can't trust them to elect leaders.' And they certainly didn't trust *women*, so they weren't about to let *them* vote."

During the lesson, boys raise their hands roughly twice as often as girls, but Ms. Nellas has a trick for making sure that girls who do volunteer are recognized; after she asks a question she looks around the room to see whose hands are up, then says, "Okay, first Randy, then Jeffrey, then Amy." If she inadvertently continues without exhausting the list, the slighted students are quick to protest. She also promotes a more tolerant culture through her classroom decor: among the encouraging messages she has posted on the classroom walls are "You Have a *Duty to Assist* Anyone Who Asks for Help" and the somewhat convoluted "Everybody Is Good at *Some* of the Abilities." Under the clock, in the most strategic spot in the room, there is a yellowed poster depicting a teacher in Renaissance garb saying to his student, "Columbus, will yer [sic] sit down and stop asking all those dumb questions?" Beneath it a caption reads: "Dumb questions lead to learning. Don't be afraid to ask." . . .

Like many teachers at Weston, Ms. Nellas is an advocate of cooperative learning: students collaborating on projects in groups, each with an assigned role. Cooperative learning—in which success is not contingent on quick response time or a loud voice—is said to be especially beneficial for girls and has become somewhat voguish in progressive schools. But, as with lab groups, the interactions if not effectively monitored, can merely reinforce the students' stereotypes. "I've noticed that when they do group work, the boys want to be the leader," Ms. Nellas says, "and the girls always take the recorder role and that's a problem. I suppose I let it happen, too, but I don't want to assign them the roles in groups because I'm afraid of my own prejudices. I think I'd pick the quick students to lead the group, and so I might end up with the boys too, although I think I'd pick more girls than they do."

"The dynamics are already in place when they get here," she continues, "and they don't improve as they get older: when I teach high school, boys put their arm around me, pat my head like I'm a pet or something because I'm a woman. It can be funny, but it's still a power play. It's all about control, about who's in charge. When they really act out, though, I'll just stop the class and wait, even if it takes thirty seconds and it's driving me crazy. That sounds like a long time, but it's less of a waste, in the end, than sending them to the principal or yelling at the student. That way, they don't get the power. And *maybe* you can make it a little more equal."

"But What Do You Mean?" Women and Men in Conversation

Deborah Tannen

introduction ▪ ▪ ▪ ▪

In many ways, men and women live parallel lives. Although they interact with one an-other and even live with one another, seldom are they in the same mental space. It often is difficult to perceive this distinction. If you look at men and women as they interact, you see them talking and laughing with one another. They discuss values, life, goals, and problems. But when given a chance—except when they are seeking sex—they generally go in separate directions. You can easily see this in almost any non-mating activity. Take out the sex, and men cluster together, as do women. In their separate groups, they talk and laugh about different things: For men, the topic is often sports or some sort of competi-tion; for women, it is often clothing or fashion or appearance of some sort. It is not that there is no crossing. There is, but this separative tendency is strong. It represents deep distinctions in the interior lives of men and women.

Men often find themselves uncomfortable around women—except when it comes to sex. They don't know quite what to say, and they don't know how women will take what they do say. Men and women find many of the same things to be humorous, for exam-ple, but a nagging difference remains. Consequently, men like to retreat into their own world constructed around their ideas of masculinity. In this world, competition, even ruthlessness and violence, are acknowledged and even given appreciation. The common form that this masculinizing of interaction takes is contact sports, with a lot of joking, bragging, and bravado demonstrated around football—but also baseball, basketball, boxing, hockey, and soccer. This is an imaginary world that offers refuge from a feminine world that men find strange and threatening.

To analyze or even acknowledge such gender distinctions runs the risk of stereotyping men and women. Yet such differences exist and persist. They show up in unexpected, and often unperceived, ways, such as those described by Deborah Tannen in this selection.

Thinking Critically

As you read this selection, ask yourself:

1. This selection should sensitize you to differences in the ways that men and women talk with one another. Start to listen to conversations to see if what Tannen analyzes is really true.

2. If Tannen's analysis is correct, what are the implications for couples who are "going together" and for husbands and wives? What problems that they experience can be attributed to honest, unintended miscommunications? How can they resolve them?

3. Are men and women doomed to miscommunicate? How can communication gaps be overcome?

*C*onversation is a ritual. We say things that seem obviously the thing to say, without thinking of the literal meaning of our words, any more than we expect the question "How are you?" to call forth a detailed account of aches and pains.

Unfortunately, women and men often have different ideas about what's appropriate, different ways of speaking. Many of the conversational rituals common among women are designed to take the other person's feelings into account, while many of the conversational rituals common among men are designed to maintain the one-up position, or at least avoid appearing one-down. As a result, when men and women interact—especially at work—it's often women who are at the disadvantage. Because women are not trying to avoid the one-down position, that is unfortunately where they may end up.

Here, the biggest areas of miscommunication.

■ ■ ■ 1. APOLOGIES

Women are often told they apologize too much. The reason they're told to stop doing it is that, to many men, apologizing seems synonymous with putting oneself down. But there are many times when "I'm sorry' isn't self-deprecating, or even an apology; it's an automatic way of keeping both speakers on an equal footing. For example, a well-known columnist once interviewed me and gave me her phone number in case I needed to call her back. I misplaced the number and had to go through the newspaper's main switchboard. When our conversation was winding

From *Talking from 9 to 5* by Deborah Tannen. "'But What Do You Mean?' Women and Men in Conversation" adapted for *Redbook*, October 1994, pp. 91–93, 145–147. Copyright © 1994 by Deborah Tannen. Reprinted by permission of HarperCollins Publishers, Inc.

down and we'd both made ending-type remarks, I added "Oh, I almost forgot—I lost your direct number, can I get it again?" "Oh, I'm sorry," she came back instantly, even though she had done nothing wrong and *I* was the one who'd lost the number. But I understood she wasn't really apologizing; she was just automatically reassuring me she had no intention of denying me her number.

Even when "I'm sorry" *is* an apology, women often assume it will be the first step in a two-step ritual: I say "I'm sorry" and take half the blame, then you take the other half. At work, it might go something like this:

A. When you typed this letter, you missed this phrase I inserted.
B. Oh, I'm sorry. I'll fix it.
A. Well, I wrote it so small it was easy to miss.

When both parties share blame, it's a mutual face-saving device. But if one person, usually the woman, utters frequent apologies and the other doesn't, she ends up looking as if she's taking the blame for mishaps that aren't her fault. When she's only partially to blame, she looks entirely in the wrong.

I recently sat in on a meeting at an insurance company where the sole woman, Helen, said "I'm sorry" or "I apologize" repeatedly. At one point she said, "I'm thinking out loud. I apologize." Yet the meeting was intended to be an informal brain-storming session, and *everyone* was thinking out loud.

The reason Helen's apologies stood out was that she was the only person in the room making so many. And the reason I was concerned was that Helen felt the annual bonus she had received was unfair. When I interviewed her colleagues, they said that Helen was one of the best and most productive workers—yet she got one of the smallest bonuses. Although the problem might have been outright sexism, I suspect her speech style, which differs from that of her male colleagues, masks her competence.

Unfortunately, not apologizing can have its price too. Since so many women use ritual apologies, those who don't may be seen as hard-edged. What's important is to be aware of how often you say you're sorry (and why), and to monitor your speech based on the reaction you get.

■ ■ ■   2. CRITICISM

A woman who cowrote a report with a male colleague was hurt when she read a rough draft to him and he leapt into a critical response—"Oh, that's too dry! You have to make it snappier!" She herself would have been more likely to say, "That's a really good start. Of course, you'll want to make it a little snappier when you revise."

Whether criticism is given straight or softened is a matter of convention. In general, women use more softeners. I noticed this difference when talking to an editor about an essay I'd written. While going over changes she wanted to make, she said, "There's one more thing. I know you may not agree with me. The reason I noticed the problem is that your other points are so lucid and elegant." She went on hedging for several more sentences until I put her out of her misery: "Do you want to cut that part?" I asked—and of course she did. But I appreciated her tentativeness. In contrast, another editor (a man) I once called summarily rejected my idea for an article by barking, "Call me when you have something new to say."

Those who are used to ways of talking that soften the impact of criticism may find it hard to deal with the right-between-the-eyes style. It has its own logic, however, and neither style is intrinsically better. People who prefer criticism given straight are operating on an assumption that feelings aren't involved. "Here's the dope. I know you're good; you can take it."

■ ■ ■ 3. THANK-YOUS

A woman manager I know starts meetings by thanking everyone for coming, even though it's clearly their job to do so. Her "thank-you" is simply a ritual.

A novelist received a fax from an assistant in her publisher's office; it contained suggested catalogue copy for her book. She immediately faxed him her suggested changes and said, "Thanks for running this by me," even though her contract gave her the right to approve all copy. When she thanked the assistant, she fully expected him to reciprocate: "Thanks for giving me such a quick response." Instead, he said, "You're welcome." Suddenly, rather than an equal exchange of pleasantries, she found herself positioned as the recipient of a favor. This made her feel like responding, "Thanks for nothing!"

Many women use "thanks" as an automatic conversation starter and closer; there's nothing literally to thank you for. Like many rituals typical of women's conversation, it depends on the goodwill of the other to restore the balance. When the other speaker doesn't reciprocate, a woman may feel like someone on a seesaw whose partner abandoned his end. Instead of balancing in the air, she has plopped to the ground, wondering how she got there.

■ ■ ■ 4. FIGHTING

Many men expect the discussion of ideas to be a ritual fight—explored through verbal opposition. They state their ideas in the strongest possible terms, thinking that if there are weaknesses someone will point them out, and by trying to argue against those objections, they will see how well their ideas hold up.

Those who expect their own ideas to be challenged will respond to another's ideas by trying to poke holes and find weak links—as a way of *helping*. The logic is that when you are challenged you will rise to the occasion: Adrenaline makes your mind sharper, you get ideas and insights you would not have thought of without the spur of battle.

But many women take this approach as a personal attack. Worse, they find it impossible to do their best work in such a contentious environment. If you're not used to ritual fighting, you begin to hear criticism of your ideas as soon as they are formed. Rather than making you think more clearly, it makes you doubt what you know. When you state your ideas, you hedge in order to fend off potential attacks. Ironically, this is more likely to *invite* attack because it makes you look weak.

Although you may never enjoy verbal sparring, some women find it helpful to learn how to do it. An engineer who was the only woman among four men in a small company found that as soon as she learned to argue, she was accepted and taken seriously. A doctor attending a hospital staff meeting made a similar discovery. She was becoming more and more angry with a male colleague who'd loudly disagreed with a point she'd made. Her better judgment told her to hold her tongue, to avoid making an enemy of this powerful senior colleague. But finally she couldn't hold it any longer, and she rose to her feet and delivered an impassioned attack on his position. She sat down in a panic, certain she had permanently damaged her relationship with him. To her amazement, he came up to her afterward and said, "That was a great rebuttal. I'm really impressed. Let's go out for a beer after work and hash out our approaches to this problem."

■ ■ ■ ■ 5. PRAISE

A manager I'll call Lester had been on his new job six months when he heard that the women reporting to him were deeply dissatisfied. When he talked to them about it, their feelings erupted; two said they were on the verge of quitting because he didn't appreciate their work, and they didn't want to wait to be fired. Lester was dumbfounded: He believed they were doing a fine job. Surely, he thought, he had said nothing to give them the impression he didn't like their work. And indeed he hadn't. That was the problem. He had said *nothing*—and the women assumed he was following the adage "If you can't say something nice, don't say anything." He thought he was showing confidence in them by leaving them alone.

Men and women have different habits in regard to giving praise. For example, Deidre and her colleague William both gave presentations at a conference. Afterward, Deidre told William, "That was a great talk." He thanked her. Then she asked, "What did you think of mine?" and he gave her a lengthy and detailed critique. She found it uncomfortable to listen to his comments. But she assured herself that he meant well, and that his honesty was a signal that she, too, should be honest when he asked for a critique of his performance. As a matter of fact, she had noticed quite a few ways in which he could have improved his presentation. But she never got a chance to tell him because he never asked—and she felt put down. The worst part was that it seemed she had only herself to blame, since she *had* asked what he thought of her talk.

But had she really asked for his critique? The truth is, when she asked for his opinion, she was expecting a compliment, which she felt was more or less required following anyone's talk. When he responded with criticism, she figured, Oh, he's playing "Let's critique each other"—not a game she'd initiated, but one which she was willing to play. Had she realized he was going to criticize her and not ask her to reciprocate, she would never have asked in the first place.

It would be easy to assume that Deidre was insecure, whether she was fishing for a compliment or soliciting a critique. But she was simply talking automatically, performing one of the many conversational rituals that allow us to get through the day. William may have sincerely misunderstood Deidre's intention—or may have been unable to pass up a chance to one-up her when given the opportunity.

■ ■ ■ ■ 6. COMPLAINTS

"Troubles talk" can be a way to establish rapport with a colleague. You complain about a problem (which shows that you are just folks) and the other person responds with a similar problem (which puts you on equal footing). But while such commiserating is common among women, men are likely to hear it as a request to *solve* the problem.

One woman told me she would frequently initiate what she thought would be pleasant complaint-airing sessions at work. She'd just talk about situations that bothered her just to talk about them, maybe to understand them better. But her male office mate would quickly tell her how she could improve the situation. This left her feeling condescended to and frustrated. She was delighted to see this very impasse in a section in my book *You Just Don't Understand,* and showed it to him. "Oh," he said, "I see the problem. How can we solve it?" Then they both laughed, because it had happened again: He short-circuited the detailed discussion she'd hoped for and cut to the chase of finding a solution.

Sometimes the consequences of complaining are more serious: A man might take a woman's lighthearted griping literally, and she can get a reputation as a chronic malcontent. Furthermore, she may be seen as not up to solving the problems that arise on the job.

■ ■ ■ ■ 7. JOKES

I heard a man call in to a talk show and say, "I've worked for two women and neither one had a sense of humor. You know, when you work with men, there's a lot of joking and teasing." The show's host and the guest (both women) took his comment at face value and assumed the women this man worked for were humorless. The guest said, "Isn't it sad that women don't feel comfortable enough with authority to see the humor?" The host said, "Maybe when more women are in authority roles, they'll be more comfortable with power." But although the women this man worked for *may* have taken themselves too seriously, it's just as likely that they each had a terrific sense of humor, but maybe the humor wasn't the type he was used to. They may have been like the woman who wrote to me: "When I'm with men, my wit or cleverness seems inappropriate (or lost!) so I don't bother. When I'm with my women friends, however, there's no hold on puns or cracks and my humor is fully appreciated."

The types of humor women and men tend to prefer differ. Research has shown that the most common form of humor among men is razzing, teasing, and mock-hostile attacks, while among women it's self-mocking. Women often mistake men's teasing as genuinely hostile. Men often mistake women's mock self-deprecation as truly putting themselves down.

Women have told me they were taken more seriously when they learned to joke the way the guys did. For example, a teacher who went to a national conference with seven other teachers (mostly women) and a group of administrators (mostly men) was annoyed that the administrators always found reasons to leave boring seminars, while the teachers felt they had to stay and take notes. One evening, when the group met at a bar in the hotel, the principal asked her how one such seminar had turned out. She retorted, "As soon as you left, it got much better." He laughed out loud at her response. The playful insult appealed to the men—but there was a trade-off. The women seemed to back off from her after this. (Perhaps they were put off by her using joking to align herself with the bosses.)

There is no "right" way to talk. When problems arise, the culprit may be style differences—and *all* styles will at times fail with others who don't share or understand them, just as English won't do you much good if you try to speak to someone who knows only French. If you want to get your message across, it's not a question of being "right"; it's a question of using language that's shared—or at least understood.

Inside Organized Racism

Kathleen M. Blee

introduction

One of the most common research methods that sociologists use is interviewing, which is more powerful when it is combined with participant observation. These two methods, interviewing and participant observation, fit together very well. Participant observation gives the researcher insight into the social dynamics of group members (such as their motivations, the group's hierarchy, and what the group members find significant and rewarding). This, in turn, suggests areas to investigate, even specific questions that should be asked. Similarly, what people talk about in response to open-ended questions cues the researcher into what to look for during participant observation.

In this selection, Blee reports on her research with women who are members of the organized hate movement. As she discusses how she did this study, she takes us behind-the-scenes of her research. You will see, for example, how fearful she became. You will also see how her fears sharpened her research skills, how they even helped her gain a better understanding of racist women.

As I have stated in the text, I admire the research that my fellow sociologists do, especially research that takes us behind the scenes of human groups to give us insight into why people in those groups think and behave as they do. I have special admiration for sociologists who do creative, risk-taking research, for it gives us understandings that cannot be gained in any other way. This research is one such example. I think you will enjoy this account.

Thinking Critically

As you read this selection, ask yourself:

1. Why would a sociologist risk her life to do this kind of research? Why would people who lead such subterranean lives even talk to a researcher?

2. Blee used participant observation and interviews to study women in hate groups. What types of information was she able to get that she could not have collected by other research methods?

3. Why do women (or men) join the organized hate movement?

At a racist gathering on the West Coast, Frank, a skinhead from Texas, sidled up to me to share his disgust at an event so mild it was "something you could see on the family channel." At his side, Liz echoed his sentiment, complaining that she felt trapped in a "Baptist church social." We chatted some more. Frank boasted that this was nothing like he expected. He made the long trip to "get his juices going," not to be part of something concocted by "wimps." Liz agreed, pointing with disdain to a group of women hauling boxes of hamburger buns over to a large grill.

I found their reactions baffling. To me, the scene was horrifying, anything but mundane. Frank's arms were covered with swastika tattoos. On his head was a baseball cap with a comic-like depiction of an African American man being lynched. Liz's black skirt, hose, and boots accentuated the small Klan cross embroidered on her white tailored shirt. The rituals of historical hatred being enacted in front of us seemed far from disappointingly "tame," as Frank and Liz's complaints suggested. A cross was doused with gasoline and set ablaze. People spoke casually of the need to "get rid" of African Americans, immigrants, Jews, gay men and lesbians, and Asian Americans, or exchanged historical trivia purporting to expose the Holocaust as a Zionist hoax....

Only much later did I understand how Frank and Liz could compare a racist rally to a community social gathering. It was years before I could bring myself to read my notes on this rally, written on sheets of paper to which faint scents of smoke and kerosene still seemed to cling. Yet with time and psychic distance from my encounters with Frank, Liz, and others like them, I came to see that aspects of racist gatherings do mirror church socials or neighborhood picnics, albeit in a distorted, perverse fashion. I remember a card table piled high with racist children's books, bumper stickers, and index cards of "white power recipes"; sessions on self-help for disgruntled or substance-addicted members; hymns sung as background to speeches about strengthening the "racialist movement"; and the pancake breakfast and "social hour."

It was with an eerie sense of the familiar colliding with the bizarre that I crossed the boundary that divides the racist underground from the mainstream to write this book. Much about racist groups appears disturbingly ordinary, especially their evocation of community, family, and social ties. One woman gushed that a Ku Klux Klan rally "was a blast. I had fun. And it was just like a big family get-together. We played volleyball. And you had your little church thing on Sunday. For the longest time I thought I would be bored. But I wasn't bored at all."...

Some of the ideas voiced by racist groups can seem unremarkable, as evident in the scary similarity to mainstream right-wing stands on such issues as gun control. Still, the watershed that divides racist activism from the rest of society is striking. The beliefs of racist groups are not just extreme variants of mainstream racism, xenophobia, or anti-Semitism. Rather, their conspiratorial logic and zeal for activism separate members of racist groups from those on "the outside," as racist activists call it. By combining the aberrant with the ordinary, the peculiar with the prosaic, modern racist groups gain strength. To design effective strategies to combat racist groups, we must understand this combination.

…Women are the newest recruiting targets of racist groups, and they provide a key to these groups' campaign for racial supremacy. "We are very picky when we come to girls," one woman told me. "We don't like sluts. The girls must know their place but take care of business and contribute a lot too. Our girls have a clean slate. Nobody could disrespect us if they tried. We want girls [who are] well educated, the whole bit. And tough…"

The groups and networks that espouse and promote openly racist and anti-Semitic, and often xenophobic and homophobic, views and actions are what I call "organized racism." Organized racism is more than the aggregation of individual racist sentiments. It is a social milieu in which venomous ideas—about African Americans, Jews, Hispanics, Asians, gay men and lesbians, and others—take shape. Through networks of groups and activists, it channels personal sentiments of hatred into collective racist acts.…

Today, organized racism in the United States is rife with paradox. While racist groups are becoming more visible, their messages of racial hatred and white supremacy find little support in the rest of society. Racist groups increasingly have anti-Semitism as their core belief, though anti-Semitic attitudes in America as a whole are at their lowest ebb. Despite proclaiming bizarre and illogical views of race and religion, racist groups attract not only those who are ignorant, irrational, socially isolated, or marginal, but also intelligent, educated people, those with resources and social connections, those with something to lose. Organized racists trade in a currency of racist stereotyping little changed from the views of the nineteenth-century Klan and of anti-Semitism recycled from World War II–era Nazi propaganda, yet they recruit successfully among the young who have little or no knowledge of that history. They seize on racist rituals from the past to foment rage about the conditions of the present, appealing to teenagers whose lives are scarred by familial abuse and terror as well as the sons and daughters of stable and loving families, the offspring of privilege and the beneficiaries of parental attention. Racist groups project a sense of hypermasculinity in their militaristic swagger and tactics of bullying and intimidation, but they increasingly are able to bring women into their ranks.

When I began my research, I wanted to understand the paradoxes of organized racism. Were, I wondered, the increased numbers of women changing the masculine cast of racist groups? Why, I asked myself, did racist activists continue to see Jews, African Americans, and others as enemies, and why did they regard violence as a racial solution? Convinced that we can defeat organized racism only if we know how it recruits and retains its members, I also wanted to learn why people join organized racism and how being in racist groups affects them.…

■ ■ ■ FOCUSING ON RACIST WOMEN

To understand organized racism from the inside—from the experiences and beliefs of its members—I decided that I needed to talk with racist activists. I chose to interview women for a variety of reasons. On a practical level, I found that I could get access to women racists and develop some measure of rapport with them. More substantively, I wanted to study women racists because we know so little about them. Since 1980 women have been actively recruited by U.S. racist groups both because racist leaders see them as unlikely to have criminal records that would draw the attention of police and because they help augment membership rolls. Today, women are estimated to constitute nearly 50 percent of new members in some racist groups, leading some antiracist monitoring groups to claim that they are the "fastest growing part of the racist movement." Yet this new group of racist activists has been ignored, as researchers have tended to view racism as male-dominated and racist women as more interested in domestic and personal concerns than in its politics.

Eventually, I persuaded thirty-four women from a variety of racist and anti-Semitic groups across the country to talk to me at length about themselves and their racist activities. Fourteen women were in neo-Nazi but not skinhead groups, six were members of Ku Klux Klans, eight were white power skinheads, and six were in Christian Identity or related groups. What they told me shatters many common ideas about what racist activists are like.

Among the women I interviewed there was no single racist *type*. The media depict unkempt, surly women in faded T-shirts, but the reality is different. One of my first interviews was with Mary, a vivacious Klanswoman who met me at her door with a big smile and ushered me into her large, inviting kitchen. Her blond hair was pulled back into a long ponytail and tied with a large green bow. She wore dangling gold hoop earrings, blue jeans, a modest flowered blouse, and no visible tattoos or other racist insignia. Her only other jewelry was a simple gold-colored necklace. Perhaps sensing my surprise at her unremarkable appearance, she joked that her suburban appearance was her "undercover uniform."

Trudy, an elderly Nazi activist I interviewed somewhat later, lived in a one-story, almost shabby ranch house on a lower-middle-class street in a small town in the Midwest. Her house was furnished plainly. Moving cautiously with the aid of a walker, she brought out tea and cookies prepared for my visit. Meeting her reminded me of the phrase "old country women," which I had once heard from a southern policeman characterizing the rural Klanswomen in his area....

My encounters with skinhead women were more guarded, although some were quite animated and articulate. Not one invited me into her home—all I got was a quick glance when I picked her up for an interview in some other location. Most seemed to live at or barely above the level of squatters, in dirty, poorly equipped spaces that were nearly uninhabitable. Their appearance varied. Molly sported five ear piercings that held silver hoops and a silver female sign, an attractive and professionally cut punk hairstyle, fine features, and intense eyes. Others were ghostly figures, with empty eyes and visible scars poorly hidden behind heavy makeup and garish lipstick.

Over a two-year period I spent considerable time with these women, talking to them about their racist commitments and getting them to tell me their life stories. Listening to them describe their backgrounds, I realized that many did not fit common stereotypes about racist women as uneducated, marginal members of society raised in terrible families and lured into racist groups by boyfriends and husbands....

Why were these racist women willing to talk to me? They had a variety of reasons. Some hoped to generate publicity for their groups or themselves—a common motivation for granting interviews to the media. Many saw an opportunity to explain their racial politics to a white outsider, even one decidedly unsympathetic to their arguments. In a racist variant on the religious imperative to "bear witness" to the unconverted, they wanted the outside world to have an accurate (even if negative) account to counter superficial media reports. As one young woman put it, "I don't know what your political affiliations are, but I trust that you'll try to be as objective as possible." Others wished to support or challenge what they imagined I had been told in earlier interviews with racist comrades or competitors. And, despite their deep antagonism toward authority figures, some young women were flattered to have their opinions solicited by a university professor. They had rarely encountered someone older who talked with them without being patronizing, threatening, or directive.

From the beginning, when I asked women if I could interview them, I made it clear that I did not share the racial convictions of these groups. I explicitly said that my views were quite opposed to theirs, that they should not hope to convert me to their views, but that I would try to depict women racist activists accurately. I revealed my critical stance but made it clear that I had no intent to portray them as crazy and did not plan to turn them over to law enforcement or mental health agencies.

I was prepared to elaborate on my disagreements with organized racism in my interviews, but in nearly every case the women cut me short, eager to talk about themselves. Recognizing the extreme marginalization of the racist movement in the American political landscape, these women had no doubt that an ideological gulf divided them from me—it separates their beliefs from nearly all political ideas deemed acceptable in modern public life. They were accustomed to having people disagree with them, and they rarely tried to sway those who openly opposed their opinions. They were interested in me not as a potential convert, but rather as a recorder of their lives and thoughts. Their desire, at once personal and politically evangelical, was that someone outside the small racist groups to which they belong hear and record their words.

Indeed, such eagerness to talk underscores the ethical dilemma of inadvertently providing a platform for racist propaganda. Studies on racist extremists have the power to publicize even as they scrutinize. The problem was brought to the fore as I considered the issue of anonymity for my interviewees. Although the inclusion of more biographical details about the racist women activists I interviewed would be useful, I decided that doing so would unavoidably reveal their identities and thus give further publicity to them and their groups. For this reason, I have used pseudonyms for interviewees and their groups and changed all identifying details, while rendering quotations verbatim. Most people interviewed by scholars desire to remain anonymous, but these women wanted to be known. Some tried to demand that I use their names or the names of their groups. When an older Ku Klux Klan woman thanked me "for writing an article that might inspire others," however, I was convinced that my decision to disguise identities was correct. . . .

Walking a tightrope in my interviews, I kept a balance between maintaining enough distance to make it clear that I rejected their ideas and creating sufficient rapport to encourage women to talk to me. A successful interview needs some conversational common ground. Each party needs to feel understood, if not entirely accepted, by the other. These racist women were unlikely to reveal much about themselves if they did not have some trust in me, if I could not manage to express interest in their lives and refrain from repeatedly condemning them.

Usually a researcher can establish rapport with interviewees by proffering details of his or her personal life or expressing agreement with their choices and beliefs. Because I was unwilling to do either, I was forced to rely on more indirect and fragile measures. Like those at family gatherings and office parties who strain toward congeniality across known lines of disagreement, I seized on any experiences or values that we shared, no matter how trivial. When they expressed dissatisfaction with their bodies, I let them know that I had the same concerns. I commented positively when they talked of their children in parental rather than political terms—for example, when they worried about having enough time to be good mothers—and hoped that my sympathy would lead them to overlook my silence when they discussed such things as the "racial education" they planned for their children....

A researcher can be simultaneously an "insider" and an "outsider" to the culture of those being studied. As a white person I had access that no nonwhite researcher could enjoy. As a woman, I had a store of shared experiences that could support a stream of conversational banter about bodies, men, food, and clothing in which a male researcher would be unlikely to engage. Certainly, both I and the women I interviewed realized that I was an outsider to the world of organized racism. But even the obvious barriers between us gave me insight into their convoluted racial beliefs. For example, my contradictory status as both a racial outsider (to their politics) and an apparent racial insider (as white) helped me understand their ambivalent descriptions of their racial and racist identities.

Yet a reliance on rapport is problematic when scholars do not share a worldview with those they study. Trying to understand the world through the eyes of someone for whom you have even a little sympathy is one thing, but the prospect of developing empathy for a racist activist whose life is given meaning and purpose by the desire to annihilate you or others like you is a very different matter....

There are uncomfortable emotional complexities to this kind of research. Interviewing members of racist groups is dangerous but also intriguing, even offering a voyeuristic thrill. Though I'm embarrassed to admit it, I found meeting racist activists to be exciting as well as horrifying. The ethnographer Barrie Thorne captures this sense of fieldwork as adventure: it consists of "venturing into exciting, taboo, dangerous, perhaps enticing social circumstances; getting the flavor of participation, living out moments of high drama; but in some ultimate way having a cop-out, a built-in escape, a point of outside leverage that full participants lack."[1]

Fieldwork with "unloved groups" also poses the problem of seduction. As Antonius Robben, an anthropologist of Argentinean fascism, notes, even when researchers and interviewees begin as wary opponents, scholars can be drawn into "trad[ing] our critical stance as observers for an illusion of congeniality with cultural insiders."[2] Indeed, others who study loathsome political groups cite the pain of discovering that participants in some of history's most dreadful social movements can be charming and engaging in interviews.[3]

My time with Linda, a white power skinhead from the West, illustrates one instance of emotional seduction. Before our formal interview, our relationship was tense. With every phone call Linda insisted on changing the place and conditions of the interview, demanding ever more evidence that I was not with the police. She repeatedly threatened to bring her boyfriend and a gun to the interview, in violation of our agreement. Each of her demands required more negotiation and gave Linda another opportunity to remind me that she would not hesitate to hurt anyone who betrayed her or her group. Indeed, I had ample reason to take her threats seriously: both Linda and her boyfriend had served prison sentences for assault, selling drugs, and other offenses. I came to the interview frightened and prepared for hostile confrontation. In person, however, Linda confounded my expectations. She was charming, soft-spoken, and concerned for my comfort during the interview. Although quite willing to express appalling attitudes, Linda prefaced many of her statements by apologizing for what I might find offensive. My fear eased, replaced by a seductive, false rapport as Linda set the parameters of our interaction and I responded to her. Off-guard, I pressed Linda less aggressively than the other women to explain contradictions in the chronology and logic of her story. In retrospect, the field notes that I taped immediately after the interview make me uneasy. They show how disarming emotional manipulation can be, even when one is on guard against it:

> I found the [negotiation and preparation for the] interview with Linda to be the most emotionally stressful, maybe with the exception of [another] interview during which I was fearing for my life. Actually with Linda and [her boyfriend] there was no indication that they might try to harm me at all. In fact, quite the contrary. I actually was afraid of that before they came because they both have very violent reputations, but in person they were extremely cordial and very friendly, not trying to intimidate me in any way. Perhaps trying to cultivate me.

Researchers often talk informally about the emotional side of doing fieldwork, but it is a subject rarely discussed in print. Pondering one's own emotional state may seem narcissistic—yet it also can be analytically revealing. In the early stages of this research, I experienced a great deal of fear. The violent reputations of some of the women I wanted to interview, including the skinhead organizer whose comrades referred to her as "Ms. Icepick," did little to dispel my concerns. As I got to know some people in the racist world, I became somewhat less afraid. As I began to see them in more complicated, less stereotyped ways, I no longer worried that every interaction would end in disaster. It also became clear that as a woman in that male-dominated world I was safer because I seemed to pose little threat: male researchers were seen as more personally challenging to male racists and more likely to be covert police operatives.

But in other respects, I grew more afraid as I became less naive. For one thing, I came to realize that my white skin color would provide me little protection. Many racist activists who have faced criminal charges were turned in by other whites, sometimes even members of their own groups. Moreover…some racists see race as determined by commitment to white power politics rather than by genetics. I could not assume that those I interviewed would view me either as white or as nonhostile. I could not count on racial immunity from violence.

As I was contacting and interviewing racist women, the structure of the racist movement also changed in two ways that increased my risk. First, the 1995 bombing of the Alfred P. Murrah Federal Building in Oklahoma City occurred midway through my interviewing. In its wake, the racist movement went further underground. Racist groups were subject to investigation and members became increasingly sensitive to the possibility of police informants and infiltrators. Second, as a result of the heightened scrutiny of hate groups after the Oklahoma City bombing, the racist movement became less organized. Some adopted a strategy known as "leaderless resistance," which was designed to make the racist movement less vulnerable to investigation and prosecution. Racist activists began to operate in small units or cells, sometimes in pairs or even alone, to avoid detection by authorities. While adhering to a common agenda of Aryan supremacism, they were able to develop their own strategies, even select enemies, without answering to formal leaders; they used the Internet or other anonymous means to disseminate their ideas rather than relying on organized groups.

Leaderless resistance makes studying the racist movement scarier because it reduces the accountability of individual racists. When I attended a racist rally in the later stages of my research, I came with the permission of the rally's leader. I felt, or at least hoped, that his invitation would ensure my safety. Yet a significant number of those in attendance felt no allegiance to him; they did not care whether their words or actions might reflect on the group or implicate its leader. The *organization* of organized racism, I realized, was double-pronged. It channeled the racist beliefs of members into collective strategies of terrorism, building an agenda of racist practices that could be catastrophic. But it could also curb the violence of particular individuals, unruly members whose actions could bring the collective and its leaders to the attention of the authorities. Without leaders, such restraints do not exist.

My fear was caused by more than simple proximity to racist groups. It was deliberately fed by the women I interviewed, who hoped to limit the scope of my study and shape my analysis…. The racist women constantly drew attention to my vulnerability to them, asking whether I was afraid to come see them, whether I was afraid to be in their homes…. Even a woman in prison on death row, who was brought to our interview in handcuffs, found a way to undermine any power I had over her by noting that she could call on gangs of allies in and outside the prison walls. "I'm not scared of anybody," she told me, "so I'm not gonna worry about it. I'll say what I got to say… 'cause I got the Jamaican Posse and the Cuban Posse all behind me, they gonna kick ass."

Some women were more indirect in their intimidation. Many bragged of their group's violence, making it clear that they treated enemies harshly. An Aryan supremacist boasted that the racist movement attracted people who were "totally messed up and totally mindless," people who were prone to "fight and kill, rip off armored cars, get guns."... Even now, years after completing the interviews, I receive signed and anonymous letters warning that they "are watching" me, that I had better tell "the truth" about them and their movement.

Often the women saw even the selection of where we would conduct the interview as an opening to use intimidation. Usually, I asked each woman to choose a place where she would feel comfortable, although I reminded her that I did not want to be interrupted by family members or racist group comrades. Several suggested their homes, saying that they would be most at ease there but also warning that their houses contained weapons and that other comrades (presumably less trustworthy than themselves) might appear at the house during the interview. Others picked a public place but indicated that they would station armed comrades nearby in case the interview did not "proceed as planned." On only two occasions did I refuse a suggestion for an interview site, both for safety reasons. One woman wanted me to be blindfolded and transported to an unknown destination in the back of a truck. Another proposed a meeting in a very remote racist compound to which I would have to be driven by a racist group member. And even in these cases, when my concerns for personal safety denied them their choice, they continued the implicit threats. For example, after the woman who had wanted me to be blindfolded agreed on a more visible site, she assured me that I should not be concerned for my safety there because "men with guns" would be hidden along the street "in case of a police raid."...

But fear went both ways. These women were afraid of me. I could betray their confidences to the police, to enemies, or to family members who were not aware of their activities. Telling me about their journey into organized racism could feel empowering to them, but it could also expose them to retribution. One Washington racist skinhead worried that I might secretly funnel information to violent gangs of antiracist skinheads about buildings occupied by racist skinheads: "[After you leave], well, uh, I wonder if some skin's house is gonna get Molotov-cocktailed and the [antiracist skinheads] are doing this in retaliation." An older neo-Nazi was concerned that my tape recording of her interview "could be used against me in a court of law." Many expressed suspicions about how I had found them at all. Throughout the interview a woman from the East repeatedly asked, "Just how did you become aware of the group that I'm in?" Worried that such fears could derail the interview, I assured each woman that her interview would be confidential and that I would not ask questions about illegal activities.... [Yet]...I had to interrupt several of these women to keep them from telling me about their illegal activities or plans. A young Nazi activist in California, for example, deflected nearly all my inquiries about her family by saying that she was being constantly watched by the police, who could use such information against her, yet she repeatedly returned to an unsolicited story about her friends who "buried their guns in oil drums up in the hills for when the race war comes."

Racists also used their own fear to create rapport to keep the interview moving. Usually the task of creating rapport falls to the researcher, who generally has the most to gain from a successful interview. But many of these women were highly motivated to have me hear their stories. Thus, even as they tried to make me more afraid, they often pointed to their vulnerability to me; a woman might emphasize my exposure in the well-guarded living room of a racist leader, and at the same time observe that I probably had "really good connections to the police." At times, this tempering became nearly comical; one interviewee repeatedly made note of the guns and sketches of lynchings that lay around her living room but then sought to assure me that although "the average person has an idea that the Klan is very military [violent] and they're afraid," she was no threat, because she "wasn't aware of [that reputation] until just recently." But fear did help bring our sense of risk to the same level, making plain the stalemate in which we at least seemed to be equally unsafe.

Although the danger of engaging with racist activists actually increased while I was interviewing these women, I became less afraid over time, for reasons that are disturbing. The first interviews, conducted largely with members of the Ku Klux Klan, left me nearly paralyzed with fear. My field journal is full of notes on how to increase my own safety. Before each interview, I made elaborate preparations, giving friends instructions on what to do if I did not return on schedule. Yet my field notes on the last interviews, conducted largely with neo-Nazis and white power skinheads—members of groups that in recent years have been more likely than the Klan to engage in overt violence—show that my fears had largely abated. I took personal risks that earlier I would have found unthinkable. I had become more numb to tales of assaults and boasts of preparing for "race war."

It is terrifying to realize that you find it difficult to be shocked. But gradually my dealings with racist women became like a business transaction, with both parties parrying for favorable terms. I was not unafraid, but I took fewer precautions based on fear. Perhaps this change in attitude explains why my later interviews were less productive. In the earlier interviews, the tension created by fear made me think hard. As it subsided, some of my analytical edge slipped away as well. I was becoming anesthetized to the horrors of organized racism, a numbness that was personally dismaying and that also signaled my need to regain emotional distance from this research before writing about it—a process that took years....

My experience suggests something about what it must feel to be inside a racist group: how the bizarre begins to feel normal, taken-for-granted, both unquestioned and unquestionable; how Jews or African Americans or gay men might come to seem so demonic and so personally threatening that group members could be moved to actions that seem incomprehensible to those on the outside. This state of mind results from a perceptual contraction that is all but imperceptible to the actor.

My feelings of fear also provide insight into the internal workings of racist groups. Fear is highly salient in the racist movement. Since they are greatly outnumbered by the racial, sexual, religious, and political groups they seek to destroy, organized racists use physical intimidation and the threat of violence to gain power over their opponents. Demonstrations, marches, violent propaganda, cross burnings, and terroristic actions are meant to demonstrate the strength of the racial movement and induce fear among enemies. So are the shocking cartoons and graphics that are the mainstay of racist propaganda. Racists pay close attention to their opponents' reactions, noting with glee any indication that they are feared by other groups or by the public. And fear is wielded within their groups as well. Members are warned repeatedly of the dire consequences that might befall them if they defect, particularly if they betray the group to the outside. These are not idle threats, as those who leave racist groups often risk violence at the hands of their former comrades. While I was doing these interviews, police on the East Coast were investigating the chilling abduction, assault, and near-murder of a young girl by a mixed-sex gang of skinheads who feared that she would defect from the group....

The emotional world of organized racism becomes clearer when I consider the emotional work I needed to do to study racist groups. In the course of interviewing, I constantly sensed the need to display certain feelings. Sometimes I mimicked what I did not feel, forcing myself to laugh along with the more innocuous comments, hoping to establish rapport and fend off anecdotes that might be more offensive. At other times I withheld the emotions I did feel, maintaining a blank and studied expression when confronted with cross burnings or propaganda that glorified Nazi atrocities or even the interviewee's warped take on current events. In an interview done right after the Oklahoma City bombing, as the sickening images of the bombing were still in the newspapers and fresh in my mind, a woman told me that the people in her group "were happy about what happened in Oklahoma. There's a lot of anger out there. The people, some felt sorry for the [white] children but the rest of them got what they deserved, the government deserved. The government provoked this.... It's like in Germany when the skinheads went on the streets and burned down the refugee centers and the townspeople poured out and applauded. It could reach that point here." Throughout, I had to feign interest in the women's intricate stories of hatred, to ask questions in a neutral tone, and to be responsive when I wanted to flee or scream. But by examining my emotional work, I gained some insight into how the racist movement manipulates the emotions of its members, evoking not just fear but also awe.

Individual and political needs collide in writing about racism. As we acknowledge the rationality of racist women, we must never forget the evil they do. Yet writing from, and about, the stories of racist women runs the risk of personalizing them too much, making their ideas more sympathetic or less odious. It may subtly lend an academic gloss to the importance of racist activists, empowering them to work harder on behalf of their beliefs. These are dangerous outcomes—but the consequences of not learning from and about racists are worse.

If we stand too far back from racist groups and fail to look carefully at the women and men in organized racism, we are likely to draw politically misleading conclusions. Superficial studies simply caricature racist activists and make organized racism a foil against which we see ourselves as righteous and tolerant. We cannot simply comb the backgrounds of racist activists in search of a flaw—an absent parent, childhood victimization, or economic hard times—that "explains" their racist commitment. Moreover, we cannot use Germany in the 1930s as a prototype for all movements of the extreme right. Economic distress and social dislocation may explain the rise of such large-scale, powerful movements as the German Nazis or earlier American racist organizations, but such factors play only a small role in the tiny and politically marginal racist movement in the United States today.

We gain far more by taking a direct, hard look at the members of modern racist groups, acknowledging the commonalities between them and mainstream groups as well as the differences. In this book I tell the story of modern organized racism from the inside, focusing on how racist activists understand themselves and their worldviews....

REFERENCES

1. Barrie Thorne, "Political Activist as Participant Observer: Conflicts of Commitment in a Study of the Draft Resistance Movement of the 1960s." In *Contemporary Field Research: A Collection of Readings,* Robert M. Emerson, ed. Prospect Heights, Ill: Waveland Press, 1983:235–252.

2. Antonius C. G. M. Robben, "The Politics of Truth and Emotion among Victims and Perpetrators of Violence." In *Fieldwork Under Fire: Contemporary Studies of Violence and Survival.* Canolyn Nordstrom and Antonius C. G. M. Robben, eds. Berkeley: University of California Press, 1995:81–104.

3. See Claudia Koonz. *Mothers in the Fatherland: Women, Family Life, and Nazi Politics.* New York: St. Martin's Press, 1987; and Robben, "Politics of Truth and Emotion."

READING **18** ■

Invisible Man

Lawrence Otis Graham

introduction ■ ■ ■ ■

As you know, the circumstances we inherit at birth have serious consequences for what happens to us in life. Some of us are born poor, others rich, most of us in between. Each of us is born into a racial–ethnic group. Some of us are born to single mothers, others to married parents; some to parents who are college graduates, others to parents who have not finished high school. Even our geography (South, West, rural, urban) sets up background factors that play a significant role in our orientations to life. Sociologists use the term *life chances* to refer to how the background factors that surround our birth affect our fate in life.

A major issue in the sociology of race–ethnic relations is the relative significance of race-ethnicity and social class in determining people's life chances. Is the color of our skin more important than social class for setting us on a course in life? More specifically, does social class or race-ethnicity play a greater role in our everyday lives? Although not providing *the* answer to these provocative questions, this selection sheds light on some of the intricate interconnections between race-ethnicity and social class. As Lawrence Graham found, racism is far from dead, and race-ethnicity continues to play a pivotal role in what happens to us in everyday life.

Thinking Critically

As you read this selection, ask yourself:

1. Since Graham is an African American, he should know about racism. Why, then, do you think he did this research?

2. What do you think Graham's most eye-opening experiences were?

3. What situation do you think embarrassed Graham the most? Why?

I drive up the winding lane past a long stone wall and beneath an archway of sixty-foot maples. At one bend of the drive, a freshly clipped lawn and a trail of yellow daffodils slope gently up to the four-pillared portico of a white Georgian colonial. The building's six huge chimneys, the two wings with slate gray shutters, and the white-brick facade loom over a luxuriant golf course. Before me stands the one-hundred-year-old Greenwich Country Club—*the* country club—in the affluent, patrician, and very white town of Greenwich, Connecticut, where there are eight clubs for fifty nine thousand people.

I'm a thirty-year-old corporate lawyer at a Midtown Manhattan firm, and I make $105,000 a year. I'm a graduate of Princeton University (1983) and Harvard Law School (1988), and I've written ten nonfiction books. Although these may seem like impressive credentials, they're not the ones that brought me here. Quite frankly, I got into this country club the only way that a black man like me could—as a $7-an-hour busboy.

After seeing dozens of news stories about Dan Quayle, Billy Graham, Ross Perot, and others who either belonged to or frequented white country clubs, I decided to find out what things were really like at a club where I heard there were no black members.

I remember stepping up to the pool at the country club when I was ten and setting off a chain reaction: Several irate parents dragged their children out of the water and fled. When the other kids ran out of the pool, so did I—foolishly thinking that there was something in the water that was going to harm all of us. Back then, in 1972, I saw these clubs only as places where families socialized. I grew up in an affluent white neighborhood in Westchester, and all my playmates and neighbors belonged to one or more of these private institutions. Across the street, my best friend introduced me to the Westchester Country Club before he left for Groton and Yale. My teenage tennis partner from Scarsdale introduced me to the Beach Point Club on weekends before he left for Harvard. The family next door belonged to the Scarsdale Golf Club. In my crowd, the question wasn't "Do you belong?" It was "Where?"

My grandparents owned a Memphis trucking firm, and as far back as I can remember, our family was well off and we had little trouble fitting in even though I was the only black kid on the high school tennis team, the only one in the orchestra, the only one in my Roman Catholic confirmation class.

Today, I'm back where I started—on a street of five- and six-bedroom colonials with expensive cars and neighbors who all belong somewhere. Through my experience as a young lawyer, I have come to realize that these clubs are where business people network, where lawyers and investment bankers meet potential clients and arrange deals. How many clients and deals am I going to line up on the asphalt parking lot of my local public tennis courts?

I am not ashamed to admit that I one day want to be a partner and a part of this network. When I talk to my black lawyer or investment-banker friends or my wife, a brilliant black woman who has degrees from Harvard College, Harvard Law School, and Harvard Business School, I learn that our white counterparts are being accepted by dozens of these elite institutions. So why shouldn't we—especially when we have the same credentials, salaries, social graces, and ambitions?

My black Ivy League friends and I know of black company vice presidents who have to ask white subordinates to invite them out for golf or tennis. We talk about the club in Westchester that rejected black Scarsdale resident and millionaire magazine publisher Earl Graves, who sits on *Fortune* 500 boards, owns a Pepsi distribution franchise, raised three bright Ivy League children, and holds prestigious honorary degrees. We talk about all the clubs that face a scandal and then run out to sign up one quiet, deferential black man who will accept a special "limited-status" membership, remove the taint, and deflect further scrutiny.

I wanted some answers. I knew I could never be treated as an equal at this Greenwich oasis—a place so insular that the word *Negro* is still used in conversation. But I figured I could get close enough to understand what these people were thinking and why country clubs were so set on excluding people like me.

■ ■ ■ ■ **MARCH 28 TO APRIL 7, 1992**

I invented a completely new résumé for myself. I erased Harvard, Princeton, and my upper-middle-class suburban childhood from my life. So that I'd have to account for fewer years, I made myself seven years younger—an innocent twenty-three. I used my real name and made myself a graduate of the actual high school I attended. Since it would be difficult to pretend that I was from "the street," I decided to become a sophomore-year dropout from Tufts University, a midsize college in suburban Boston. My years at nearby Harvard and the fact that my brother had gone there had given me enough knowledge about the school to pull it off. I contacted some older friends who owned large companies and restaurants in the Boston and New York areas and asked them to serve as references. I was already on a short leave of absence from my law firm to work on a book.

I pieced together a wardrobe that consisted of a blue polyester blazer, white oxford shirt, ironed blue slacks, black loafers, and a horrendous pink, black, and silver tie, and I set up interviews at clubs. Over the telephone, five of the eight said that I sounded as if I would make a great waiter. During each of my phone conversations, I made sure that I spoke to the person who would make the hiring decision. I also confirmed exactly how many waiter positions were available, and I arranged a personal interview within forty minutes to an hour of the conversation, just to be sure that they could not tell me that no such job was available.

"We don't have any job openings—and if you don't leave the building, I will have to call security," the receptionist said at the first club I visited in Greenwich.

I was astounded by the speed with which she made this remark, particularly when I saw that she had just handed an application to a young-looking Hispanic man wearing jeans, sneakers, a T-shirt, and sunglasses. "I'm here to see Donna, your maître d'," I added defensively as I forced a smile at the pasty-looking woman who sat behind a window.

"There's no Donna here."

"But I just spoke to her thirty minutes ago and she said to come by to discuss the waiter job."

"Sorry, but there are no jobs and no one here named Donna."

After convincing the woman to give me an application, I completed it and then walked back into the dining room, which was visible from the foyer.

I came upon a white male waiter and asked him, "Is there a Donna here?"

"The maître d'?" he asked. "Yeah, she's in the kitchen."

When I found Donna and explained that I was the one she had talked to on the phone forty minutes earlier, she crossed her arms and shook her head. "You're the 'Larry' I talked to on the phone?"

"Yes," I answered.

"No way."

"I beg your pardon," I said.

"No. No way," she said while refusing to take the application I waved in front of her.

"We just talked on the phone less than an hour ago. You said I sounded perfect. And I've waited in three different restaurants—I've had two years of college—You said you have five waiter jobs open—I filled out the application—I can start right away—"

She still shook her head. And held her hands behind her back—unwilling to even touch my application. "No," she said. "Can't do it."

My talking did no good. It was 1992. This was the Northeast. If I hadn't been involved, I would never have believed it. I suddenly thought about all the times I quietly disbelieved certain poor blacks who said they had tried to get jobs but no one would hire them. I wanted to say then and there, "Not even as a waiter?"

Only an hour earlier, this woman had enthusiastically urged me to come right over for an interview. Now, as two white kitchen workers looked on, she would only hold her hands tightly behind her back and shake her head emphatically. So I left.

There were three other clubs to go to. When I met them, the club managers told me I "would probably make a much better busboy."

"Busboy? Over the phone, you said you needed a waiter," I argued.

"Yes, I know I said that, but you seem very alert, and I think you'd make an excellent busboy instead."

In his heavy Irish brogue, the club manager said he needed to give me a "perception test." He explained it this way: "This ten-question test will give us an idea of your perception, intellectual strength, and conscious ability to perform the duties assigned to you as a busboy."

I had no idea how much intellectual strength and conscious ability (whatever that meant) could be required of a busboy, but here are some of the questions he asked me:

1. If there are three apples and you take two away, how many do you have?
2. How many of each species of animal did Moses put on his new ark?
3. It's 1963 and you set your digital clock to ring at 9:00 A.M. when you go to bed at 8:00 P.M. How many hours will you sleep?
4. If a house gets southern exposure on all four sides, what color is the bear that walks by the house?

And the responses…

1. I answered "one apple" because I thought this was a simple math question, as in "three minus two equals one," but the correct answer was "two" because, as the manager said, "You've got to think, Larry—if you take away two apples and put them in your pocket, you've got two apples, not one."
2. Fortunately, I answered this question as it was presumably designed to smoke out any applicants who hadn't been raised in a Judeo-Christian culture. It was Noah, not Moses, who built an ark.
3. I scored major credibility points here by lying and saying, "Wow, I wasn't even born yet in 1963…." The "right" answer was that there were no digital clocks in 1963. I took his word for it.
4. Although I believed that a house could get southern exposure on all four sides only at the South Pole—and thus the bear had to be a white polar bear—I was told that I was "trying to act too smart" and that all bears are, of course, brown.

■ ■ ■ APRIL 8 TO 11

After interviewing for advertised waiter jobs at five clubs, I had gotten only two offers—both for non-waiter jobs. One offer was to split my time as a towel boy in the locker room and a busboy in the dining room. The second offer—which followed a callback interview—was to work as a busboy. When I told the club manager that I had only wanted a waiter job, he responded, "Well, we've discussed it here and everyone would feel more comfortable if you took a busboy job instead."

"But I've never worked as a busboy," I reminded him.

He nodded sympathetically. "People here have decided that it's busboy or nothing."

Given these choices I made my final job selection in much the way I had decided on a college and a law school: I went for prestige. Not only was the Greenwich Country Club celebrating its hundredth anniversary but its roster boasted former president Gerald Ford, baseball star Tom Seaver, former Securities and Exchange Commission chairman and U.S. ambassador to the Netherlands John Shad, as well as former Timex spokesman John Cameron Swayze. Add to that a few dozen *Fortune* 500 executives, bankers, Wall Street lawyers, European entrepreneurs, a Presbyterian minister, and cartoonist Mort Walker, who does *Beetle Bailey*. (The Greenwich Country Club did not respond to any questions about the club and its members.)

For three days, I worked on my upper-arm muscles by walking around the house with a sterling-silver tray stacked high with heavy dictionaries. I allowed a mustache to grow in, then added a pair of arrestingly ugly Coke-bottle reading glasses.

■ ■ ■ APRIL 12 (SUNDAY)

Today was my first day at work. My shift didn't start until 10:30 A.M., so I laid out my clothes at home: a white button-down shirt, freshly ironed cotton khaki pants, white socks, and white leather sneakers. I'd get my official club uniform in two days. Looking in my wallet, I removed my American Express Gold Card, my Harvard club membership ID, and all of my business cards.

When I arrived at the club, I entered under the large portico, stepping through the heavy doors and onto the black-and-white checkerboard tiles of the entry hall.

A distracted receptionist pointed me toward Mr. Ryan's office. (*All names of club members and personnel have been changed.*) I walked past glistening silver trophies and a guest book on a pedestal to a windowless office with three desks. My new boss waved me in and abruptly hung up the phone.

"Good morning, Larry," he said with a sufficiently warm smile. The tight knot in his green tie made him look more fastidious than I had remembered from the interview.

"Hi, Mr. Ryan. How's it going?"

Glancing at his watch to check my punctuality, he shook my hand and handed me some papers. "Oh, and by the way, where'd you park?"

"In front, near the tennis courts."

Already shaking his head, he tossed his pencil onto the desk. "That's off-limits to you. You should always park in the back, enter in the back, and leave from the back. No exceptions."

"I'll do the forms right now," I said. "And then I'll be an official busboy."

Mr. Ryan threw me an ominous nod. "And Larry, let me stop you now. We don't like that term busboy. We find it demeaning. We prefer to call you busmen."

Leading me down the center stairwell to the basement, he added, "And in the future, you will always use the back stairway by the back entrance." He continued to talk as we trotted through a maze of hallways. "I think I'll have you trail with Carlos or Hector—no, Carlos. Unless you speak Spanish?"

"No." I ran to keep up with Mr. Ryan.

"That's the dishwasher room, where Juan works. And over here is where you'll be working." I looked at the brass sign. MEN'S GRILL.

It was a dark room with a mahogany finish, and it looked like a library in a large Victorian home. Dark walls, dark wood-beamed ceilings. Deep-green wool carpeting. Along one side of the room stood a long, highly polished mahogany bar with liquor bottles, wineglasses, and a two-and-a-half-foot-high silver trophy. Fifteen heavy round wooden tables, each encircled with four to six broad wooden armchairs padded with green leather on the backs and seats, broke up the room. A big-screen TV was set into the wall along with two shelves of books.

"This is the Men's Grill," Mr. Ryan said. "Ladies are not allowed except on Friday evenings."

Next was the brightly lit connecting kitchen. "Our kitchen serves hot and cold foods. You'll work six days a week here. The club is closed on Mondays. The kitchen serves the Men's Grill and an adjoining room called the Mixed Grill. That's where the ladies and kids can eat."

"And what about men? Can they eat in there, too?"

This elicited a laugh. "Of course they can. Time and place restrictions apply only to women and kids."

He showed me the Mixed Grill, a well-lit pastel-blue room with glass French doors and white wood trim.

"Guys, say hello to Larry. He's a new busman at the club."

I waved.

"And this is Rick, Stephen, Drew, Buddy, and Lee." Five white waiters dressed in white polo shirts with blue "1892" club insignias nodded while busily slicing lemons.

"And this is Hector, and Carlos, the other two busmen." Hector, Carlos, and I were the only nonwhites on the serving staff. They greeted me in a mix of English and Spanish.

"Nice to meet all of you," I responded.

"Thank God," one of the taller waiters cried out. "Finally—somebody who can speak English."

Mr. Ryan took me and Carlos through a hall lined with old black-and-white portraits of former presidents of the club. "This is our one hundredth year, so you're joining the club at an important time," Mr. Ryan added before walking off. "Carlos, I'm going to leave Larry to trail with you—and no funny stuff."

Standing outside the ice room, Carlos and I talked about our pasts. He was twenty-five, originally from Colombia, and hadn't finished school. I said I had dropped out, too.

As I stood there talking, Carlos suddenly gestured for me to move out of the hallway. I looked behind me and noticed something staring at us. "A video camera?"

"They're around," Carlos remarked quietly while scooping ice into large white tubs. "Now watch me scoop ice."

After we carried the heavy tubs back to the grill, I saw another video camera point down at us. I dropped my head.

"You gonna live in the Monkey House?" Carlos asked.

"What's that?"

We climbed the stairs to take our ten-minute lunch break before work began. "Monkey House is where workers live here," Carlos said.

I followed him through a rather filthy utility room and into a huge white kitchen. We got in line behind about twenty Hispanic men and women—all dressed in varying uniforms. At the head of the line were the white waiters I'd met earlier.

I was soon handed a hot plate with two red lumps of rice and some kind of sausage-shaped meat. There were two string beans, several pieces of zucchini, and a thin, broken slice of dried meat loaf that looked as if it had been cooked, burned, frozen, and then reheated. Lurking at the very edge of my dish was an ice-cream-scoop-sized helping of yellowish mashed potatoes.

I followed Carlos, plate in hand, out of the kitchen. To my surprise, we walked back into the dank and dingy utility room, which turned out to be the workers' dining area.

The white waiters huddled together at one end of the table, while the Hispanic workers ate quietly at the other end. Before I could decide which end to integrate, Carlos directed me to sit with him on the Hispanic end.

I was soon back downstairs working in the grill. At my first few tables, I tried to avoid making eye contact with members as I removed dirty plates and wiped down tables and chairs. Having known so many people who belonged to these clubs, I was sure I'd be recognized by someone from childhood, college, or work.

At around 1:15, four men who looked to be in their mid- to late fifties sat down at a six-chair table. They pulled off their cotton windbreakers and golf sweaters.

"It's these damned newspeople that cause all the problems," said golfer number one, shoving his hand deep into a popcorn bowl. "These Negroes wouldn't even be thinking about golf. They can't afford to join a club, anyway."

Golfer number two squirmed out of his navy blue sweater and nodded in agreement. "My big problem with this Clinton fellow is that he apologized." As I stood watching from the corner of the bar, I realized the men were talking about then-governor Bill Clinton's recent apology for playing at an all-white golf club in Little Rock, Arkansas.

"Holt, I couldn't agree with you more," added golfer number three, a hefty man who was biting off the end of a cigar.

"You got any iced tea?" golfer number one asked as I put the silverware and menus around the table. Popcorn flew out of his mouth as he attempted to speak and chew at the same time.

"Yes, we certainly do."

Golfer number three removed a beat-up Rolex from his wrist. "It just sets a bad precedent. Instead of apologizing, he should try to discredit them—undercut them somehow. What's to apologize for?" I cleared my throat and backed away from the table.

Suddenly, golfer number one waved me back to his side. "Should we get four iced teas or just a pitcher and four glasses?"

"I'd be happy to bring whatever you'd like, sir."

Throughout the day, I carried "bus buckets" filled with dirty dishes from the grill to the dishwasher room. And each time I returned to the grill, I scanned the room for recognizable faces. Fortunately, I saw none. After almost four hours of running back and forth, clearing dishes, wiping down tables, and thanking departing members who left spilled coffee, dirty napkins, and unwanted business cards in their wake, I helped out in the coed Mixed Grill.

"Oh, busboy," a voice called out as I made the rounds with two pots of coffee. "Here, busboy. Here, busboy," the woman called out. "Busboy, my coffee is cold. Give me a refill."

"Certainly, I would be happy to." I reached over for her cup.

The fiftyish woman pushed her hand through her straw blond hair and turned to look me in the face. "Decaf, thank you."

"You are quite welcome."

Before I turned toward the kitchen, the woman leaned over to her companion. "My goodness. Did you hear that? That busboy has diction like an educated white person."

A curly-haired waiter walked up to me in the kitchen. "Larry, are you living in the Monkey House?"

"No, but why do they call it that?"

"Well, no offense against you, but it got that name since it's the house where the workers have lived at the club. And since the workers used to be Negroes— blacks—it was nicknamed the Monkey House. And the name just stuck—even though Negroes have been replaced by Hispanics."

■ ■ ■ **APRIL 13 (MONDAY)**

I woke up and felt a pain shooting up my calves. As I turned to the clock, I realized I'd slept for eleven hours. I was thankful the club was closed on Mondays.

■ ■ ■ **APRIL 14 (TUESDAY)**

Rosa, the club seamstress, measured me for a uniform in the basement laundry room while her barking gray poodle jumped up on my feet and pants. "Down, Margarita, down," Rosa cried with pins in her mouth and marking chalk in her hand. But Margarita ignored her and continued to bark and do tiny pirouettes until I left with all of my new country-club polo shirts and pants.

Today, I worked exclusively with the "veterans," including sixty-five-year-old Sam, the Polish bartender in the Men's Grill. Hazel, an older waitress at the club, is quick, charming, and smart—the kind of waitress who makes any restaurant a success. She has worked for the club nearly twenty years and has become quite territorial with certain older male members. Whenever I was on my way to hand out menus or clear dishes at a table, Hazel would either outrun me or grab me by the arm when she saw that the table contained important male members. Inevitably, Hazel would say, "Oh, Larry, let me take care of Dr. Collingsworth. You go fill this salt shaker," or "Larry, I'll take Judge Wilson's dirty dish. You go slice some lemons in the kitchen," or "Larry, I'll clean up Reverend Gundersen's cracker crumbs. You go find some peanut oil."

During a lull, Sam, who I swear reminded me of a Norman Lear creation circa 1972, asked me to run out and get some supplies from a Mr. Chang.

"Who is Mr. Chang?" I asked.

"You know, the Chinaman. Mr. Chang."

I had recalled seeing an elderly Asian man with a gray uniform in the halls, but we had not been introduced.

"And where would I find him?"

"He's down at the other end of the hall beyond the stairs." Sam handed me a list of items on a printed form. "He's the Chinaman and it's easy to remember 'cause he's right next to the laundry room."

Hector came along and warned me not to lose the signed form because I could be accused of stealing food and supplies if the signed list wasn't given to Mr. Chang.

Down a dark, shadowy hall, we found Mr. Chang, who, in Spanish, shouted phrases at me while swinging his arms in the air.

"Do you understand him?" I asked Hector.

"He said to follow him and bring a cart."

We followed the methodical Mr. Chang from storage room to storage room, where he pulled out various items like a magician. Lemons were stored with paper goods, cans of ketchup were stored with pretzels and simultaneously served as shelves for large sacks of onions. Bottles of soda were stored with old boxes that had "Monkey House" written on them. Combustible popcorn oil and boxes of matches were stored with Styrofoam cups in the furnace room. It was all in a disorder that seemed to make complete sense to Mr. Chang.

Back in the Mixed Grill, members were talking about hotel queen and Greenwich resident Leona Helmsley, who was on the clubhouse TV because of her upcoming prison term for tax evasion.

"I'd like to see them haul her off to jail," one irate woman said to the rest of her table. "She's nothing but a garish you-know-what."

"In every sense of the word," nodded her companion as she adjusted a pink headband in her blondish white hair. "She makes the whole town look bad. The TV keeps showing those aerial shots of Greenwich and that dreadful house of hers."

A third woman shrugged her shoulders and looked into her bowl of salad. "Well, it is a beautiful piece of property."

"Yes, it is, except for those dreadful lampposts all over the lawn," said the first woman. "But why here? She should be in those other places like Beverly Hills or Scarsdale or Long Island, with the rest of them. What's she doing here?"

Woman number three looked up. "Well, you know, *he's* not Jewish."

"Really?"

"So that explains it," said the first woman with an understanding expression on her tanned forehead. "Because, you know, the name didn't sound Jewish."

The second woman agreed: "I can usually tell."

■ ■ ■ APRIL 15 (WEDNESDAY)

Today, we introduced a new, extended menu in the two grill rooms. We added shrimp quesadillas ($6) to the appetizer list—and neither the members nor Hazel could pronounce the name of the dish or fathom what it was. One man pounded on the table and demanded to know which country the dish had come from. He told Hazel how much he hated "changes like this. I like to know that some things are going to stay the same."

Another addition was the "New Dog in Town" ($3.50). It was billed as knockwurst, but one woman of German descent sent the dish back: "This is not knockwurst—this is just a big hot dog."

As I wiped down the length of the men's bar, I noticed a tall stack of postcards with color photos of nude busty women waving hello from sunny faraway beaches. I saw they had been sent from vacationing members with fond regards to Sam or Hazel. Several had come from married couples. One glossy photo boasted a detailed frontal shot of a red-haired beauty who was naked except for a shoestring around her waist. On the back, the message said, *Dear Sam, Pull string in an emergency. Love always, The Atkinson Family.*

■ ■ ■ APRIL 16 (THURSDAY)

This afternoon, I realized I was learning the routine. I was fairly comfortable with my few "serving" responsibilities and the rules that related to them:

- When a member is seated, bring out the silverware, cloth napkin, and a menu.
- Never take an order for food, but always bring water or iced tea if it is requested by a member or waiter.

- When a waiter takes a chili or salad order, bring out a basket of warm rolls and crackers along with a scoop of butter.
- When getting iced tea, fill a tall glass with ice and serve it with a long spoon, a napkin on the bottom, and a lemon on the rim.
- When a member wants his alcoholic drink refilled, politely respond, "Certainly, I will have your waiter come right over."
- Remember that the member is always right.
- Never make offensive eye contact with a member or his guest.
- When serving a member fresh popcorn, serve to the left.
- When a member is finished with a dish or a glass, clear it from the right.
- Never tell a member that the kitchen is out of something.

But there were also some "informal" rules that I discovered (but did not follow) while watching the more experienced waiters and kitchen staff in action:

- If you drop a hot roll on the floor in front of a member, apologize and throw it out. If you drop a hot roll on the floor in the kitchen, pick it up and put it back in the bread warmer.
- If you have cleared a table and are 75 percent sure that the member did not use the fork, put it back in the bin with the other clean forks.
- If, after pouring one glass of Coke and one of diet Coke, you get distracted and can't remember which is which, stick your finger in one of them to taste it.
- If a member asks for decaffeinated coffee and you have no time to make it, use regular coffee and add water to cut the flavor.
- When members complain that the chili is too hot and spicy, instead of making a new batch, take the sting out by adding some chocolate syrup.
- If you're making tuna on toasted wheat and you accidentally burn one side of the bread, don't throw it out. Instead, put the tuna on the burnt side and lather on some extra mayo.

■ ■ ■ APRIL 17 (FRIDAY)

Today, I heard the word "nigger" four times. And it came from someone on the staff.

In the grill, several members were discussing Arthur Ashe, who had recently announced that he had contracted AIDS through a blood transfusion.

"It's a shame that poor man has to be humiliated like this," one woman golfer remarked to a friend over pasta-and-vegetable salad. "He's been such a good example for his people."

"Well, quite frankly," added a woman in a white sunvisor, "I always knew he was gay. There was something about him that just seemed too perfect."

"No, Anne, he's not gay. It came from a blood transfusion."

"Ohh," said the woman. "I suppose that's a good reason to stay out of all those big-city hospitals. All that bad blood moving around."

Later that afternoon, one of the waiters, who had worked in the Mixed Grill for two years, told me that Tom Seaver and Gerald Ford were members. Of his brush with greatness, he added, "You know, Tom's real first name is George."

"That's something."

"And I've seen O. J. Simpson here, too."

"O. J. belongs here too?" I asked.

"Oh, no, there aren't any black members here. No way. I actually don't even think there are any Jews here either."

"Really? Why is that?" I asked.

"I don't know. I guess it's just that the members probably want to have a place where they can go and not have to think about Jews, blacks, and other minorities. It's not really hurting anyone. It's really a WASP club.... But now that I think of it, there's a guy here who some people think is Jewish, but I can't really tell. Upstairs, there's a Jewish secretary too."

"And what about O. J.?"

"Oh, yeah, it was so funny to see him out there playing golf on the eighteenth hole." The waiter paused and pointed outside the window. "It never occurred to me before, but it seemed so odd to see a black man with a golf club here on this course."

■ ■ ■ APRIL 18 (SATURDAY)

When I arrived, Stephen, one of the waiters, was hanging a poster and sign-up sheet for a soccer league whose main purpose was to "bridge the ethnic and language gap" between white and Hispanic workers at the country clubs in the Greenwich area. I congratulated Stephen on his idea. He said he was tired of seeing the whites and Hispanics split up during meals, breaks, and evening activities. "We even go to separate bars and diners," he explained. "I think a weekly soccer game might bring us all closer together."

Later, while I was wiping down a table, I heard a member snap his fingers in my direction. I turned to see a group of young men smoking cigars. They seemed to be my age or a couple of years younger. "Hey, do I know you?" the voice asked.

As I turned slowly toward the voice, I could hear my own heartbeat. I was sure it was someone I knew.

"No," I said, approaching the blond cigar smoker. He had on light green khaki pants and a light yellow V-neck cotton sweater adorned with a tiny green alligator. As I looked at the other men seated around the table, I noticed that all but one had alligators on their sweaters or shirts. Each one of them was a stranger to me.

"I didn't think so. You must be new—what's your name?"

"My name is Larry. I just started a few days ago."

The cigar-smoking host grabbed me by the wrist while looking at his guests. "Well, Larry, welcome to the club. I'm Mr. Billings. And this is Mr. Dennis, a friend and new member."

"Hello, Mr. Dennis," I heard myself saying to a freckle-faced young man who puffed uncomfortably on his fat roll of tobacco.

The first cigar smoker gestured for me to bend over as if he were about to share some important confidence. "Now, Larry, here's what I want you to do. Go get us some of those peanuts and then give my guests and me a fresh ashtray. Can you manage that?"

My workday ended at 4:20.

■ ■ ■ **EVENING OF APRIL 18 (SATURDAY)**

After changing back into my street clothes at around 8:00 P.M., I drove back to the club to get together with Stephen and Lillie, two of the friendlier waiters (and the only ones willing to socialize with a busboy), in Stephen's room on the grounds. We sat, ate Hostess donuts, drank wine, watched the Saturday-night NBC-TV lineup, and talked about what it would be like to be a rich member of the club.

Squeezed into the tiny room and sitting on the bed, which was pushed against the wall, we each promised to look out for and warn the others if anyone else tried to backstab us in the grill. Stephen was talking about his plans for the intercultural soccer league and what it could do for all eight clubs in the area.

"After spending a couple semesters in Japan," Stephen explained, "I realized how afraid Americans are of other cultures." Stephen told me that he was working at the club to pay for the rest of his college education. He was taking a two-year break between his sophomore and junior years at a midwestern university, where he was majoring in Japanese.

Lillie talked about the formal dinner that she had just worked at that evening. It was then that I learned she was half South American. Her father, who was from Colombia, was an outdoor groundskeeper at the club. "I'm taking college courses now," she explained. "And maybe I'm crazy to say this, but I think I'd like to go into broadcasting." Given her nearly flawless English and her very white skin, I wondered if the members were aware of her Hispanic background. She felt very strong about her South American heritage, and she often acted as interpreter for some of the club workers who spoke only Spanish.

They were both such nice people, I felt terrible for intruding under such fraudulent circumstances.

■ ■ ■ **APRIL 19 (SUNDAY)**

It was Easter Sunday and the Easter-egg hunt began with dozens of small children scampering around the tulips and daffodils while well-dressed parents watched from the rear patio of the club. A giant Easter bunny gave out little baskets filled with jelly beans to parents and then hopped over to the bushes, where he hugged the children. As we peered out from the closed blinds in the grill, we saw women in mink, husbands in gray suits, children in Ralph Lauren and Laura Ashley. Hazel let out a sigh. "Aren't they beautiful?" she said. For just a moment, I found myself agreeing.

"So, Larry." Sam laughed as I poured fresh oil into the popcorn machine's heated pan. It was my second day at the machine in the Men's Grill. "When you decide to move on from the club, you'll be able to get yourself a job at the popcorn counter in one of those big movie theaters."

I forced a smile.

"And you can tell them," he continued, "that you just about have a master's degree in popcorn popping. Tell 'em you learned everything you know from Sam at the country club."

I laughed. "Sure, Sam."

"Yeah, tell them I awarded you a master's degree."

I had already become an expert at yucking it up with Sam.

As I raced around taking out orders of coffee and baskets of hot rolls, I got a chance to see groups of families. The men seemed to be uniformly taller than six feet. Most of them were wearing blue blazers, white shirts, and incredibly out-of-style silk ties—the kind with little blue whales or little green ducks floating downward. They were bespectacled and conspicuously clean-shaven.

The "ladies," as the club prefers to call them, almost invariably had straight blond hair. Whether or not they had brown roots and whether they were twenty-five or forty-eight, they wore their hair blond, straight, and off the face. No dangling earrings, five-carat diamonds, or designer handbags. Black velvet or pastel headbands were de rigueur.

There were also groups of high school kids who wore torn jeans, sneakers, or unlaced L.L. Bean shoes, and sweatshirts that said things like "Hotchkiss Lacrosse" or "Andover Crew." At one table, two boys sat talking to two girls.

"No way, J.C.," one of the girls cried in disbelief while playing with the straw in her diet Coke.

The strawberry blond girl next to her flashed her unpainted nails in the air. "Way. She said that if she didn't get her grades up by this spring, they were going to take her out altogether."

"And where would they send her?" one of the guys asked.

The strawberry blond's grin disappeared as she leaned in close. "Public school."

The group, in hysterics, shook the table. The guys stomped their feet.

"Oh, my God, J.C., oh, J.C., J.C.," the diet-Coke girl cried.

Sitting in a tableless corner of the room beneath the TV set was a young, dark-skinned black woman dressed in a white uniform and a thick wool coat. On her lap was a baby with silky white blond hair. The woman sat patiently, shifting the baby in her lap while glancing over to where the baby's family ate, two tables away.

I ran to the kitchen, brought back a glass of tea, and offered it to her. The woman looked up at me, shook her head, and then turned back to the gurgling infant.

■ ■ ■ APRIL 21 (TUESDAY)

The TV in the Men's Grill was tuned to one of the all-day cable news channels and was reporting on the violent confrontations between pro-choice marchers and right-to-life protesters in Buffalo, New York.

"Look at all those women running around," a man in his late forties commented as he sat by himself at one of the larger tables in the Men's Grill.

At 11:10 A.M., the grill wasn't even officially opened yet.

As I walked around doing a final wipe of the tables, the man cried out into the empty room. "That's just a damned shame," he said while shaking his head and pulling at his yellow polo shirt in disbelief.

I nodded as he looked at me over his bowl of peanuts. "I agree with you."

He removed his sun visor and dropped it onto a table closer to the television. We both watched images of police dragging women who lay sprawled in the middle of a Buffalo city street.

"You know, it just scares me to see all these women running around like that," the middle-aged member continued as we both watched screaming crowds of placard-carrying activists and hand-cuffed protesters. "Someone's gotta keep these women reined in. A good, hard law that forces them to have those babies when they get pregnant will teach them to be responsible."

I looked at the man as he sat there hypnotized by the screen.

"All this equal rights bull," he finally added. "Running around getting pregnant and then running around doing what they want. Enough to make you sick."

Later, while Hector and I stood inside a deep walk-in freezer, we scooped balls of butter into separate butter dishes and talked about our life plans. "Will you go finish school sometime?" he asked as I dug deep into a vat of frozen butter.

"Maybe. In a couple of years, when I save more money, but I'm not sure." I felt lousy about having to lie.

"Maybe? If I had money, I'd go now—and I'm twenty-three years old." He shook his head in disapproval. "In my country, I had education. But here I don't because I don't know much English. It's tough because we have no work in South America. And here, there's work, but you need English to get it and make money."

We agreed that since 75 percent of the club employees were Spanish-speaking South Americans, the club really needed a bilingual manager or someone on staff who understood their concerns.

"Well," I offered. "I'll help you with English if you teach me some Spanish."

He joked that my Spanish was a lot worse than his English. After all, I only knew the words *gracias, buenos dias,* and *por favor.* So, during an illegal twelve-minute break, he ran through a quick vocabulary lesson while we walked to his minuscule room just across the sweaty congested halls of the noisy squash courts.

The room he took me into overlooked the driving range and was the size of a walk-in closet. The single bed touched three walls of the room. The quarter-sized refrigerator served as a stand for a stereo. There were a small dresser and a small desk plastered with many different pictures of a young Spanish-looking woman and a cute baby girl.

"My family" is all Hector would say in explanation while simultaneously pushing me out of the room and into the sweaty hall. "We go now—before we lose our job."

Just as we were leaving for the day, Mr. Ryan came down to hand out the new policies for those who were going to live in the Monkey House. Amazingly, without a trace of discomfort, he and everyone else referred to the building as "the Monkey House." Many of the workers had been living temporarily in the squash building. Since it had recently been renovated, the club was requiring all new residents to sign the form. The policy included a rule that forbade the employees to have overnight guests. Rule 14 stated that the club management had the right to enter an employee's locked bedroom at any time, without permission and without giving notice.

As I was making rounds with my coffeepots, I overheard a raspy-voiced woman talking to a mother and daughter who were thumbing through a catalog of infants' clothing.

"The problem with au pairs is that they're usually only in the country for a year."

The mother and daughter nodded in agreement.

"But getting one that is a citizen has its own problems. For example, if you ever have to choose between a Negro and one of these Spanish people, always go for the Negro."

One of the women frowned, confused. "Really?"

"Yes," the raspy-voiced woman responded with cold logic, "Even though you can't trust either one, at least the Negroes can speak English and follow your directions."

Before I could refill the final cup, the raspy-voiced woman looked up at me and smiled. "Oh, thanks for the refill, Larry."

■ ■ ■ APRIL 22 (WEDNESDAY)

"This is our country, and don't forget it. They came here and have to live by our rules!" Hazel pounded her fist into the palm of her pale white hand.

I had made the mistake of telling her I had learned a few Spanish phrases to help me communicate better with some of my coworkers. She wasn't impressed.

"I'll be damned if I'm going to learn or speak one word of Spanish. And I'd suggest you do the same," she said. She took a long drag on her cigarette while I loaded the empty shelves with clean glasses.

Today, the TV was tuned to testimony and closing arguments from the Rodney King police-beating trial in California.

"I am so sick of seeing this awful videotape," one woman said to friends at her table. "It shouldn't be on TV."

At around two, Lois, the club's official secretary, asked me to help her send out a mailing to six hundred members after my shift. It seemed that none of the waiters wanted to stay late. And since the only other choice was the non-English-speaking bus staff and dishwashers, I was it.

She took me up to her office on the main floor and introduced me to the two women who sat with her.

"Larry, this is Marge, whom you'll talk with in three months, because she's in charge of employee benefits."

I smiled at the brunette.

"And Larry, this is Sandy, whom you'll talk with after you become a member at the club, because she's in charge of members' accounts."

Both Sandy and I looked up at Lois with shocked expressions.

Lois winked, and at the same moment, the three jovial women burst out laughing.

Lois sat me down at a table in the middle of the club's cavernous ballroom and had me stamp "Annual Member Guest" on the bottom of small postcards and stuff them into envelopes.

As I sat in the empty ballroom, I looked around at the mirrors and the silver-and-crystal chandeliers that dripped from the high ceiling. I thought about all the beautiful weddings and debutante balls that must have taken place in that room. I could imagine members asking themselves, "Why would anybody who is not like us want to join a club where they're not wanted?"

I stuffed my last envelope, forgot to clock out, and drove back to the Merritt Parkway and into New York.

■ ■ ■ ■ APRIL 23 (THURSDAY)

"Wow, that's great," I said to Mr. Ryan as he posted a memo entitled "Employee Relations Policy Statement: Employee Golf Privileges."

After quickly reading the memo, I realized this "policy" was a crock. The memo opened optimistically. "The club provides golf privileges for staff.... Current employees will be allowed golf privileges as outlined below." Unfortunately, the only employees the memo listed "below" were department heads, golf-management personnel, teaching assistants, the general manager, and "key staff that appear on the club's organizational chart."

At the end of the day, Mr. Ryan handed me my first paycheck. Perhaps now the backbreaking work would seem worthwhile. When I opened the envelope and saw what I'd earned—$174.04 for five days—I laughed out loud.

Back in the security of a bathroom stall, where I had periodically been taking notes since my arrival, I studied the check and thought about how many hours—and how hard—I'd worked for so little money. It was less than one-tenth of what I'd make in the same time at my law firm. I went upstairs and asked Mr. Ryan about my paycheck.

"Well, we decided to give you $7 an hour," he said in a tone overflowing with generosity. I had never actually been told my hourly rate. "But if the check looks especially big, that's because you got some extra pay in there for all of your terrific work on Good Friday. And by the way, Larry, don't tell the others what you're getting, because we're giving you a special deal and it's really nobody else's business."

I nodded and thanked him for his largesse. I stuffed some more envelopes, emptied out my locker, and left.

The next morning, I was scheduled to work a double shift. Instead, I called and explained that I had a family emergency and would have to quit immediately. Mr. Ryan was very sympathetic and said I could return when things settled down. I told him, "No thanks," but asked that he send my last paycheck to my home. I put my uniform and the key to my locker in a brown padded envelope, and I mailed it all to Mr. Ryan.

Somehow it took two months of phone calls for me to get my final paycheck ($123.74 after taxes and a $30 deduction for my uniform).

I'm back at my law firm now, dressed in one of my dark gray Paul Stuart suits, sitting in a handsome office thirty floors above Midtown. While it's a long way from the Monkey House, we still have a long way to go.

19▪▪▪▪▪ ▪ ▪ ▪ ▪ ▪ ▪ ▪ ▪ ▪ ▪ ▪ ▪ ▪ ▪

The American Family

Stephanie Coontz

introduction ▪ ▪ ▪ ▪ ▪

The family is the social institution that introduces us to society. It is within the family that we learn our basic orientations to social life; the family is considered to be the basic building block of society. Within this great socializer, we learn our language and the basic norms that guide our behavior. It is here that we are introduced to ways of eating and dressing, to ideas of punctuality and neatness, and to highly refined norms that are difficult to put into words, such as how much self-centeredness we are allowed to display as we interact with others. Our family also teaches us its views of gender, race–ethnicity, social class, religion, people with disabilities, the elderly. From our family, we even learn attitudes about our own intelligence and our body. This early socialization becomes part of our basic outlook on life, the ways we evaluate others and ourselves.

Like our other social institutions, U.S. families are changing. They have become smaller, they have more disposable income, parental authority has decreased, people are marrying later, more children are reared by single mothers and single fathers, and divorce has made families fragile. (Some sociologists point out that because parents used to die much younger, today's children have about the same chance of living through childhood with both their biological parents as did children of two hundred years ago. Either way, marriage *is* fragile.) Sometimes, we look at the past with nostalgia. If only we could have family life like it used to be in those *Leave It to Beaver* years! The comparisons that Coontz makes between family life today and back then might hold a few surprises.

Thinking Critically

As you read this selection, ask yourself:

1. Do you think you would prefer the family life of the 1950s to that of today? Why?

2. What does Coontz mean when she says that "much nostalgia for the 1950s is a result of selective amnesia"?

3. What major differences are there between family life of the 1950s and that of today?

As the century comes to an end, many observers fear for the future of America's families. Our divorce rate is the highest in the world, and the percentage of unmarried women is significantly higher than in 1960. Educated women are having fewer babies, while immigrant children flood the schools, demanding to be taught in their native language. Harvard University reports that only 4 percent of its applicants can write a proper sentence.

There's an epidemic of sexually transmitted diseases among men. Many streets in urban neighborhoods are littered with cocaine vials. Youths call heroin "happy dust." Even in small towns, people have easy access to addictive drugs, and drug abuse by middle-class wives is skyrocketing. Police see 16-year-old killers, 12-year-old prostitutes, and gang members as young as 11.

America [today]? No, America at the end of the 1890s.

The litany of complaints may sound familiar, but the truth is that many things were worse at the start of this century than they are today. Then, thousands of children worked full-time in mines, mills and sweatshops. Most workers labored 10 hours a day, often six days a week, which left them little time or energy for family life. Race riots were more frequent and more deadly than those experienced by recent generations. Women couldn't vote, and their wages were so low that many turned to prostitution.

In 1990 a white child had one chance in three of losing a brother or sister before age 15, and a black child had a fifty-fifty chance of seeing a sibling die. Children's-aid groups reported widespread abuse and neglect by parents. Men who deserted or divorced their wives rarely paid child support. And only 6 percent of the children graduated from high school, compared with 88 percent today.

Why do so many people think American families are facing worse problems now than in the past? Partly it's because we compare the complex and diverse families of the 1990s with the seemingly more standard-issue ones of the 1950s, a unique decade when every long-term trend of the 20th century was temporarily reversed. In the 1950s, for the first time in 100 years, the divorce rate fell while marriage and fertility rates soared, creating a boom in nuclear-family living. The percentage of foreign-born individuals in the country decreased. And the debates over social and cultural issues that had divided Americans for 150 years were silenced, suggesting a national consensus on family values and norms.

Some nostalgia for the 1950s is understandable: Life looked pretty good in comparison with the hardship of the Great Depression and World War II. The GI Bill gave a generation of young fathers a college education and a subsidized mortgage on a new house. For the first time, a majority of men could support a family and buy a home without pooling their earnings with those of other family members. Many Americans built a stable family life on these foundations.

But much nostalgia for the 1950s is a result of selective amnesia—the same process that makes childhood memories of summer vacations grow sunnier with each passing year. The superficial sameness of 1950s family life was achieved through censorship, coercion and discrimination. People with unconventional beliefs faced governmental investigation and arbitrary firings. African Americans and Mexican Americans were prevented from voting in some states by literacy tests that were not administered to whites. Individuals who didn't follow the rigid gender and sexual rules of the day were ostracized.

Leave It to Beaver did not reflect the real-life experience of most American families. While many moved into the middle class during the 1950s, poverty remained more widespread than in the worst of our last three recessions. More children went hungry, and poverty rates for the elderly were more than twice as high as today's.

Even in the white middle class, not every woman was as serenely happy with her lot as June Cleaver was on TV. Housewives of the 1950s may have been less rushed than today's working mothers, but they were more likely to suffer anxiety and depression. In many states, women couldn't serve on juries or get loans or credit cards in their own names.

And not every kid was as wholesome as Beaver Cleaver, whose mischievous antics could be handled by Dad at the dinner table. In 1955 alone, Congress discussed 200 bills aimed at curbing juvenile delinquency. Three years later, LIFE reported that urban teachers were being terrorized by their students. The drugs that were so freely available in 1900 had been outlawed, but many children grew up in families ravaged by alcohol and barbiturate abuse.

Rates of unwed childbearing tripled between 1940 and 1958, but most Americans didn't notice because unwed mothers generally left town, gave their babies up for adoption and returned home as if nothing had happened. Troubled youths were encouraged to drop out of high school. Mentally handicapped children were warehoused in institutions like the Home for Idiotic and Imbecilic Children in Kansas, where a woman whose sister had lived there for most of the 1950s once took me. Wives routinely told pollsters that being disparaged or ignored by their husbands was a normal part of a happier than-average marriage.

Denial extended to other areas of life as well. In the early 1900s, doctors refused to believe that the cases of gonorrhea and syphilis they saw in young girls could have been caused by sexual abuse. Instead, they reasoned, girls could get these diseases from toilet seats, a myth that terrified generations of mothers and daughters. In the 1950s, psychiatrists dismissed incest reports as Oedipal fantasies on the part of children.

Spousal rape was legal throughout the period and wife beating was not taken seriously by authorities. Much of what we now label child abuse was accepted as a normal part of parental discipline. Physicians saw no reason to question parents who claimed that their child's broken bones had been caused by a fall from a tree.

There are plenty of stresses in modern family life, but one reason they seem worse is that we no longer sweep them under the rug. Another is that we have higher expectations of parenting and marriage. That's a good thing. We're right to be concerned about inattentive parents, conflicted marriages, antisocial values, teen violence and child abuse. But we need to realize that many of our worries reflect how much better we want to be, not how much better we *used* to be.

Fathers in intact families are spending more time with their children than at any other point in the past 100 years. Although the number of hours the average woman spends at home with her children has declined since the early 1900s, there has been a decrease in the number of children per family and an increase in individ-

American Mirror

Muncie, Ind. (pop. 67,476), calls itself America's Hometown. But to generations of sociologists it is better known as America's Middletown—the most studied place in the 20th century American landscape. "Muncie has nothing extraordinary about it," says University of Virginia professor Theodore Caplow, which is why, for the past 75 years, researchers have gone there to observe the typical American family. Muncie's averageness first drew sociologists Robert and Helen Lynd in 1924. They returned in 1935 (their follow-up study was featured in a LIFE photo essay by Margaret Bourke-White). And in 1976, armed with the Lynds' original questionnaires, Caplow launched yet another survey of the town's citizens.

Caplow discovered that family life in Muncie was much healthier in the 1970s than in the 1920s. No only were husbands and wives communicating more, but unlike married couples in the 1920s, they were also shopping, eating out, exercising and going to movies and concerts together. More than 90 percent of Muncie's couples characterized their marriages as "happy" or "very happy." In 1929 the Lynds had described partnerships of a drearier kind, "marked by sober accommodation of each partner to his share in the joint undertaking of children, paying off the mortgage and generally 'getting on.'"

Caplow's five-year study, which inspired a six-part PBS series, found that even though more moms were working outside the home, two thirds of them spent at least two hours a day with their children; in 1924 fewer than half did. In 1924 most children expected their mothers to be good cooks and housekeepers, and wanted their fathers to spend time with them and respect their opinions. Fifty years later, expectations of fathers were unchanged, but children wanted the same—time and respect—from their mothers. . . .

—Sora Song

ual attention to each child. As a result, mothers today, including working moms, spend almost twice as much time with each child as mothers did in the 1920s. People who raised children in the 1940s and 1950s typically report that their own adult children and grandchildren communicate far better with their kids and spend more time helping with homework than they did—even as they complain that other parents today are doing a worse job than in the past.

Despite the rise in youth violence from the 1960s to the early 1990s, America's children are also safer now than they've ever been. An infant was four times more likely to die in the 1950s than today. A parent then was three times more likely than a modern one to preside at the funeral of a child under the age of 15, and 27 percent more likely to lose an older teen to death.

If we look back over the last millennium, we can see that families have always been diverse and in flux. In each period, families have solved one set of problems only to face a new array of challenges. What works for a family in one economic and cultural setting doesn't work for a family in another. What's helpful at one stage of a family's life may be destructive at the next stage. If there is one lesson to be drawn from the last millennium of family history, it's that families are always having to play catch-up with a changing world.

Take the issue of working mothers. Families in which mothers spend as much time earning a living as they do raising children are nothing new. They were the norm throughout most of the last two millennia. In the 19th century, married women in the United States began a withdrawal from the workforce, but for most families this was made possible only by sending their children out to work instead. When child labor was abolished, married women began reentering the workforce in ever large numbers.

For a few decades, the decline in child labor was greater than the growth of women's employment. The result was an aberration: the male-breadwinner family. In the 1920s, for the first time, a bare majority of American children grew up in families where the husband provided all the income, the wife stayed home full-time, and they and their siblings went to school instead of work. During the 1950s, almost two thirds of children grew up in such families, an all-time high. Yet that same decade saw an acceleration of workforce participation by wives and mothers that soon made the dual-earner family the norm, a trend not likely to be reversed in the next century.

What's new is not that women make half their families' living, but that for the first time they have substantial control over their own income, along with the social freedom to remain single or to leave an unsatisfactory marriage. Also new is the declining proportion of their lives that people devote to rearing children, both because they have fewer kids and because they are living longer. Until about 1940, the typical marriage was broken by the death of one partner within a few years after the last child left home. Today, couples can look forward to spending more than two decades together after the children leave.

The growing length of time partners spend with only each other for company has made many individuals less willing to put up with an unhappy marriage, while women's economic independence makes it less essential for them to do so. It is no wonder that divorce has risen steadily since 1900. Disregarding a spurt in 1946, a dip in the 1950s and another peak around 1980, the divorce rate is just where you'd expect to find it, based on the rate of increase from 1900 to 1950. Today, 40 percent of all marriages will end in divorce before a couple's 40th anniversary. Yet despite this high divorce rate, expanded life expectancies mean that more couples are reaching that anniversary than ever before.

Families and individuals in contemporary America have more life choices than in the past. That makes it easier for some to consider dangerous or unpopular options. But it also makes success easier for many families that never would have had a chance before—interracial, gay or lesbian, and single-mother families, for example. And it expands horizons for most families.

Women's new options are good not just for themselves but for their children. While some people say that women who choose to work are selfish, it turns out that maternal self-sacrifice is not good for children. Kids do better when their mothers are happy with their lives, whether their satisfaction comes from being a full-time homemaker or from having a job.

Largely because of women's new roles at work, men are doing more at home. Although most men still do less housework than their wives, the gap has been halved since the 1960s. Today, 49 percent of couples say they share childcare equally, compared with 25 percent of 1985.

Men's greater involvement at home is good for their relationships with their parents, and also good for their children. Hands-on fathers make better parents than men who let their wives do all the nurturing and childcare: They raise sons who are more expressive and daughters who are more likely to do well in school, especially in math and science.

In 1900, life expectancy was 47 years, and only 4 percent of the population was 65 or older. Today, life expectancy is 76 years, and by 2025, about 20 percent of Americans will be 65 or older. For the first time, a generation of adults must plan for the needs of both their parents and their children. Most Americans are responding with remarkable grace. One in four households gives the equivalent of a full day a week or more in unpaid care to an aging relative, and more than half say they expect to do so in the next 10 years. Older people are less likely to be impoverished or incapacitated by illness than in the past, and they have more opportunity to develop a relationship with their grandchildren.

Even some of the choices that worry us the most are turning out to be manageable. Divorce rates are likely to remain high, but more non-custodial parents are staying in touch with their children. Child-support receipts are up. And a lower proportion of kids from divorced families are exhibiting problems than in earlier decades. Step-families are learning to maximize children's access to supportive adults rather than cutting them off from one side of the family.

Out-of-wedlock births are also high, however, and this will probably continue because the age of first marriage for women has risen to an all-time high of 25, almost five years above what it was in the 1950s. Women who marry at an older age are less likely to divorce, but they have more years when they are at risk—or at choice—for a nonmarital birth.

Nevertheless, births to teenagers have fallen from 50 percent of all nonmarital births in the late 1970s to just 30 percent today. A growing proportion of women who have a nonmarital birth are in their twenties and thirties and usually have more economic and educational resources than unwed mothers of the past. While two involved parents are generally better than one, a mother's personal maturity, along with her educational and economic status, is a better predictor of how well her child will turn out than her marital status. We should no longer assume that children raised by single parents face debilitating disadvantages.

As we begin to understand the range of sizes, shapes and colors that today's families come in, we find that the differences *within* family types are more important than the differences *between* them. No particular family form guarantees success, and no particular form is doomed to fail. How a family functions on the inside is more important than how it looks from the outside.

The biggest problem facing most families as this century draws to a close is not that our families have changed too much but that our institutions have changed too little. America's work policies are 50 years out of date, designed for a time when most moms weren't in the workforce and most dads didn't understand the joys of being involved in childcare. Our school schedules are 150 years out of date, designed for a time when kids needed to be home to help with the milking and haying. And many political leaders feel they have to decide whether to help parents stay home longer with their kids or invest in better childcare, preschool and afterschool programs, when most industrialized nations have long since learned it's possible to do both.

So America's social institutions have some Y2K bugs to iron out. But for the most part, our families are ready for the next millennium.

The Transformation of Family Life

Lillian B. Rubin

introduction

Marriage has to be one of the most difficult endeavors of human life. There are many reasons for the difficulties of holding marriage together, not the least of which are the high—some would say, exaggerated—expectations that we attach to marriage. The two people who marry come from diverse backgrounds. (Consider just the conversational differences discussed by Tannen in Reading 16.) The couple is expected to "fall in love" (for that is the ideal, and for some the only legitimate reason to marry). In that emotional state, they are expected to unite not just their bodies but also their minds, goals, attitudes, and ways of thinking. They are supposed to meet almost every need of the other person, and to make that person happy for the rest of his or her life.

What unrealistic expectations we have of marriage. There is no way to accomplish such lofty goals. Even if the couple has attached the label of love to their feelings, emotions are temporary. They come and go, reach heights and depths. The couple will inevitably have problems, for the requirements to get through everyday life are highly demanding—doing what a job requires to earn money, paying bills, keeping the cars and appliances running, buying groceries, doing shopping. These are wearisome tasks—and I haven't even mentioned housework. Then, in the typical case, come kids—and when they do, the obligations and responsibilities multiply.

And when the couple has problems, whom do they blame? Typically, they see the spouse as the source of the problems: It was on that person that they had placed such great hopes for life's happiness, but something—they often don't know quite what it is—isn't working out. In the preceding paragraph, I mentioned some of what sociologists call structural reasons for marital tensions. In this selection, Lillian Rubin analyzes others—the changes in marriage and family that lead to problems between couples.

Thinking Critically

As you read this selection, ask yourself:

1. What structural reasons (those that are built into marriage) does Rubin give for marital problems?

2. How can the structural reasons for problems in marriage be overcome?

3. How does Rubin's analysis match your own experience (that of yourself if you are married, or that of your parents, friends, or relatives if you are not married)?

"I know my wife works all day, just like I do," says Gary Braunswig, a twenty-nine-year-old white drill press operator, "but it's not the same. She doesn't have to do it. I mean, she has to because we need the money, but it's different. It's not really her job to have to be working; it's mine." He stops, irritated with himself because he can't find exactly the words he wants, and asks, "Know what I mean? I'm not saying it right; I mean, it's the man who's supposed to support his family, so I've got to be responsible for that, not her. And that makes one damn big difference.

"I mean, women complain all the time about how hard they work with the house and the kids and all. I'm not saying it's not hard, but that's her responsibility, just like the finances are mine."

"But she's now sharing that burden with you, isn't she?" I remark.

"Yeah, and I do my share around the house, only she doesn't see it that way. Maybe if you add it all up, I don't do as much as she does, but then she doesn't bring in as much money as I do. And she doesn't always have to be looking for overtime to make an extra buck. I got no complaints about that, so how come she's always complaining about me? I mean, she helps me out financially, and I help her out with the kids and stuff. What's wrong with that? It seems pretty equal to me."

Cast that way, his formulation seems reasonable: They're each responsible for one part of family life; they each help out with the other. But the abstract formula doesn't square with the lived reality. For him, helping her adds relatively little to the burden of household tasks he must do each day. A study by University of Wisconsin researchers, for example, found that in families where both wife and husband work full-time, the women average over twenty-six hours a week in household labor, while the men do about ten. That's because there's nothing in the family system to force him to accountability or responsibility on a daily basis. He may "help her out with the kids and stuff" one day and be too busy or preoccupied the next. But for Gary's wife, Irene, helping him means an extra eight hours every working day. Consequently, she wants something, more consistent from him than a helping hand with a particular task when he has the time, desire, or feels guilty enough. "Sure, he helps me out," she says, her words tinged with resentment. "Hell give the kids a bath or help with the dishes. But only when I ask him. He doesn't have to ask me to go to work every day, does he? Why should I have to ask him?"

"Why should I have to ask him?"—words that suggest a radically different consciousness from the working-class women I met twenty years ago. Then, they counted their blessings. "He's a steady worker; he doesn't drink; he doesn't hit me," they told me by way of explaining why they had "no right to complain." True, these words were reminders to themselves that life could be worse, that they shouldn't take these things for granted—reminders that didn't wholly work to obscure their discontent with other aspects of the marriage. But they were nevertheless meaningful statements of value that put a brake on the kinds of demands they felt they could make of their men, whether about the unequal division of household tasks or about the emotional content of their lives together.

Now, the same women who reminded themselves to be thankful two decades ago speak openly about their dissatisfaction with the role divisions in the family. Some husbands, especially the younger ones, greet their wives' demands sympathetically. "I try to do as much as I can for Sue, and when I can't, I feel bad about it," says twenty-nine-year-old Don Dominguez, a Latino, father of three children, who is a construction worker.

Others are more ambivalent. "I don't know, as long as she's got a job, too, I guess it's right that I should help out in the house. But that doesn't mean I've got to like it," says twenty-eight-year-old Joe Kempinski, a white warehouse worker with two children.

Some men are hostile, insisting that their wives' complaints are unreasonable, unjust, and oppressive. "I'm damn tired of women griping all the time; it's nothing but nags and complaints," Ralph Danesen, a thirty-six-year-old white factory worker and the father of three children, says indignantly. "It's enough! You'd think they're the only ones who've got it hard. What about me? I'm not living in a bed of roses either. . . . What does she want? It's not like I don't do anything to help her out, but it's never enough."

In the past there was a clear understanding about the obligations and entitlements each partner took on when they married. He was obliged to work outside the home; she would take care of life inside. He was entitled to her ministrations, she to his financial support. But this neat division of labor with its clearcut separation of rights and obligations no longer works. Now, women feel obliged to hold up their share of the family economy—a partnership men welcome. In return, women believe they're entitled to their husband's full participation in domestic labor. And here is the rub. For while men enjoy the fruits of their wives' paid work outside the home, they have been slow to accept the reciprocal responsibilities—that is, to become real partners in the work inside the home.

The women, exhausted from doing two days' work in one, angry at the need to assume obligations without corresponding entitlements, push their men in ways unknown before. The men, battered by economic uncertainty and by the escalating demands of their wives, feel embattled and victimized on two fronts—one outside the home, the other inside. Consequently, when their wives seem not to see the family work they do, when they don't acknowledge and credit it, when they fail to appreciate them, the men feel violated and betrayed. "You come home and you want to be appreciated a little. But it doesn't work that way, leastwise not here anymore," complains Gary Braunswig his angry words at odds with sadness in his eyes. "There's no peace, I guess that's the real problem; there's no peace anywhere anymore."

The women often understand what motivates their husbands' sense of victimization and even speak sympathetically about it at times. But to understand and sympathize is not to condone, especially when they feel equally assaulted on both the home and the economic fronts. "I know I complain a lot, but I really don't ask for that much. I just want him to help out a little more," explains Ralph Danesen's wife, Helen, a thirty-five-year-old office worker. "It isn't like I'm asking him to cook the meals or anything like that. I know he can't do that, and I don't expect him to. But every time I try to talk to him, you know, to ask him if I couldn't get a little more help around here, there's a fight."

One of the ways the men excuse their behavior toward family work is by insisting that their responsibility as breadwinner burdens them in ways that are alien to their wives. "The plant's laying off people left and right; it could be me tomorrow. Then what'll we do? Isn't it enough I got to worry about that? I'm the one who's got all the worries; she doesn't. How come that doesn't count?" demands Bob Duckworth, a twenty-nine-year-old factory worker.

But, in fact, the women don't take second place to their men in worrying about what will happen to the family if the husband loses his job. True, the burden of finding another one that will pay the bills isn't theirs—not a trivial difference. But the other side of this truth is that women are stuck with the reality that the financial welfare of the family is out of their control, that they're helpless to do anything to prevent its economic collapse or to rectify it should it happen. "He thinks I've got it easy because it's not my job to support the family," says Bob's wife, Ruthanne. "But sometimes I think it's worse for me. I worry all the time that he's going to get laid off, just like he does. But I can't do anything about it. And if I try to talk to him about it, you know, like maybe make a plan in case it happens, he won't even listen. How does he think *that* makes me feel? It's my life, too, and I can't even talk to him about it...."

Not surprisingly, there are generational differences in what fuels the conflict around the division of labor in these families. For the older couples—those who grew up in a different time, whose marriages started with another set of ground rules—the struggle is not simply around how much men do or about whether they take responsibility for the daily tasks of living without being pushed, prodded, and reminded. That's the overt manifestation of the discord, the trigger that starts the fight. But the noise of the explosion when it comes serves to conceal the more fundamental issue underlying the dissention: legitimacy. What does she have a right to expect? "What do I know about doing stuff around the house?" asks Frank Moreno, a forty-eight-year-old foreman in a warehouse. "I wasn't brought up like that...."

For the younger couples, those under forty, the problem is somewhat different. The men may complain about the expectation that they'll participate more fully in the care and feeding of the family, but talk to them about it quietly and they'll usually admit that it's not really unfair, given that their wives also work outside the home. In these homes, the issue between husband and wife isn't only who does what. That's there, and it's a source of more or less conflict, depending upon what the men actually do and how forceful their wives are in their demands. But in most of these families there's at least a verbal consensus that men *ought* to participate in the tasks of daily life. Which raises the next and perhaps more difficult issue in contest between them: Who feels responsible for getting the tasks done? Who re-gards them as a duty, and for whom are they an option? On this, tradition rules.

Even in families where husbands now share many of the tasks, their wives still bear full responsibility for the organization of family life. A man may help cook the meal these days, but a woman is most likely to be the one who has planned it. He may take the children to child care, but she virtually always has had to arrange it. It's she also who is accountable for the emotional life of the family, for monitoring the emotional temperature of its members and making the necessary corrections. It's this need to be responsible for it all that often feels as burdensome as the tasks them-selves. "It's not just doing all the stuff that needs doing," explains Maria Jankowicz, a white twenty-eight-year-old assembler in an electronics factory. "It's worrying all the time about everything and always having to arrange everything, you know what I mean. It's like I run the whole show. If I don't stay on top of it all, things fall apart because nobody else is going to do it. The kids can't and Nick, well, forget it," she concludes angrily. . . .

Virtually all the men do some work inside the family—tending the children, washing dishes, running the vacuum, going to the market. And they generally also remain responsible for those tasks that have always been traditionally male—mow-ing the lawn, shoveling the snow, fixing the car, cleaning the garage, doing repairs around the house. Among the white families in this study, 16 percent of the men share the family work relatively equally, almost always those who live in families where they and their wives work different shifts or where the men are unemployed. "What choice do I have?" asks Don Bartlett, a thirty-year-old white handyman who works days while his wife is on the swing shift. "I'm the only one here, so I do what's got to be done."

Asian and Latino men of all ages, however, tend to operate more often on the old male model, even when they work different shifts or are unemployed, a finding that puzzled me at first. Why, I wondered, did I find only two Asian men and one Latino who are real partners in the work of the family? Aren't these men subject to the same social and personal pressures others experience?

The answer is both yes and no. The pressures are there but, depending upon where they live, there's more or less support for resisting them. The Latino and Asian men who live in ethnic neighborhoods—settings where they are embedded in an intergenerational community and where the language and culture of the home country is kept alive by a steady stream of new immigrants—find strong support for clinging to the old ways. Therefore, change comes much more slowly in those fami-lies. The men who live outside the ethnic quarter are freer from the mandates and constraints of these often tight-knit communities, therefore are more responsive to the winds of change in the larger society.

These distinctions notwithstanding, it's clear that Asian and Latino men gener-ally participate least in the work of the household and are the least likely to believe they have much responsibility there beyond bringing home a paycheck. "Taking care of the house and kids is my wife's job, that's all," says Joe Gomez flatly.

"A Chinese man mopping a floor? I've never seen it yet," says Amy Lee an-grily. Her husband, Dennis, trying to make a joke of the conflict with his wife, says with a smile, "In Chinese families men don't do floors and windows. I help with the dishes sometimes if she needs me to or," he laughs, "if she screams loud enough. The rest, well, it's pretty much her job."

The commonly held stereotype about black men abandoning women and children, however, doesn't square with the families in this study. In fact, black men are the most likely to be real participants in the daily life of the family and are more intimately involved in raising their children than any of the others. True, the men's family work load doesn't always match their wives', and the women are articulate in their complaints about this. Nevertheless, compared to their white, Asian, or Latino counterparts, the black families look like models of egalitarianism.

Nearly three-quarters of the men in the African-American families in this study do a substantial amount of the cooking, cleaning, and child care, sometimes even more than their wives. All explain it by saying one version or another of: "I just figure it's my job, too." Which simply says what is, without explaining how it came to be that way.

To understand that, we have to look at family histories that tell the story of generations of African-American women who could find work and men who could not, and to the family culture that grew from this difficult and painful reality. "My mother worked six days a week cleaning other people's houses, and my father was an ordinary laborer, when he could find work, which wasn't very often," explains thirty-two-year-old Troy Payne, a black waiter and father of two children. "So he was home a lot more than she was, and he'd do what he had to do around the house. The kids all had to do their share, too. It seemed only fair, I guess."

Difficult as the conflict around the division of labor is, it's only one of the many issues that have become flash points in family life since mother went to work. Most important, perhaps, is the question: Who will care for the children? For the lack of decent, affordable facilities for the care of the children creates unbearable problems and tensions for these working-class families.

It's hardly news that child care is an enormous headache and expense for all two job families. In many professional middle-class families, where the child-care bill can be $1,500–2,000 a month, it competes with the mortgage payment as the biggest single monthly expenditure. Problematic as this may be, however, these families are the lucky ones when compared to working-class families, many of whom don't earn much more than the cost of child care in these upper middle-class families. Even the families in this study at the highest end of the earnings scale, those who earn $42,000 a year, can't dream of such costly arrangements.

For most working-class families, therefore, child care often is patched together in ways that leave parents anxious and children in jeopardy. "Care for the little ones, that's a real big problem," says Beverly Waldov, a thirty-year-old white mother of three children, the youngest two, products of a second marriage, under three years old. "My oldest girl is nine, so she's not such a problem. I hate the idea of her being a latchkey kid, but what can I do? We don't even have the money to put the little ones in one of those good day-care places, so I don't have any choice with her. She's just got to be able to take care of herself after school," she says, her words a contest between anxiety and hope.

"We have a kind of complicated arrangement for the little kids. Two days a week, my mom takes care of them. We pay her, but at least I don't have to worry when they're with her; I know it's fine. But she works the rest of the time, so the other days we take them to this woman's house. It's the best we can afford, but it's not great because she keeps too many kids, and I know they don't get good attention. Especially the little one; she's just a baby, you know." She pauses and looks away, anguished. "She's so clingy when I bring her home; she can't let go of me, like nobody's paid her any mind all day. But it's not like I have a choice. We barely make it now; if I stop working, we'd be in real trouble."...

Some have tried a variety of child-care arrangements, only to have them fail in a moment of need. "We tried a whole bunch of things, and maybe they work for a little while," says Faye Ensey, a black twenty-eight-year-old office worker. "But what happens when your kid gets sick? Or when the baby sitter's kids get sick? I lost two jobs in a row because my kids kept getting sick and I couldn't go to work. Or else I couldn't take my little one to the baby sitter because her kids were sick. They finally fired me for absenteeism. I didn't really blame them, but it felt terrible anyway. It's such a hassle, I sometimes think I'd be glad to just stay home. But we can't afford for me not to work, so we had to figure out something else."

For such families, that "something else" is the decision to take jobs on different shifts—a decision made by one-fifth of the families in this study. With one working days and the other on swing or graveyard, one parent is home with the children at all times. "We were getting along okay before Daryl junior was born, because Shona, my daughter, was getting on. You know, she didn't need somebody with her all the time, so we could both work days," explains Daryl Adams, a black thirty-year-old postal clerk with a ten-year-old daughter and a nine-month-old son. "I used to work the early shift—seven to three—so I'd get home a little bit after she got here. It worked out okay. But then this here big surprise came along." He stops, smiles down fondly at his young son and runs his hand over his nearly bald head.

"Now between the two of us working, we don't make enough money to pay for child care and have anything left over, so this is the only way we can manage. Besides, both of us, Alesha and me, we think it's better for one of us to be here, not just for the baby, for my daughter, too. She's growing up and, you know, I think maybe they need even more watching than when they were younger. She's coming to the time when she could get into all kinds of trouble if we're not here to put the brakes on."

But the cost such arrangements exact on a marriage can be very high. When I asked these husbands and wives when they have time to talk, more often than not I got a look of annoyance at a question that, on its face, seemed stupid to them. "Talk? How can we talk when we hardly see each other?" "Talk? What's that?" "Talk? Ha, that's a joke."

Mostly, conversation is limited to the logistics that take place at shift-changing time when children and chores are handed off from one to the other. With children dancing around underfoot, the incoming parent gets a quick summary of the day's or night's events, a list of reminders about things to be done, perhaps about what's cooking in the pot on the stove. "Sometimes when I'm coming home and it's been a hard day, I think: Wouldn't it be wonderful if I could just sit down with Leon for half an hour and we could have a quiet beer together?" thirty-one-year-old Emma Guerrero, a Latina baker, says wistfully.

But it's not to be. If the arriving spouse gets home early enough, there may be an hour when both are there together. But with the pressures of the workday fresh for one and awaiting the other, and with children clamoring for parental attention, this isn't a promising moment for any serious conversation. "I usually get home about forty-five minutes or so before my wife has to leave for work," says Ralph Jo, a thirty-six-year-old Asian repairman whose children, ages three and five, are the product of a second marriage. "So we try to take a few minutes just to make contact. But it's hard with the kids and all. Most days the whole time gets spent with taking care of business—you know, who did what, what the kids need, what's for supper, what bill collector was hassling her while I was gone—all the damn garbage of living. It makes me nuts."

Most of the time even this brief hour isn't available. Then the ritual changing of the guard takes only a few minutes—a quick peck on the cheek in greeting, a few words, and it's over. "It's like we pass each other. He comes in; I go out; that's it."

Some of the luckier couples work different shifts on the same days, so they're home together on weekends. But even in these families there's so little time for normal family life that there's hardly any room for anyone or anything outside. "There's so much to do when I get home that there's no time for anything but the chores and the kids," says Daryl's wife, Alesha Adams. "I never get to see anybody or do anything else anymore and, even so, I'm always feeling upset and guilty because there's not enough time for them. Daryl leaves a few minutes after I get home, and the rest of the night is like a blur—Shona's homework, getting the kids fed and down for the night, cleaning up, getting everything ready for tomorrow. I don't know; there's always something I'm running around doing. I sometimes feel like— What do you call them?—one of those whirling dervishes, rushing around all the time and never getting everything done.

"Then on the weekends, you sort of want to make things nice for the kids— and for us, too. It's the only time we're here together, like a real family, so we always eat with the kids. And we try to take them someplace nice one of the days, like to the park or something. But sometimes we're too tired, or there's too many other catch-up things you have to do. I don't even get to see my sister anymore. She's been working weekends for the last year or so, and I'm too busy week nights, so there's no time.

"I don't mean to complain; we're lucky in a lot of ways. We've got two great kids, and we're a pretty good team, Daryl and me. But I worry sometimes. When you live on this kind of schedule, communication's not so good."

For those whose days off don't match, the problems of sustaining both the couple relationship and family life are magnified enormously. "The last two years have been hell for us," says thirty-five-year-old Tina Mulvaney, a white mother of two teenagers. "My son got into bad company and had some trouble, so Mike and I decided one of us had to be home. But we can't make it without my check, so I can't quit.

"Mike drives a cab and I work in a hospital, so we figured one of us could transfer to nights. We talked it over and decided it would be best if I was here during the day and he was here at night. He controls the kids, especially my son, better than I do. When he lays down the law, they listen." She interrupts her narrative to reflect on the difficulty of raising children. "You know, when they were little, I used to think about how much easier it would be when they got older. But now I see it's not true; that's when you really have to begin to worry about them. This is when they need someone to be here all the time to make sure they stay out of trouble."

She stops again, this time fighting tears, then takes up where she left off. "So now Mike works days and I work graveyard. I hate it, but it's the only answer; at least this way somebody's here all the time. I get home about 8:30 in the morning. The kids and Mike are gone. It's the best time of the day because it's the only time I have a little quiet here. I clean up the house a little, do the shopping and the laundry and whatever, then I go to sleep for a couple of hours until the kids come home from school.

"Mike gets home at five; we eat; then he takes over for the night, and I go back to sleep for another couple of hours. I try to get up by 9 so we can all have a little time together, but I'm so tired that I don't make it a lot of times. And by 10, he's sleeping because he has to be up by 6 in the morning. So if I don't get up, we hardly see each other at all. Mike's here on weekends, but I'm not. Right now I have Tuesday and Wednesday off. I keep hoping for a Monday-Friday shift, but it's what everybody wants, and I don't have the seniority yet. It's hard, very hard; there's no time to live or anything," she concludes with a listless sigh. . . .

Clearly, such complaints aren't unique to the working class. The pressures of time, the impoverishment of social life, the anxieties about child care, the fear that children will live in a world of increasing scarcity, the threat of divorce—all these are part of family life today, regardless of class. Nevertheless, there are important differences between those in the higher reaches of the class structure and the families of the working class. The simple fact that middle-class families have more discretionary income is enough to make a big difference in the quality of their social life. For they generally have enough money to pay for a baby-sitter once in a while so that parents can have some time to themselves; enough, too, for a family vacation, for tickets to a concert, a play, or a movie. At $7.50 a ticket in a New York or San Francisco movie house, a working-class couple will settle for a $3.00 rental that the whole family can watch together.

Finding time and energy for sex is also a problem, one that's obviously an issue for two-job families of any class. But it's harder to resolve in working-class families because they have so few resources with which to buy some time and privacy for themselves. Ask about their sex lives and you'll be met with an angry, "What's that?" or a wistful, "I wish." When it happens, it is, as one woman put it, "on the run"—a situation that's particularly unsatisfactory for most women. For them, the pleasure of sex is related to the whole of the interaction—to a sense of intimacy and connection, to at least a few relaxed, loving moments. When they can't have these, they're likely to avoid sex altogether—a situation the men find equally unsatisfactory.

"Sex?" asks Lisa Scranton, a white twenty-nine-year-old mother of three who feigns a puzzled frown, as if she doesn't quite know the meaning of the word. "Oh yeah, that; I remember now," she says, her lips smiling, her eyes sad. "At the beginning, when we first got together, it was, WOW, real hot, great. But after a while it cools down, doesn't it? Right now, it's down the toilet. I wonder, does it happen to everybody like that?" she asks dejectedly.

"I guess the worst is when you work different shifts like we do and you get to see each other maybe six minutes a day. There's no time for sex. Sometimes we try to steal a few minutes for ourselves but, I don't know, I can't get into it that way. He can. You know how men are; they can do it any time. Give them two minutes, and they can get off. But it takes me time; I mean, I like to feel close, and you can't do that in three minutes. And there's the kids; they're right here all the time. I don't want to do it if it means being interrupted. Then he gets mad, so sometimes I do. But it's a problem, a real problem."

The men aren't content with these quick sexual exchanges either. But for them it's generally better than no sex at all, while for the women it's often the other way around. "You want to talk about sex, huh?" asks Lisa's husband, Chuck, his voice crackling with anger. "Yeah, I don't mind; it's fine, only I got nothing to talk about. Far as I'm concerned, that's one of the things I found out about marriage. You get married, you give up sex. We hardly ever do it anymore, and when we do, it's like she's doing me a favor.

"...I know the way we've got to do things now isn't great," he protests, running a hand through his hair agitatedly. "We don't see each other but a few minutes a day, but I don't see why we can't take five and have a little fun in the sack. Sure, I like it better when we've got more time, too. But for her, if it can't be perfect, she gets all wound and uptight...."

Once such conflicts arise, spontaneity takes flight and sex becomes a problem that needs attention rather than a time out for pleasure and renewal. Between times, therefore, he's busy calculating how much time has passed: "It's been over two weeks;" nursing his wounds: "I don't want to have to beg her;" feeling deprived and angry: "I don't know why I got married." When they finally do come together, he's disappointed. How could it be otherwise, given the mix of feelings he brings to the bed with him—the frustration and anger, the humiliation of feeling he has to beg her, the wounded sense of manhood.

Meanwhile, she, too, is preoccupied with sex, not with thoughts of pleasure but with figuring out how much time she has before, as she puts it, "he walks around with his mouth stuck out. I know I'm in real big trouble if we don't do it once a week. So I make sure we do, even if I don't want to." She doesn't say those words to him, of course. But he knows. And it's precisely this, the knowledge that she's servicing him rather than desiring him that's so hard for him to take.

The sexual arena is one of the most common places to find a "his and her" marriage—one marriage, two different sex lives. Each partner has a different story to tell; each is convinced that his or her version is the real one. A husband says mournfully, "I'm lucky if we get to make love once a week." His wife reports with irritation, "It's two, sometimes three times a week." It's impossible to know whose account is closest to the reality. And it's irrelevant. If that's what they were after, they could keep tabs and get it straight. But facts and feelings are often at war in family life. And nowhere does right or wrong, true or false count for less than in their sexual interactions. It isn't that people arbitrarily distort the truth. They simply report their experience, and it's feeling, not fact, that dominates that experience; feeling, not fact, that is their truth.

But it's also true that, especially for women, the difference in frequency of sexual desire can be a response—sometimes conscious, sometimes not—to other conflicts in the marriage. It isn't that men never withhold sex as a weapon in the family wars, only that they're much more likely than women to be able to split sex from emotion, to feel their anger and still experience sexual desire. For a man, too, a sexual connection with his wife can relieve the pressures and tensions of the day, can make him feel whole again, even if they've barely spoken a word to each other.

For a woman it's different. What happens—or, more likely, what doesn't happen—in the kitchen, the living room, and the laundry room profoundly affects what's possible in the bedroom. When she feels distant, unconnected, angry; when her pressured life leaves her feeling fragmented; when she hasn't had a real conversation with her husband for a couple of days, sex is very far from either her mind or her loins. "I run around busy all the time, and he just sits there, so by the time we go to bed, I'm too tired," explains Linda Bloodworth, a white thirty-one-year-old telephone operator.

"Do you think your lack of sexual response has something to do with your anger at your husband's refusal to participate more fully in the household?" I ask.

Her eyes smoldering, her voice tight, she snaps, "No, I'm just tired, that's all." Then noticing something in my response, she adds, "I know what you're thinking; I saw that look. But really, I don't think it's because I'm angry; I really am tired. I have to admit, though, that I tell him if he helped more, maybe I wouldn't be so tired all the time. And," she adds defiantly, "maybe I wouldn't be."...

Time and money—precious commodities in short supply. These are the twin plagues of family life, the missing ingredients that combine to create families that are both frantic and fragile. Yet there's no mystery about what would alleviate the crisis that now threatens to engulf them: A job that pays a living wage, quality child-care facilities at rates people can pay, health care for all, parental leave, flexible work schedules, decent and affordable housing, a shorter work week so that parents and children have time to spend together, tax breaks for those in need rather than for those in greed, to mention just a few. These are the policies we need to put in place if we're to have any hope of making our families stable and healthy.

What we have, instead, are families in which mother goes to work to relieve financial distress, only to find that time takes its place next to money as a source of strain, tension, and conflict. Time for the children, time for the couple's relationship, time for self, time for social life—none of it easily available for anyone in two-job families, not even for the children, who are hurried along at every step of the way. And money! Never enough, not for the clothes children need, not for the doctor's bill, not for a vacation, not even for the kind of child care that would allow parents to go to work in peace. But large as these problems loom in the lives of working-class families, difficult as they are to manage, they pale beside those they face when unemployment strikes, especially if it's father who loses his job.

Name Index

Subject Index